ASSIGNMENT: WILDLIFE

Anne LaBastille

Anne LaBastille

ASSIGNMENT: WILDLIFE

E. P. Dutton   New York

For information contact:
Elsevier-Dutton, 2 Park Avenue,
New York, N.Y. 10016

Library of Congress Cataloging in Publication Data
LaBastille, Anne.
Assignment, wildlife.
1. LaBastille, Anne. 2. Nature conservation—Latin
America. 3. Conservationists—United States—Biography.
I. Title.
QH31.L15A32   1980   333.95′092′4 [B]   80-445

ISBN: 0-525-05910-5

Published simultaneously in Canada by
Clarke, Irwin & Company
Limited, Toronto and Vancouver

Designed by Barbara Cohen

10 9 8 7 6 5 4 3 2 1

First Edition

To Manuel

🗿 Contents

# Foreword

Anne LaBastille is a remarkable woman, a vitally important conservationist, and a very good writer. We have, over the last few years, been treated to a spate of conservation books, some good, some bad, some indifferent. This book definitely falls into the first category.

We should remember how new, relatively speaking, the idea of conservation is and how there is still enormous ignorance of its importance.

Not too long ago, a major British newspaper devoted its entire editorial to castigating a well-known and respected scientist for suggesting that we—the human race—were treating our planet in a profligate and, indeed, suicidal way. With all the arrogant ignorance so frequently displayed by journalists, the paper stated that there was no room for such dangerous and subversive talk about the world's dwindling resources. The scientist was accused of lacking a sense of scientific responsibility to suggest that our almost maniacal destruction of the forests of the world and our disgusting pollution of the air, the rivers, lakes, and sea were evils, and that our ratlike overbreeding could only end in disaster. There were, the newspaper informed its readers, more than enough resources in the world to cope with fifty times the world population at that time.

Shortly after this, I was in Australia, where there was a fierce controversy going on about the desirability of drilling for oil on the Great Barrier Reef. Fortunately, the conservationists won the day. However, during the course of the debate, a—one presumed—responsible minister in the Queensland government made a statement to the press that forever enshrined him in my memory. This gentleman, the Minister for Mines, said he could not understand the conservationists' unrest, since an oil slick (in the unlikely event of there being one) would cause no harm, for, "as every schoolboy knew," oil floated on top of the water and coral lived underneath, so no damage could ensue.

If we are thus informed by our press and so guided by our politicians, it is scarcely surprising that our world's biological predicaments (infinitely more worrying and dangerous than any ideological traumas) are so appalling.

It is for this reason that we so urgently need people like Anne LaBastille, people who not only care deeply about our plight but actually go out and do something about it. With her knowledge and tact—and these two virtues do not always go hand in hand—she has helped world conservation immeasurably. She is in the very forefront of that small but dedicated band of conservationists to whom future generations will owe an enormous debt.

This is the story of her work, beautifully and modestly written. It is a book that should be read not only by serious scientists but by everyone interested in the future of our species and all other species that share this world with us.

GERALD DURRELL
San José, Costa Rica
March 15, 1979

🐾 Introduction

I became a woodswoman and wildlife woman because I love the outdoors. That's it—pure and simple. Yet my childhood in suburban New Jersey, playing Indian in vacant lots and on golf courses, hardly prepared me for my first ecological research and conservation campaign in Central America. As a youngster I had fantasized about living in the woods and watching wildlife—notions fed by such books as *Enchanted Vagabonds* and *Quest for a Lost City* by Dana and Ginger Lamb, *After You, Marco Polo* by Jean Bowie Shor, *Driftwood Valley* by Theodora Stanwell-Fletcher, and *The Yearling* by Marjorie Kinnan Rawlings. On top of that, my mother never let me go camping, which only nourished my hunger to tramp wilderness trails and travel in wild places far away. Early on, I vowed resolutely that I would do so one day.

College opened the door to the realm of natural history. I discovered the dozens of "ologies" which make up the study of nature and the outdoor world. There were marine biology, ornithology, mammalogy, woodland ecology, meteorology, entomology, geology, ichthyology, herpetology, as well as some of the "un-ologies" like oceanography, forestry, and anatomy of vertebrate animals. In my undergraduate days at Cornell University, what was called natural history was really a type of field biology, or early ecology. As students, we spent a lot of time identifying different organisms in their habitats, poking about living systems to see how they functioned, and making collections. We became avid bird watchers, snake collectors, frog-song and wildflower identifiers: Field guides and scientific keys were our bibles.

But I did see that ecologists had to be generalists as well as specialists, gleaning knowledge from many scientific disciplines, and this made the field even more interesting to me. Instead of examining things at the cellular level as other biologists did, we probed into organisms, populations, and whole ecosystems. Best of all, most ecologists worked outside laboratories, using the outdoors as their "ultimate test tube" and wearing muddy boots and old shirts instead of starched white lab coats. That, I decided, was for me.

But how would I get there? I had all the instincts. I knew, for example, that many of the environmental ills that ecosystems faced, and would confront in the future, are manmade, yet they still belong to the field of ecology. Human beings are a part of nature and are now the dominant force in the natural world. I was filled with zeal to conserve wildlife and wildlands.

But I knew too that without the formal education and field work—much as I would hate some of it—I could not become a wildlife ecologist. Those credentials were necessary, even crucial, to the profession. Without academic degrees, I'd probably stay in New Jersey, raising parakeets, monkeys, and guppies, maybe camping overnight in my backyard occasionally, and dutifully sending in my dues to the S.P.C.A., National Audubon Society, and the Wilderness Society. Of course, I would no doubt also be fighting vigorously for clean air, a local bird sanctuary, and good conservation education in the schools.

Thus, I went through the course work for a bachelor's, a master's, and finally a doctor's degree. I developed from being a lister of birds and tropical fishes to an investigator of ecosystems, and as a natural outgrowth, becoming a conservationist and protector of wildlife and wildlands.

Another descriptive term for what I am professionally is "environmental doctor." Ecologists are the scientists who evaluate ecosystems or wildlife/fish/forest populations, diagnose their problems, prescribe the cure, and sometimes treat the malady. "Ecology" derives from the Greek *oikos* (meaning "home" or "place to live"), and ecologists try to keep the natural environment—our place to live—healthy.

I also had a few lucky breaks along the way. One university wildlife professor encouraged me to study deer food habits on a remote hillside near Ithaca, New York; another let me fondle a Siberian tiger skin in his office; an Audubon tour leader gave me a pair of binoculars for my birthday and took me out to watch waterbirds in the Florida Keys; an older zoology instructor lent me fins and face mask and introduced me to the fairyland of a coral reef; a wildlife research unit leader at Colorado State University allowed me to conduct a survey of mule deer winter range high in the Rockies for two years. But the strongest impetus to persevere came from the eminent ornithologist who warned me that if I pursued a scientific career, I'd end up as a sad, neurotic old maid. Fightin' words!

At any rate, I've come to the conclusion that, with or without degrees, with or without lucky breaks, *anyone, anywhere, at any time, and at any level* can fight to conserve natural resources.

This book might be called a sequel to my earlier book, *Woodswoman,* since it tells what I do when I'm not at my Adirondack wilderness cabin. It tells what it's like to be a wildlife woman. Looking back over the past fifteen years, I see that my childhood dreams have come true. Despite my mother's early protests, I've camped all over the world. I do "live in the woods" and "watch wildlife,"—although it would be more accurate to say that I watch out for wildlife and wildlands.

If I could make a wish for the next fifteen years, it would be to help developing countries obtain more wildlands and create more national parks and wildlife reserves from them and train the people to be good stewards of their natural resources. This way I could leave a large, safe heritage for others who also dream of traveling to the wild places of our earth and seeing, studying, and conserving whatsoever things wild.

ASSIGNMENT: WILDLIFE

Giant Grebes and Big Waters

The *chocomil*—"fury of the demons"—was beginning early. Hot noonday air was rising from the Pacific coast to meet the main mountain mass of Guatemala. Ivory-headed, black-boweled thunderheads were building quickly above the lofty volcanoes. I took one more look through my binoculars at a jaunty black-and-white diving waterbird and clicked off my stopwatch. Strong winds were funneling among the three volcanoes which backdrop Lake Atitlán and whipping its cobalt waters to whitecaps. I started my ancient outboard engine and backed out of the reeds. Time to head back across the 1,200-foot-deep lake to one of the few safe anchorages on its precipitous shoreline. My rickety wooden rowboat chugged down the wind-ruffled Bay of Santiago Atitlán, passed a jagged shoal known as the Lion's Rocks, and headed out into the main body of water.

Suddenly, the chocomil caught the little craft in its grip. Here, in the middle of Lake Atitlán, over its deepest part, the water was angry blue and turbulent. Crosswinds collided and waves leaped every which way. The boat creaked and groaned as it bucked up and sidled down each crest. My straw hat had long since blown overboard and my jeans were soaking wet. The nearest land lay miles away and I had no other course than to plow on toward the village of Panajachel straight ahead.

Many people consider Lake Atitlán one of the most beautiful lakes in the world. However, as I knelt in the bottom of that old scow, clutching the motor handle, a tropical midday sun baking my head, I could well consider it one of the more dangerous. Its Indian name means "big water." At least a dozen people drown here each year, and bodies that go down can never be recovered at those depths. Hundreds of people succumb to severe sunburns and sunstroke at the 5,200-foot altitude.

Abruptly, the motor faltered, then died. A large wave broke over the transom, leaving the floorboards awash. Slowly my boat veered sideways and began rolling heavily in the troughs. More water spilled over the gunwales. My binoculars, tape recorder, and camera fell off the seats into the bilge water. I was only halfway across Atitlán. The southerly chocomil would get worse the closer I approached the north shore. Without power, I doubted that I could safely reach the small inn and dock where I moored my rented boat. Rowing or drifting, I would probably end up smashing against the rocky shoreline.

After pumping the gas tank, checking the fuel line, and repeatedly choking the motor, I got it to cough reluctantly. As soon as I was under way again, I lunged forward to retrieve my field gear and began bailing vigorously. The next hour was a struggle to keep the engine running, make my equipment safe, and stave off flooding. The trip which normally took twenty minutes one way on the satin-smooth surface at dawn, stretched into two and a half hours. I came close to sinking at least twice.

When I finally reached Panajachel and tied up, I was shaking from fright and exertion. No one met me. I stood for some moments on the shore, letting the volcanoes and lake stop rocking in my head. The wind and the brilliant sun began to dry my clothes. What was I doing risking my life like this? The boat's owner never should have let that craft and motor out in such condition to someone who knew as little about mechanics as I did. There had to be a better and safer way to do research—even on one of the rarest, oddest waterbirds in the world. Yet this old rowboat was all I could afford at present. Larger speedboats cost as much per day as I was paying per week.

I reflected further. Why was I really here at all? My professional reason for choosing Lake Atitlán was that it is the home of a strange waterbird, the giant pied-billed grebe, which is unable to fly, scarcely capable of walking, and lives nowhere else on earth. Few birds are truly flightless. Only two other grebes share this distinction—the short-winged grebe of Lake Titicaca, Bolivia, and the puna grebe of Lake Junin, Peru. All three species are confined to high-altitude lakes and show fascinating evolutionary changes. As far as I could find out in the library, the Atitlán grebe had never been photographed or written up beyond the briefest scientific description. What a find! It's unusual and challenging in this day and age to find a totally new wildlife subject to study. I reasoned that an illustrated article about the handsome bird with its neat white eye-ring and heavy striped beak might make interesting reading and pay my expenses in Guatemala for a month or two. Furthermore, the ecological aspects tickled my scientific curiosity and would augment my academic training and field experience in wildlife ecology.

On the personal side, the decision to go to Guatemala had been strictly intuitive. A pending divorce had left me on my own with little cash and no family to turn to. I had built and was living in a little log cabin in the Adirondacks, but now another harsh winter was approaching. I felt I should get out. I should go to Guatemala, spend a few weeks in this sunny, spectacular land where I had already conducted several wildlife tours with my naturalist ex-husband, Morgan. Ours were the first natural-history tours to operate outside of the United States. We had spent several winters searching for tropical birds, climbing Indian ruins, skin-diving on coral reefs, and photographing indigenous peoples. Of all the countries we had visited with our small, select groups, one stood out: Guatemala. And so I had come here a few days ago, speaking little Spanish, and knowing only three people in the town of Panajachel. Never did I imagine that one bird would have a profound impact on my life and that I would spend four years saving it from extinction.

The sun was beginning to burn my already peeling face and arms, so I walked down the beach toward the small room I was renting at Doña Rosa's house. Glumly I kicked at white pieces of pumice which had floated ashore. Rounding a hedge of hibiscus, I looked up and was startled to see a tall, lean, white-bearded man gazing out over the lake. He had on a faded blue cotton shirt, scuffed leather boots, and the red sash of a Basque. It was 1:30 P.M.—time for all good Guatemalans to be taking a siesta. I murmured, "*Buenas tardes, Señor.*"

He turned and tipped his wide straw sombrero politely. "*Buenas tardes,*" he replied in a deep voice. "*Malo, muy malo, el lago*" ("Bad, very bad, the lake"), he said; then he told me that his name was Don Emilio.

I stopped to introduce myself. The old man admitted he had been watching me battle my way across the lake, that it was particularly rough today. Then he sternly chastised me for being out in a boat alone at all. I shrugged helplessly.

"What can I do? The motor is very old and the owner does not care. I can't afford to rent a fancy speedboat from the big hotel."

The old Basque glared down the beach toward the inn and dock, and muttered something under his breath. "A señorita should not go out alone on this lake," he continued in a louder tone. "It is not safe. I have lived here for over seventy years since I came from Spain when I was a boy. I know how capricious Atitlán can be."

"But I want to go out every morning to study the *zambullidor*" (a diving duck-like bird)," I protested. "It's not possible to see them from the shore because of the thick reed beds, and there's no road around much of the lake. Besides, I don't know anyone who would enjoy sitting out there with me for six or seven hours in the sun without making noise. And, then, crossing back in the chocomil."

"I know, I know," Don Emilio said testily. "You are the crazy bird lady, the little *gringita* (Yankee girl) who goes barefoot and wears pigtails like an Indian woman and loves animals."

I grinned to myself at the description, marveling at the speed of small-town gossip.

"I will speak to my son about you," stated Don Emilio flatly. "Perhaps Armando can fix you a good boat and motor." Then he turned abruptly and strode back to the simple adobe-and-tile house which commanded a magnificent view of the aquamarine lake and its three symmetrical volcanoes. A child was crying inside. A short time later, I learned that Don Emilio had several children; the youngest had recently been born—on his eighty-second birthday. The tough Basque still rode up into the hills to supervise his properties where a few cattle were raised and coffee was grown.

Next morning I was lugging a full five-gallon gas tank and my knapsack down to the dock when a Land Rover pulled up beside me on the dirt road. Its driver was a short, muscular man with a deep tan and twinkling blue eyes. *"Ola,"* he greeted me, pearly white teeth flashing. "Do you want a ride, señorita?" He leaped out and offered his hand. "I'm Armando," he said courteously. "My father said you are having troubles with the boat and motor you are renting. Perhaps I can help?"

He took the gas tank from me and placed it in the back of the jeep, then chivalrously opened the door for me.

"Oh, thank you, yes," I answered, flustered by the sudden courtesy and kindness.

As we drove to the dock, I explained the erratic behavior of the motor and the leaks in the boat. Armando shook his head in disapproval.

"The owner is very wrong to let you go out in such a boat, señorita. The spark plugs are probably old and fouled, the carburetor dirty, and the tank full of water. You must not take these chances with the lake. You must not go out alone."

I was rapidly learning that most Latins are accustomed to go around in groups and are very protective toward women. They could not understand how or why I worked alone. I found this concern touching. Living among the rugged and independent people of the Adirondacks, I was quite used to fending for myself. Needless to say, though, I did need a reliable boat to continue daily observations and to carry out a complete census around Lake Atitlán's 70-mile shoreline. So I told Armando something about my work plan.

The number of these flightless birds was estimated by ornithologists Alexander Wetmore and Ludlow Griscom almost fifty years ago at a stable 200 or more. Theirs were the only estimates and descriptions ever made of the grebes. It was definitely time to renew the population count. And, besides, the grebes are superb divers and veritable submarines; I had already discovered just how hard it was to track them on the surface and almost impossible underwater. Local folklore proclaimed that grebes can duck a shotgun blast, stay submerged for half an hour, and swim underwater for half a mile. Another legend explained how grebes commit suicide if they are wounded or know they are being hunted. The Indians say that a bird dives down to a waterweed patch, grabs on, and drowns itself. Could any of these stories be true? I had to find out. Also I was intrigued by the deep, commanding lake itself. What animals and plants composed its aquatic ecosystem, its food chains?

After I explained all this to Armando, he offered to dig out an old outboard engine and refinish a boat he had in storage. The repairs would be free, he volunteered, because he had long wanted to get his boat back in service but had been too lazy. The rent would be $45 a month. That was considerably more than the dollar a day I had been paying and $5 more than I was paying for room and board for myself. It left me only $15 for gas and oil, from the $100 a month I lived on. However, I accepted eagerly because Armando agreed to stand behind his work and take care of any new repairs.

"Just give me a week or so," he said as he politely opened my door and deposited the gas tank on the dock.

The next week passed slowly. The old boat continued to break down. I learned how to strain gas, clean out the fuel tank, and change plugs. I now always carried a pair of pliers in my hip pocket for emergencies. Gradually I became accustomed to the rhythms of Lake Atitlán's weather and water. The November mornings would dawn crystal-clear, not a cloud in the sky. The mile-high lake was a perfect mirror reflecting the great green-and-gray volcanoes. Although Guatemala is only 14 degrees above the equator, I had to wear a wool jacket and windbreaker until the sun had dispelled the night's chill. By 11 o'clock, the first southerly breezes were wafting across the lake and fluffy clouds were forming. By noon, the chocomil started. If I left the Bay of Santiago Atitlán, where most grebes lived, by noon, I could beat the heavy waves and wind home. (There was also the *norte*, which blew in from the north, but I had yet to experience that.)

I visited Don Emilio one afternoon that week to ask him what he knew about my birds. We sat on his shady porch, slapping fleas which hopped onto our pants from his German shepherds. "Yes, yes," he reminisced, "the zambullidors were all around the lake when I was young. I could barely sleep on full-moon nights for their serenading. There must have been hundreds. But, lately, it seems there are not so many birds and not so many reeds. Too many people nowadays."

A census was imperative to see if the birds were really decreasing in number. But the new boat was not yet ready. Parts had to be sent for from Guatemala City, 75 miles away. So, trusting to luck, I began edging my way around the lake in the old rowboat, checking a new section of reeds and cattails early each morning while the lake was calm. When I finished my first census a week later, Armando was putting the final touches of paint on his boat. "Tomorrow," he said proudly, waving his brush, "you can begin using it. See! I named the boat *Xelaju,* the beautiful one, just for you, Anita."

I was charmed but also troubled. My census had yielded only 80 birds instead of the 200 to 300 the two ornithologists had found in the 1930s. I had stopped by every stretch of shoreline vegetation and scanned the water carefully. I'd kept track of every grebe, American coot, Florida gallinule, and duck seen. Something was wrong. I asked Armando what he thought.

"You should do it again—at night," he counseled. "With a full moon, quiet, no wind. It will be better. You may have missed some birds by day with the waves and wind."

"But how will I see them?" I asked, perplexed. "It's hard enough to spot them in sunlight."

"You won't. You'll hear them," he answered cryptically. "The grebes always call with the full moon. You can call back, then make sure how many answer and where each one is roosting."

I stared at Armando in admiration. It was a brilliant idea. My mind raced. If I used the tape recorder on which I noted my observations and had a real taped grebe call, I could be sure of getting better responses. Armando read my mind.

"You have the recorder. Why not spend the next few days trying to get a good call on tape? The moon will be full November twenty-fifth," he added, excitement in his voice. "I will go with you and help count the zambullidors."

Four nights later, Armando and I were steering toward a pitch-black bed of reeds in a remote corner of Lake Atitlán. A cold moon silhouetted the volcanic cones of Atitlán, Tolimán, and San Pedro. Their huge shadows were lacquered upon the quicksilver of the lake. Cutting the motor, I switched on the recorder and played the male grebe's call used to delineate and defend territory. At once, a challenging *caow, caow, caow-uh, caow-uh* responded near shore. Armando placed a dot on the map, and I checked off one adult male. Seconds later, a soft warbling duet floated on the air. The male had met his mate. I had often noted this greeting call between pairs during the early days of my observations. I checked off one adult female, then played the recording again. No more replies. Methodically, I waited another minute and repeated the process. Silence.

"That's all there are here," whispered Armando. "Let's go on." And he started the engine. We cruised past miles of steep, rocky shoreline, keeping well offshore until we reached another reed patch. This tall emergent vegetation is the only habitat where grebes and other waterbirds can roost, nest, and hide on the craggy, often-violent, mountain lake. Again we went through the precise routine—three plays, three waits, totaling five minutes per stop to give the grebes time to answer. Then we'd move 100 yards, or roughly the width of a pair's territory, and repeat the process until we ran out of reeds or cattails.

By 3 A.M. I was shivering from cold. Armando was yawning. "Shall we go back?" he asked. "Not yet," I pleaded. "It's such a perfect night, and we still have two hours of moon and darkness. I just wish I could get warm."

"Let's go to the hot springs," he suggested. "That will warm you up fast."

"Hot springs?" I was puzzled. "In the lake?"

"Yes, sulfur springs that bubble up from the bottom. We can soak in them a while. You'll feel terrific afterward."

He pointed the boat toward a jagged escarpment and eased close to shore. The rank odor of sulfur fumes invaded my nose. Armando threw an anchor overboard and pulled off his jacket. "I wore my bathing suit, just in case," he said courteously. "I'll swim in and find the spot. You wait here." With an almost splashless dive, he plunged into the black lake. I shuddered. How could he stand the cold? How could I? In a couple of minutes his voice echoed back from the cliffside and I could hear him splashing along the edge. After about five minutes he called to me.

"Here they are, Anita. There's a little rock wall protecting the springs from the main lake. It's like a bathtub. The water is as hot as anything. Come on in."

I couldn't disappoint the companion who was being such a help in my work. On the other hand, I had never done a crazier thing in my life—swim through a cold lake 1,200 feet deep in the moonlight at 3 A.M. to reach a hot sulfur spring with a Guatemalan man I scarcely knew. Stripping to my cotton shirt and underwear, I slid over the side, gasping with shock. Although Atitlán stays about 72 degrees F year-round, I was already too chilled to feel anything but colder. A few swift strokes and I was next to Armando and grasping my way over the low wall.

"Sit here," he commanded. Instantly I felt the upwelling of hot water. The springs were so well situated that I could sit on the pebbly lake bottom and be bathed in warm water right up to my neck. The view out across the lake was magnificent. I stopped shivering and relaxed, watching the corn-colored moon slowly set toward the wild western skyline. It was a magical night.

After an hour of steeping, both Armando and I were limp with muscle relaxation from the sulfur. We swam back to the boat, reviving at once in the cold water, scrambled in and dried ourselves briskly. Then we bundled back up to finish our census before first light.

Thus we canvassed the entire grebe population of Lake Atitlán. When we had finished, that dawn in late 1964, we had counted only 80 birds. The nighttime number matched too well with my daylight census to be a mistake. Something was definitely amiss in this beautiful, bizarre lake. How could the world's only population of these flightless birds have been cut by more than half? What was wrong with them or their habitat? I resolved to find out.

Binoculars and Shamans

I didn't know where to start. My graduate wildlife-management classes at Colorado State University had not prepared me for this. We had learned the theoretical techniques of studying and censusing wildlife populations, but here I was dealing with a total of 80 wary, endangered birds. Probably no one else around the lake realized they were declining, or cared. Most of the local inhabitants are Mayan Indians, living in twelve villages along the shoreline and seven others at higher elevations. They are totally engrossed in corn farming, light fishing, weaving, and cutting firewood. There were only a handful of *ladinos* (Guatemalans of mixed Spanish and Indian blood) who ran small shops and pensions; a smattering of retired Americans and Europeans loafing and sunning in Panajachel; and a few wealthy Guatemalans who spent their weekends at lovely chalets scattered about the lake. No large conservation or natural resource departments such as we know in the United States existed in this country. There were no departments of wildlife, forestry, or ecology in any of the universities. And so I had no one to turn to for advice, information, or ideas.

In the four weeks I had been at the lake, all my observations had been made from a small boat in open water or along the edge of the reeds. Those birds I had seen seemed healthy and non-suicidal. They spent their mornings preening and floating leisurely above the submerged beds of pondweed, stonewort, and other aquatic plants, or diving and fishing. The grebes I had timed during the past month never stayed underwater longer than 90 seconds. I had also determined that they traveled submerged no farther than 300 feet and at a top speed of about 5 miles per hour. Every bird that went down came back up. So much for all those quaint folk tales and exaggerations.

Furthermore, I had never seen a grebe fly. They did try to patter across the water, beating their wings valiantly, but never became airborne. Giant grebes have bodies two to three times as heavy as those of common pied-billed grebes, yet their wings are almost the same size. Also their wing bones are small and the pectoral muscles poorly developed, so it is impossible for them actually to fly.

That was the extent of my knowledge so far. Clearly I had to find out what went on inside the thick band of shoreline vegetation and underwater. I still should watch grebes courting, mating, and nesting; find a breeding platform, nest, eggs, and chicks. And what exactly did they eat? More important, what ate them? Something had reduced a seemingly stable group of 200 or more birds down to less than half. Were any other animals disappearing around the lake? The more I pondered these unanswered questions, the more important it seemed to obtain basic field data, and the more anxious I was to stay at Atitlán a little longer. I canceled my air ticket, renewed my tourist card, and paid another month's rent on room, boat, and motor.

With safer water transportation, I became bolder in my field work. I decided to visit each of the dozen shoreline villages and talk to the inhabitants about the birds. Since the Mayans live so close to nature, perhaps they would have some information and clues. My first visit was to Santiago Atitlán, the lake's largest town. I tied Armando's boat to the spindly dock and started walking up the long, cobblestone main street lined with thatched houses. Inquisitive eyes watched me from small dark windows; a hundred dogs barked at me. Several children—exact replicas of their parents, all dressed in purple-and-white striped pants with red-and-purple striped shirts for males, purple-and-white striped *huipiles* (blouses) with intricate embroidery and red-and-purple skirts for females—trailed behind me. Young Indian men lounged in doorways; their black slanted eyes discreetly examining my jeans, khaki shirt, straw sombrero, and pigtails. A woman in pants was unheard of in their culture; indeed, the fashion had not then arrived even in Guatemala City or anywhere else in Central America.

As I walked toward the main plaza, groups of young barefooted girls padded softly past me with clay water jugs on their heads. Their jet-black hair hung lustrous and thick well below their waists. From their giggles and glances, it was easy to see that going for water was a special event, not a chore. Probably it was the best time to do some surreptitious courting. No wonder the boys were standing around and not working.

Unable to speak the Mayan Tzutuhil dialect, and not knowing any one in the town of 15,000, I headed for the Mayor's office. Surely someone there would speak Spanish. In the low, stone building, I met the Secretary, a ladino from near Guatemala City, as he explained. This spare, dry-skinned man seemed only too pleased to stop writing his fine, feathery script into a huge record book and talk with me. I asked him if he knew anything about the grebes.

"The *what*?" he asked.

"The small duck that dives so well and lives in the reeds," I explained.

"Ah, the *poc*," he responded with a look of relief. "Of course I do."

Evidently he considered himself a source of information in this town, being bilingual and from a larger place.

"Poc is the Tzutuhil name," he explained, noting my bewilderment. "Many pocs live in the Bay of Santiago Atitlán. The Indians hunt them with slingshots and use them for food."

"They *eat* grebes?" I asked astonished. Fish-eating birds are usually rank and sinewy.

"Certainly," he replied calmly, "and ducks, coots, gallinules, herons, any meat they can get. Eating tortillas and black beans three times a day becomes monotonous. If they're smoked, the birds are not too bad," he said a trifle disdainfully. "The Indians sell them in the market for one *quetzal* (one dollar) each." He blinked his green eyes rapidly and added importantly, "Of course, it's against the law."

"What law?"

He unbent his cadaverous frame from the desk and pulled an enormous cardboard file box off a shelf. Sucking in his breath between yellowed teeth, he riffled through sheafs of official papers. Dust gently floated into the shafts of sunshine streaming in the open door.

"Here it is," declared the Secretary with a flourish. "President Miguel Ydigoras Fuentes, on 14 January 1959, decreed that hunting or molesting the pocs and other waterbirds at Lake Atitlán was prohibited. He imposed a fine of five to twenty-five dollars, plus confiscation of firearms, on anyone breaking the law."

I was overjoyed to discover a legal basis of protecting the grebes. "Are there any game wardens working here?" I asked.

"Game wardens?" asked the Secretary, as perplexed by that word as I had been by "poc."

"You know, conservation officers; uhhh, wildlife patrolmen; uhhh, vigilantes, sort of," I ended lamely, unable to think of the Spanish equivalent.

"Ah, *vigilantes!*" exclaimed the Secretary, sucking in his breath again and blinking his eyes several times. "There are no vigilantes for birds in Guatemala," he said decisively. "Maybe for trees, and certainly for people. Our *aguaciles* (Indian policemen) are sitting right outside this room."

I glanced outside and saw six handsome, robust Indian men holding long sticks sitting along a worn wooden bench.

"Can't they also watch out for animals," I asked naïvely, "if the law protects them?"

He shrugged. "No one cares, señorita."

"But there are only eighty pocs left. They are disappearing, and this is the only place on earth where they live. I don't know why this is happening, but I'd like to find out," I countered.

The Secretary gazed at me a moment, then said most courteously, but flatly, "And what difference does that make, señorita?"

His question so shocked me that I was tongue-tied, fumbling in my inadequate Spanish for an answer. Terms like "conservation conscience," "aesthetics," "genetic pool," "a scientific enigma," and "ethics," tumbled around my tongue. But somehow I sensed without speaking that this thin, self-important official would never understand these words or my firm belief that humans have an obligation to cherish the world's wildlife. We are their stewards.

Not only is it a question of moral responsibility, a reverence for life, an insistence on animal and plant rights as well as human rights; there are also solid practical reasons for saving wildlife and wildlands. We depend ultimately on finely tuned, well-functioning ecosystems for our biological sustenance. If certain species are eliminated, then the whole system becomes impoverished and disrupted. Eventually, our life-support systems are undermined.

Furthermore, hundreds of wild things in wild places have

proved to be of enormous value to people—rubber, vaccines, contraceptives, curare. Who's to say what will still be discovered of benefit to mankind? Nothing can be gained when a species is gone. Also, animals have had profound influences on our art, literature, sports, music, religion, and recreation. To wipe out any of them is a tragedy.

Haltingly, I tried to explain some of this to the Secretary. "Señor, human beings have done so much damage to the natural world that it's up to us to manage and protect the wild things that survive. It's our duty."

For a long moment he stared at me, then shook his head impatiently and said, "I'm sorry, but there is nothing to be done about the poc."

We shook hands and I left, crossing self-consciously in front of the row of silent policemen. Each aguacile wore his straight black hair cut in a trim line, sported a new hat, rubber-soled sandals, and a billy stick. I mumbled good morning. Then I walked over to the market, curious to see how many smoked grebes were for sale. Poaching appeared to be a possible reason for the birds' decline.

Under a high tin roof supported by tall posts, I found several women kneeling on the ground next to large wicker baskets filled with foodstuffs. Scarlet tomatoes, glistening white onions, pale-green cabbages, forest-green avocados, silvery minnows, buff-colored eggs, stubby little bananas and carrots, purple eggplants, freshwater crabs, burgundy beets, watermelons—a kaleidoscope of colors and smells. Among the women squatted children and laying hens. Enormous-eyed babies wrapped in *rebozos* (shawls) were slung over their mothers' backs or breasts, sleeping or suckling. A soft murmuring filled the air. Nowhere did I hear strident hawkers or discordant shoppers. It was a gentle market.

I hopscotched my way through the marketplace down narrow aisles, shopping casually as I went. For less than $2, I soon had enough fruit and vegetables to last my landlady Doña Rosa for a week. Nowhere did I see any smoked birds. After asking a few women in Spanish if they had any pocs for sale, I gave up. Each one shook her head in total confusion and looked away shyly. Finally a fat, toothless ladino lady pointed to a stall filled with spices and cereal grains. I reviewed the *canastas* (baskets) of tiny chili peppers, coarse salt, white rice, black beans, and golden corn kernels. Then looking up at a string of garlic cloves, I spied a lone leathery bird dangling from a piece of twine. If this was the extent of smoked birds for sale, then market hunting didn't seem to be a significant drain on the wild population.

It was almost lunchtime, so I walked back to my boat and ran it out toward some reed beds to watch grebes and eat at the same time. I tied up to some stalks and sprawled out on the bottom of the boat with only my head above the gunwales. To my surprise, an Indian canoe approached, rammed itself into the reeds, and the paddler started to slash at the vegetation. With every swing of his machete, he cut several stalks and laid them carefully in the bottom of his dugout. I continued eating and trying to figure out what he was doing. The man worked methodically and quickly. Within half an hour, he had completely cleared a patch about 8 feet square and his canoe was half full of reeds. Could he be cutting a landing pathway to shore or a mooring for his boat? But he showed no sign of slowing down, as he cut deeper and deeper into the stand. Then it dawned on me that he was harvesting reeds.

Suddenly a Florida gallinule dashed out and paddled away panic-stricken. That triggered my imagination. Supposing the man was cutting during the nesting season of these waterbirds. Would he chop up their nests, eggs, chicks? And what about right now? He was destroying the only available habitat for my grebes, plus a lot of other animals like the small fishes, crabs, frogs, aquatic insects, snails, and turtles which needed the reed and cattail beds for nurseries and homes.

The man should be stopped. The law prohibited killing and molesting waterbirds. I leaped up and called to him in Spanish. Startled, he almost dropped his machete. I shouted over an explanation why he should not cut the stalks, but he acted as if he understood nothing. I shook my head and arm vigorously and yelled, "No, no," in a severe way. He kept on slashing at the reeds. I didn't quite feel like approaching any closer with that gleaming machete between us. Maybe these people didn't like foreigners. For the first time at that idyllic lake, I felt an edge of apprehension. After all, I was in a strange country and largely ignorant of Mayan customs. Perhaps I should carry a machete or a gun, or at least take a dog along for protection. With these quickly sobering thoughts, I decided it was wisest to shut up and go for help. Pushing out of the reeds, I rushed back to Santiago Atitlán and went looking for my new friend the Secretary. He was taking a siesta in the large swivel chair behind his desk, his yellow teeth bared to the ceiling. He snored quietly.

Timidly I tapped on his desk and cleared my throat. He opened one green eye and closed his mouth. Then he struggled into a sitting position and half rose to say hello. Breathlessly I explained what I'd seen. "Can't you send your aguaciles to stop the man?" I pleaded.

"To the far side of the bay?" he asked incredulously. "To stop a man cutting reeds?" He blinked a few times, then regarded me sternly. "Unfortunately, señorita, I cannot. In the first place, the police have no boat. In the second place, it is too far to walk. The man would be gone by the time anyone got there. In the third place, there is no law against cutting reeds."

"But slashing them down destroys the grebes' home and nests," I argued. "And that's the same thing as *molesting* them."

"In the fourth place, señorita," the Secretary continued coolly, "these people use the reeds for *petates* (sleeping mats) and little seats. Several families earn part of their living cutting and weaving reeds."

"You mean those reed beds aren't *wild*?" I asked astonished.

"Oh, no," he said officiously. "Every stalk either belongs to, or is rented to, an Indian reed cutter. Lake Atitlán has the best reeds in all Guatemala."

A picture blossomed in my head of hundreds of Indians slashing down all the reed and cattail beds around the lake; of grebes and gallinules homeless; of fish and crabs hopelessly looking for spawning grounds. This must be the cause of the birds' decrease. The Secretary yawned and slouched back in his chair, clearly indicating that it was time for him to resume his siesta. I thanked him and walked back to the dock. The chocomil was in full force by now, but somehow it was not as bad as that first week. Besides, I was becoming adept at handling boats in it and I barely noticed the jumbled waves as I crossed back to Panajachel. I was too busy thinking of all I'd learned and trying to fit the new pieces of the puzzle together.

Approaching Don Emilio's beach, I saw two figures standing on the shore. I glanced at my watch—it was 3:30 P.M. I'd never returned so late before, and both Armando and his father were waiting for me, mildly worried about the delay. They helped to pull my boat out of the water and reached in to take out my gear. As I began blurting out the day's events I noticed that Armando was standing very still and looking at me in a peculiar way.

"Anita," he said, "where's your tape recorder, and your cameras, your binoculars?"

"Under the bow in my knapsack, as always," I answered, surprised at the question.

"They're not there," he replied quietly.

I looked at Armando in disbelief.

"Did you leave the boat alone at the dock in Santiago?"

I nodded.

"Well, that's it. Someone stole your things. You must always pay a boy a few centavos to watch the boat."

There was no way I could replace the invaluable field equipment short of great expense and a trip to Guatemala City, maybe even to Miami. "What will I do?" I began moaning, but already Armando was tugging the boat back into the water. Don Emilio let out a series of explosive swear words and pitched in to help his son who was wet to his thighs from the waves crashing on the beach. "Get in quick!" Armando barked at me. "We're going right over to Santiago Atitlán and report this. If we offer a reward and put out a *pregon* (town crier's proclamation) there's still a chance we can get your things back." With his usual direct logic, he explained, "Either the thief will go out by bus tomorrow at dawn to pawn the stuff in the city, or the knapsack is sitting in the hut of some poor Indian who has no idea what he has and no idea what to do with it. He's probably scared stiff and consulting a shaman right now."

Don Emilio gave us a final shove and we were turned and pounding our way into the chocomil. I was too upset to talk. Here I was going for the third time the same day to this Indian village, making a nuisance of myself. Word was certainly going to spread about the "crazy bird lady." However, Armando handled everything smoothly. He immediately went into a huddle with the Secretary and the Mayor and soon persuaded them to call out the aguaciles and make a pregon. Since so few villagers read or write, or possess phones, radios, or television sets, the pregon was the best way to inform the populace about imperative or urgent matters. Armando advised them to say that the lady scientist from the States had lost very valuable things from her boat. They were of no use to anyone in the town, and only good for watching the pocs. She would pay a $5 reward to get them back.

I whispered to Armando that I would gladly pay $25, but he hushed me with a frown. "These people earn only a hundred to three hundred dollars a year," he explained softly, "so five dollars is a whole week's pay. Just keep quiet and let me manage this, Anita. Please!"

Twilight was coming on and the wind had dropped. A haze of pine-wood smoke hung over the village, as aromatic as incense. It came from hundreds of small cooking fires in the huts where Mayan women were preparing the evening meal of tortillas and black beans. Hundreds of dogs were barking as men and small boys came home from the cornfields, hoes and *morales* (string bags) over their shoulders. An incandescent pink glow flared up behind Volcano San Pedro, clear as claret. To the east, the first stars were already showing pale and winking in the darkening sky. The village quieted as suppertime began. Then I heard the low muffled boom of a drum. It reverberated eerily against the stone huts and cobblestone streets. Armando and I stepped out of the Secretary's office and saw the Indian policemen parading across the empty plaza. One beat on a large wooden drum and another carried a flaming *ocote* (pine heartwood) torch. The third was the crier. At every street and path intersection, they stopped and shouted out the news. Giant shadows were thrown against the walls, and here and there the torchlight caught a glint of eyes peeking out now-shuttered windows.

"If anyone finds a bag with black and silver metal things in it, bring it to the office of the *alcalde* (mayor). These things are of no value. The *gringa* who watches the poc will pay five quetzals to get them back," Armando translated for me.

The staccato Indian dialect sounded strange to my ears, and the night seemed very dark. My chances of ever seeing that equipment seemed slim indeed. Once again I asked myself what I was doing in a place like this? Why was I getting so wrapped up in the survival of a bird? How many other wildlife ecologists were off in other foreign lands trying to save a species? Then I caught Armando's blue eyes smiling at me.

"Do not worry, Anita," he said gently. "You'll get your things back. We must wait now. Be patient. Are you hungry?"

"Oh, yes." I suddenly realized how long the day had been—I had started out at 5 in the morning and it was now 7:30 P.M.—and how little lunch I'd eaten because of the Indian reed cutter.

"Come. We'll find a *tienda* (little store) that's still open."

We strolled along a dirt path and then toward a huge Catholic church until we saw candles flickering behind an open window. Armando tapped confidently on the window countertop with a coin. "*Muy buenas noches,*" he called. "Doña Carmela?"

A chubby ladino shopkeeper in a cheap housedress appeared with plastic curlers in her hair. How different she looked from the neat, statuesque Indian women.

"*Si, Señor? Que quiere?*" ("What do you want?") She looked up and then said, "Ah, it's you, Armando, how are you?"

Armando didn't ask her for food; he asked about her health, her son's health, the health of her nephew and his children. Meanwhile my stomach rumbled. Finally, I heard tantalizing words—*tortillas, frijoles, huevos revueltos, chiles, cerveza.* The woman nodded cheerfully and disappeared into the back of her store. Armando turned to me and thoughtfully laid his jacket over my shoulders.

"Are you cold, Anita? Come in and let's drink a beer." He pushed open a door and led me to some straight chairs inside the tiny shop. The woman came back with two lukewarm bottles of beer, some salt, and a dish of dried miniature river shrimp.

"*Momentito.*" She smiled and bustled away.

I sat down gratefully, suddenly exhausted. In those days I had not yet learned to drink anything alcoholic, but the warm beer tasted good. I was so hungry that I munched the shrimp despite thoughts of amoebas and hepatitis hovering in the back of my mind. Who knew what river they came from and how polluted the water might be since most Indian farmers use night soil (human urine, feces, and manure) on their fields and defecate on the ground.

Then stacks of hot tortillas, a plate of purple-brown beans, two plates of scrambled eggs fried in butter, and fiery little peppers arrived and drove all fears from my mind. Armando had ordered well from Doña Carmela's kitchen. We ate ravenously by candlelight, listening to the pregon's drum growing fainter. The aguaciles must have given their announcement to the whole town by now.

As soon as we finished eating, we hurried back to the Secretary's office. No knapsack, no news. My heart dropped. Without my tools I couldn't make observations, take photographs for a story, record field notes and bird calls, or make another census. I might have to stop the work and go home to New York State. The thought was chilling. It was almost 10 o'clock and the pregon was over. The village was asleep. The policemen were shuffling away. The Secretary yawned unceremoniously. There was nothing to do but return to Panajachel, for there were no overnight accommodations in Santiago. Armando left the five quetzal reward and an extra quetzal to telegraph him in Panajachel in case the bag turned up next day. Then we stumbled back toward the dock—there hadn't been time to bring flashlights. On top of that, I was tipsy from the beer. Armando had to support me down the cobblestones. Once I bumped into a dog, then almost walked off the dock. Armando chuckled and sat me firmly in the front seat with a warning not to fall out of the boat. He started the motor and we headed slowly across the immense sheet of water toward the twinkling lights of Panajachel. At that time, it was the only town around Atitlán with electricity. The other towns had generators which worked until 10 P.M. for street lights, and the people used candles and kerosene lanterns. Tiny torches flickered like fireflies along the dark shoreline. They were the pinewood flares of crab fishermen who crabbed with long gigs at night. Huge stars glowed in a velvet-black sky. All three volcanoes wore haloes of silvery clouds. A cool breeze was crinkling the lake with star-shimmer like beaten silver. I felt a nip in the air.

"A norte," said Armando, cocking his head back toward the volcano tops. "See those caps on the peaks? Tomorrow we'll have a strong north wind."

I didn't care what it did tomorrow because I couldn't go out on the lake without equipment. Depressed, I hardly spoke or looked at the magnificent night. At the beach, I dejectedly helped Armando pull out the boat. As we tugged and hauled, a dark object rolled down from under the bow. Armando grabbed it and held it up under the star glow. Then he shouted with joy. "Here are your things, Anita!"

I couldn't believe my ears. But, yes, he was holding my

prized knapsack. Inside were the binoculars, the tape recorder, and two cameras. "But, but how . . ." I stuttered.

"A shaman," said Armando sagely. "He must have advised the person who took your things to put them back and ward off an evil eye. Most shamans are very wise men and healers. It's the *brujas* (evil witch doctors) who are mischievous or malicious with their advice."

I stared at him incredulously. "Shamans, brujas. Baloney, Armando. Someone just wanted the reward."

"No," said Armando with great conviction. "No one will take your money. For one thing, this would make the whole village suspect that person of having stolen your things in the first place. For another, it is better to be rid of such mysterious objects. You must realize that these Indians have never seen a camera except in the hands of tourists. And then they will not permit their pictures to be taken unless they are paid. Otherwise the camera may steal their soul. They've never looked through binoculars and cannot comprehend that things look several times bigger, or smaller, depending on which way you look through. A tape recorder would be sheer magic to them. It might be stealing their voice." Giving me a bear hug, he said exuberantly, "Oh, yes, it was a smart shaman."

"It was just dumb luck," I muttered pompously. How could I, a university product, with a bachelor's and a master's degree in science, believe that poppycock? Things worked by cause and effect, rationally and logically, steps *a*, *b*, *c*, and *d*. Little did I know how much I was yet to learn from this experience, nor did I imagine that soon I too would admit needing the help of a shaman.

A Discovery

Next morning, as Armando had predicted, the norte was blowing so hard that I dared not go out. At Panajachel, on the leeward shore, it was calm, but across near Santiago Atitlán and all along that south shoreline, waves were 4 and 5 feet high. When I tried to launch my boat, Don Emilio ran down and sternly ordered me to stay home.

"These nortes are the tail end of your snowstorms in the States," he explained. "They usually blow for two or three days. Then it's back to the chocomil. Be patient, Anita."

How could I be patient? I was burning to find out why the grebes had decreased in number. I still had not got a single good picture for my article. And there was much more to learn about the birds' behavior and life history. But the old Basque was adamant. He tugged at the clove of garlic he always hung around his neck to ward off heart trouble and motioned me toward his house. "Come in," he ordered. "I want to show you something."

Resigned, I followed him. On the porch, he began fiddling with knobs and decorations on a 7-foot-tall wooden chest. Suddenly a door swung smoothly open from the ornate front. It was an old Spanish safe! Inside stood several tin cans of Nestlé's dried milk. Curious now, I watched him take out four tins and pry off their tops. Then he spilled cascade upon cascade of green jade stones onto the rough plank table top. I was stunned. Dozens of authentic carved faces, ear plugs, nose plugs, drilled necklace pieces and plain polished pieces lay in disarray before me—a treasure trove of Mayan artifacts.

"Where did you get them?" I asked in amazement.

The wiry old gentleman gestured vaguely toward the north and said, "Oh, up in the mountains when I ride to my farms."

More than ever I was impressed by this indomitable character. Don Emilio was in a talkative mood that morning. He picked out various ornaments with his gnarled hands and told me about their uses. Finding him in such a good humor, I settled back and decided to question him further about the grebes. So far, he was the best informant I'd found around the lake.

"Do you think that reed cutting is killing off the pocs?"

"Heavens, no," he replied. "The Indians have been using the *tul* (reeds) for centuries. They know they have to leave some standing so as to maintain the crop. There's sure to be some shelter for the birds most of the time."

"How many people cut reeds?" I asked. "Maybe they're beginning to overharvest."

"Probably sixty or seventy men. They dry the stalks in the sun for at least ten days, or until they are tawny brown. Then the old men and women weave them into petates and seats. All the villages together probably make a thousand mats a year. Remember, Anita, the Mayans don't use beds and have very few chairs. The reed industry is important here at Atitlán."

"Then what is making the pocs disappear, Don Emilio?"

"The rich hunters!" he roared. "*Picaros* (rascals)! They shoot dozens of ducks and leave them lying in the water. Most Indians don't have enough meat as it is, yet these hunters don't even retrieve the dead birds."

Hunters! I'd never thought of *that*. "But there's a law," I began.

"*Caramba!*" snorted the old Basque, scooping handfuls of jade back into a Nestlé can. "They do not care about any laws. Who even knows about it? Besides they have fast boats and motors and good guns. Who can stop them? *Muy hodida!*"

I didn't know what the old man's swear words meant, but I did think about his explanation.

"How many sportsmen are there?" I asked him.

"Who knows?" he shrugged. "More every year. Many who own vacation homes here are probably shooting birds on the weekends."

This fresh lead sent me off on a new tack of investigation. As soon as the norte blew itself out, I once again circled the entire shoreline of Lake Atitlán, counting weekend homes and looking for hunters. I found thirty-two chalets perched on the shoreline. Most owners had cut away the reeds and cattails to build docks, walls, beaches, and boathouses, and to enhance the spectacular views. Yet this didn't seem to have had much of an impact on the total environment so far. Only once on a Sunday did I hear distant shots, but they came from shore. The next weekend I saw a trio of hunters shooting from a smart fiberglass boat with a 75-horsepower motor. There was no way I could reach them with my 25-horsepower one. These were the only sportsmen I saw. The lake was not exactly crawling with hunters, as Don Emilio had led me to believe. Perhaps I should look still further for the explanation for the pocs' decline.

One morning I left Panajachel at 5:30 and sped across the flat calm lake. The sky was incredibly clear and the air chilly. I cruised past the Lion's Rocks to the far end of Santiago Atitlán bay and tied up in the same reeds where I'd been working the last few days. Opening a thermos of fragrant Guatemalan coffee, I pulled out my notebook and binoculars and prepared for another interesting day of observations. The pair of grebes that occupied this stretch of reeds was less wary than others because Indian women came to wash their clothes in the shallows and therefore these two were used to humans. The male seemed strongly territorial today, braying out his weird call every few minutes. I made fresh recordings and christened the vocalization, the "gulping cow call." One of the nice facets of being the first person to study a species is creating your own names for calls and displays. This gave me a little thrill of scientific discovery.

Yesterday, the male had executed a marvelous dive right in front of the reeds. He literally folded in the middle and sank without a ripple; his tail and head last to disappear. I immediately named this the "accordion alarm dive" because he appeared nervous about something and was obviously going off on a reconnaissance. A moment later he emerged, cautiously surveying the surroundings with only his eyes and nostrils above water like the periscope of a submarine. One needed a quick eye and a calm surface to pick up this maneuver. No wonder local folk thought the birds could stay down for half an hour.

Soon the male appeared 20 feet from the female who was fishing 100 feet offshore. Suddenly both birds hunched down in the water and puffed up their feathers. They faced each other and dived toward each other. They popped up barely 3 feet apart, now sleek and trim, and swam rapidly together. A collision seemed so imminent that I almost cried out. Then at the last second, both birds veered sideways and swam in parallel. They gave a sweet warbling call in duet. It was the same one I'd heard in the reeds on our moonlight census—the one I'd named the "hen-flicker recognition call." Altogether, this was a courtship display of surpassing grace.

I began to wonder if the reproductive season was starting. It was early March and so far I had not seen any signs of courting, nest building, or caring for chicks. As I watched, the male abruptly left his mate and performed still another new action. He faced the edge of his reed patch and bent his neck forward. The top of his crown was flattened until it almost made a straight line with the top of his beak. The neck crooked into a strong S-curve. The bird's throat swelled like a cobra's and the black patch showed clearly. The whole effect was that of a coiled snake about to strike. This metaphor flashed into my mind so I called it the "snake-head aggressive display."

Another grebe in the same posture was advancing upon my male. He approached like an angry black torpedo, body half-submerged and powerful feet kicking back a wake. A small ripple preceded the interloper like a miniature tidal wave. The two met near the reeds. They pivoted back to back, side to side, beak to beak. They looked for all the world like two street dogs bridling on a corner. Every few minutes the birds repeated this behavior along a straight line. I could almost imagine their territorial border as a barbed-wire fence between them.

Suddenly both males rose up in the water, beating their small wings mightily and each slashing at the other's neck and head. After five minutes of tussling, the invader retreated ignominiously, diving for safety in the reed bed. My victorious male swam slowly "home," kicking water back in spurts. This was the strongest show of aggression and territorial defense I'd seen. Surely a reproductive mood must have been gripping them.

As I sat glued to my seat for this spectacle, the sun had risen and warmed the day. Indians' canoes were crossing the bay bound for the cornfields on San Pedro's slopes. Each boat held a man standing near the bow paddling, one or two small boys, and a mongrel dog. (If I stretched my imagination just a bit, the canoeists looked like businessmen crossing Grand Central Station from morning trains to their offices.) The Mayan men would spend their day out on the volcano-side, tending the life-sustaining cornfields and cutting firewood. Back home, the women would be grinding corn kernels into a *masa* (dough), patting out tortillas, and baking dozens upon dozens of these nutritious corn cakes over open fires. Thus man, woman, and corn made an endless, dependent circle in the Mayan culture.

As I waited for more surprises from the pocs, two dark shapes slowly bobbed toward me at the edge of the submerged water plants. Puzzled, I trained my glasses on them. A pipe stuck up from each basket-ball-sized object. They came closer and I heard the sound of air being sucked in. Skin divers! The two paid no attention to me, and swam into a narrow channel cut through the reeds toward shore and waded out. From their belts hung two of the biggest bass I'd ever seen. One must have weighed close to 15 pounds; the other, 12. The two ladino men stood shivering and flailing their arms for warmth. As they began taking off their fins and masks, I rowed in to talk to them.

"*Buenas días*," I greeted the divers. "Where did you get such beautiful fish?"

They smiled and one held out the larger bass for inspection. It had to be all of 15 pounds, deep-bellied and fat. The huge jaws and mouth curved downward balefully: a largemouth bass.

"The *lobina negra* (black bass) were put in Lake Atitlán a couple of years ago," they explained. "Now the fish are all over. The big ones hide in the deep-water weeds. It's easy to spear them there. We take them to Guatemala City to sell in the fish markets."

Then it hit me. Bass might be the culprits! These carnivorous fish are notorious predators of aquatic life, including young waterbirds. They've been known to snatch red-wing blackbirds, warblers, and swallows who fly too close to the water. I had little doubt that bass of this size could also gobble up native populations of tiny minnows, crabs, frogs, and aquatic insects. As a scientist, though, I had to prove my suspicions. How, I was not sure.

As I was talking to the divers, a short, swarthy young man in highly polished boots sauntered down the path beneath dense coffee trees and walked toward us. He looked quite dapper in pressed khaki pants, a green windbreaker, and wide sombrero. The divers greeted him warmly. "*Óla, Don Roberto, que tal?*" I introduced myself and learned that he was the owner of the property around the end of the bay. Beside his *finca* (farm), a high escarpment held in the lake like a natural dam between the two great volcanic masses. Beyond this escarpment, the land slanted steeply down to the Pacific lowlands, more than 3,000 feet below. The topography was impressive. From Volcano Atitlán's grim summit at 11,600 feet, to the Pacific Ocean 50 miles away, Lake Atitlán sat like a teacup balanced on a wide saucer. Thanks to the rich volcanic soil and abundant rainfall here, all of Roberto's land was enormously fertile. Though small compared to most, his finca won prize after prize for its high-quality coffee. He invited me and the divers to his modest farmhouse. His widowed mother, with whom he lived, served us demitasses of his finest essence of coffee. Delicious.

The divers were eager to be off with their fresh fish, but Roberto asked me to stay and see his farm. Judging from the efficiently run farm, I could tell that Roberto was an intelligent, well-organized young man. As we walked through the plantation, I told him why I was there.

"You mean I've had pocs living right in front of my farm all these years and I never saw them act like you did?" he asked amazed.

"Yes, indeed," I said, smiling. "There's a lot more to learn about, too. For example, no one's ever seen their nests, eggs, or chicks."

"Then why not look in my reed beds for them?" offered Roberto enthusiastically. "There must be ten or twenty birds here. I always hear them calling in March and April and I've seen young birds in May and June. I'll help you look."

I was happy to find another person taking an interest in my work and the waterbirds.

"You must stay for lunch today," he insisted. "Make my farm your home. Work here as much as you like."

This generous invitation greatly helped my field work. Here, I could zero in on established birds and have a safe place to anchor and keep things. The offer had come just in time. By late March, the grebes were definitely courting and nest building.

Both male and female would carry bits of rotten reed stalks, old cattail fronds, and fresh-water plants into the reed beds. They would twitter their little duet and other amorous-sounding calls from deep within these stands. Evidently they performed all their intimacies in this hidden realm on low, barely floating platforms, for I never saw grebes copulating in the open water. Somehow I must enter their private world.

One morning I decided to force my way into those 18-foot-tall reeds, among the tallest and densest in the world. I had quite an audience. Roberto waited well offshore in his own boat, clad in his shiny boots and a bathing suit. He directed me toward the area where we most often heard the birds. One of his Indian laborers paddled me to the edge of the reeds and stood by in case I needed to be pulled out. Roberto's mother stood on the shore under a parasol, sending shrill warnings. "Be careful of the water scorpions," she called. "Watch out for water snakes." A little later, "Do you have your hat on, Anita? The sun is very strong today." Meanwhile several Indian women who were washing clothes stopped and stared.

My trip to the center of that 50-foot-wide reed bed was not easy. I began by swimming through the tallest stalks in 10 feet of water, over a sand bottom. Then I began shoving through matted patches of reeds and sinking into oozy mud. The shallower it got, the more murky it became. Fetid odors bubbled up around me. I paused often to look for snakes and scorpions. My heart was pounding in apprehension. The sun beat down on my wet head.

"*Mas al derecho*" ("More to the right")! yelled Roberto. "*Ahora diez pies adelante*" ("Now ten feet forward").

I was practically crawling on my belly over flattened masses of dead reeds, perspiring, itching, tired. The water here was only 4 feet deep. I could see no more than 3 feet in any direction. Suddenly, there lay the nest, anchored to a few reed stalks. It measured about 18 inches in diameter with only 3 inches protruding above the water's surface. The rest hung down in a 3-foot funnel. Its very shape and size assured stability in the strong winds and waves of Atitlán. A more flimsy nest, such as the common pied-billed grebe normally builds, would have soon disintegrated. This nest would easily overflow a bushel basket and weigh 100 pounds. How did two little birds, less than 2 pounds each, manage such a feat?

After making mental notes and measurements, I began backing out of the reeds. Few, if any, predators—except man and his machete—could ever reach this inner sanctum. I remembered what Dr. Arthur A. Allen, the famed ornithologist and bird photographer, had written about the common grebes: "Few birds offer greater difficulties to the ornithologist who would become familiar with their lives." How often would I repeat these words to myself in the next two years of field work at the lake.

I left Roberto's finca that afternoon. My ride home took longer than that first frightening trip in the heavy chocomil, for a new strong norte had begun and was hurling 5-foot waves against the south shores. Armando's boat shuddered from the onslaught. Again I lost a hat overboard. Throughout the pounding crossing, a merciless sun beat down. I beached the boat about 5 o'clock and took my usual scolding from Don Emilio about being out so long alone.

I walked back to my room feeling queasy and light-headed. I couldn't eat the supper Doña Rosa had prepared for me as usual. All I wanted was cool liquids. At 8 P.M. Armando came by. He took one look at me and called to Doña Rosa for a thermometer. It showed 102 degrees F. By 9 P.M., it was 103 and I was shaking with chills. The good woman coaxed me to bed, lit a fire on the hearth, and wrapped three thick Guatemalan blankets around me. Armando sat on the edge of the bed, putting cold compresses on my head, while the landlady hurried back and forth with camomile tea, aspirin, coconut butter, and ice. Despite the deep tan I'd acquired in the last 14 weeks, 8 hours of exposure to that brilliant sun, mostly without a hat, plus the physical exertion in the reeds, had caused a sunstroke. On top of that, the foul mud had provoked a skin rash.

Three rough days passed. The village doctor was away. Armando and Doña Rosa nursed me, sitting patiently by my bed for hours, telling stories and chatting. After my fever went down, Armando warned me not to go out in the sun for several days. He was right. Waves of faintness would wash over me at the slightest exertion and bright light made my head pound.

I was able to use this enforced quiet time, however, to study up on the bass. I made a trip to Guatemala City to the Ministry of Agriculture.

Here was an entire nation just a little smaller than the State of New York (42,042 versus 49,576 square miles) whose total department of conservation/natural resources in 1965 consisted of four people. None was trained specifically in natural-resource management, nor did any have a degree higher than a B.S. in agronomy or fishery biology. They had perhaps three cars, three boats, a few fish hatcheries, and one tiny lab at their disposal; salaries were pitifully low; there were no official, uniformed, game wardens. New York State, in comparison, had a department of over 2,000 people, a few with doctorates. There were hundreds of vehicles, uniforms, firearms, and even a couple of planes and helicopters; salaries were respectable; and roughly 250 game wardens worked out of several regional offices.

This comparison is in no way meant to imply that Guatemala or any other Central American country was slack or backward but rather to illustrate that the state of the art of conservation and the science of natural-resource management were very new, unsophisticated, and of low priority in government programs. However, the comparison did spur me to devote my energies and concerns to helping this developing nation.

Guatemala's four-man Division of Fauna was mostly involved with fisheries. From them, I learned that Pan American Airways and the Panajachel Tourist Board had introduced largemouth bass and crappies into Lake Atitlán in 1958, and again in 1960, in an effort to improve sport fishing and attract more tourists. This was done without any experimentation or research and against the recommendations of a U.S. Fish and Wildlife Service technician.

During 1958–1963, the bass underwent a population explosion which deranged Lake Atitlán's aquatic ecosystem. Small native fishes, frogs, crabs, and snails appeared to be decreasing rapidly, while reports of huge bass came in from skin divers and sport fishermen. Little wonder the grebes were declining, I reasoned. The fish- and crab-eating birds were faced with unexpected competition from these introduced carnivores. Their usual sources of food were disappearing. Grebes, especially juveniles, were vulnerable and might starve unless they were able to adapt to eating largemouth bass—*if* they could catch and swallow them. It was a little like trying to change the Mayans' centuries-old diet of corn, beans, and fish to hot dogs, Cokes, and banana splits. How could one expect them to thrive?

Even more ominous, I felt, was the fact that these exotic giant fish could easily prey on the young of grebes, ducks, gallinules, coots, and other waterbirds. A tiny chick would just make a tasty hors d'oeuvre.

At last everything made sense. The unwise introduction of largemouth bass was the mysterious limiting factor I had been looking for. I felt certain that the situation was critical. At the rate the giant pied-billed grebes of Lake Atitlán were waning, they would probably be extinct in 5 to 10 years. Whereas it had taken 10,000 years of evolution to turn this once-migratory species into a flightless freak, an Ice Age relic, a scientific curiosity, it could be wiped out in a split second of that time span.

This discovery was not exactly what I'd come to Guatemala to find. But now that I had stumbled onto the life-and-death drama, what should I do about it?

Operation Protection of the Poc

I waited a month to recover from the sunstroke before venturing out on field work again. During that time, I did a lot of thinking. Daily I sermonized to Armando, Doña Rosa, and Don Emilio that it was morally unjust for the grebes to be exterminated by human mismanagement. I quoted Sir Peter Scott, a popular water fowl artist and conservationist of international fame, who wrote so eloquently, "Only natural cataclysmic forces have the right to take lives or force into extinction any wild creature."

It was Armando who finally said, "Well, why don't you save the poc?"

"Who, me?" was my startled reaction.

"Why not?" he shot back.

Armando's questions spurred me on to conceive of a conservation campaign. Aldo Leopold, the father of game management as practiced in the United States and Canada, had written that wildlife could be restored by the creative use of the same tools which had heretofore destroyed it, that land (and water) could be managed skillfully to produce sustained crops of wild animals. Controls were necessary—over hunting, predators, disease, food, the habitat—and the establishment of refuges was important, too. Maybe if I could learn more about the factors affecting the birds, I could save them, or possibly bring them back to their original numbers. Ultimately, it would take an ambitious program of enforcement, public education, habitat management, and future protection. I even thought of a name—"Operation Protection of the Poc"—as I was dreaming and scheming. (Later we condensed this to "Operation Protection Poc.")

Hesitantly, I sent letters to World Wildlife Fund International and the International Council for Bird Preservation, explaining the critical situation, giving my census figures, and asking for funds to carry on research. I desperately needed money for the boat, gas and oil, tapes, film, and developing. To my delight, I received a small grant, enough to carry me along another three or four months. Surely in that space of time I would arrive at a sound scientific plan for the management and preservation of the pocs.

The first morning I went back to the Bay of Santiago Atitlán, I felt heady with anticipation. What would I find in the nest of my favorite pair? Armando came along in case I had a relapse or was unable to force my way through the reeds. We both wore wet suits, sneakers, and bandanas to protect ourselves from mud rashes and sun. As we approached the nest site, I spotted four small eggs, stained a mottled brown from the damp vegetation. They lay in the nest's depression, only inches above the lake level. The frightened female had apparently deserted moments ago and had covered her treasures with a light blanket of pondweed and the roots of water hyacinth. To one side, peeking out from this protective camouflage, was a chick!

I let out a hoot of exultation. At last! Unwrapping my camera from several plastic bags, I snapped the first portrait ever taken of a baby Atitlán grebe. From nearby, the mother made a low, reassuring sound to her youngster—"poc-poc-poc." Now I knew where the Indian name came from. The tiny puffball stared at us audaciously. It was striped in black and white from beak to tail like a little zebra, with touches of scarlet-orange at the lores and the base of the bill. It looked only hours old, yet it was dry, fluffy, and cheeping constantly. Again, its mother called, "poc-poc." Abruptly, the little creature waddled to the nest edge and dived. Utterly astonished, we watched it swim underwater a few inches, pop to the surface like a cork, and start swimming toward its parent.

She, meanwhile, hurried through the reeds to meet it. Armando and I glimpsed her making a half turn, depressing her rear in the water, and waiting as the precocious baby scrambled onto her back. Slowly she disappeared into the reeds with the chick cuddled down out of sight between her wings. We didn't dare frighten the female further. After a few more pictures, we quietly maneuvered our way back to the boat.

Armando and I heaved ourselves in and joyfully exchanged a hug. What a glorious discovery! Excitedly, we discussed the next step. Obviously, I wanted to spend the next several weeks observing this family and recording the care of the young, food habits, feeding and diving, their growth and age of independence. Also, Armando thought it very important to find out about the bass and their predations on Atitlán's animal life. We devised a plan to survey the local Indian fishermen and crabmen and ladino scuba divers. By asking them simple nonbiased questions, perhaps I could find out what environmental effects were taking place. There seemed no other way to get this information unless a fishery biologist suddenly materialized. I also decided to check on the diet of bass by buying or collecting big fish whenever possible and dissecting their intestines.

Armando quickly had it all figured out. "You can ask the fishermen questions on the way to the bay, then make your observations, and pick up bass and examine them whenever you get a chance." All in all, an ambitious plan!

Slowly, it paid off in a wealth of information. During April, May, and June, I found twenty more nests, each with two to five eggs, never more. This is roughly half the number laid by the common pied-billed grebe, the closest cousin of the Atitlán grebe. Both parents care for the young. The chicks' insistent begging and cheeping wins them a steady supply of water insects, hellgrammites, crustaceans, and tiny fish, captured by the adults and brought to the nest during the chicks' first days of life. After the young become stronger, they fare forth with their parents to learn to dive and fish in open water. At this time, the mated pair randomly divides its brood in two and each one takes care of a group. Fish caught by adults now are either torn apart on the surface and pieces offered to the babies or are given to them whole.

Once I saw a parent present a small bass to a fledgling twenty-five times. Struggle as it might, the little bird could not swallow the thick, spiny fish. Certainly, young bass are different in shape and size from the original native small minnows and cyprinids that grebes were accustomed to catching and eating. Finally the chick gave up. This started me wondering if perhaps those zillions of young bass in the lake were not even available to my birds.

I discovered that young grebes go off on their own at roughly 10 to 12 weeks. Until then, their plumage is changing from the initial zebra-striping to all coffee-brown in color with no stripes, while the lores fade to ivory. As soon as they are independent, these juveniles skulk along the shoreline, hiding from other birds and strange objects. Probably their drab coloration protects them during this critical period of their lives when they have no home range or territory. Hand-examining three juveniles, I found them so malnourished and emaciated that they seemed half dead. Again I wondered if these somewhat older birds also were having trouble catching and eating the exotic bass. My research showed that chick survival during the first 12 weeks of life was roughly half the brood, or 47 percent; not too bad. But, thereafter, the mortality rate during the juvenile period increased greatly.

At this same time, my survey of fishermen was progressing nicely. My Spanish, though still poor, was improving rapidly. The Indians seemed to understand. Day by day I asked them these few simple questions: How are the fish here? Many? Few? Like always? How are the crabs? How many years ago did the fish and crabs change? Why? Where do you find the crabs now? What kinds of fish do you catch now? What's the largest bass you've seen?

I interviewed fifty-six men, 15 to 60 years old. Over 80 percent told me they have been catching fewer fish and crabs over the last 3 to 6 years. (This tied in perfectly with the bass introductions of 1958 and 1960.) Half the fishermen blamed the bass for ruining their fishery—a native observation I found remarkably astute. The fishermen said they used to catch 20 to 50 pounds of tiny fish a day in stick corrals and wicker traps baited with corn. This had been the traditional way of fishing at Atitlán for centuries, and fish had been a major source of protein for the people. These days they caught only 2 to 4 pounds of bass and crappies, with small hooks and string lines, as they had no experience in using nets. And now the villagers seldom had fish to eat, thus little protein other than that in corn and beans.

Likewise, the crab fishermen told a tale of woe. In the old days, a night's catch yielded five dozen to six dozen crabs, captured by torchlight along the shoreline with gigs or baited strings, in depths up to 75 feet. Now the nightly catch averaged only a dozen or two dozen crabs taken from water as deep as 300 feet.

The largest bass anyone had caught weighed 25 pounds, with the average 9 pounds. Every indication was that these fish grew from fingerlings to near-record-growth adults in only 27 months.

An incredible situation became clear from this survey data: The huge bass population in Lake Atitlán was virtually untouched and untouchable by the local Indians because they had neither means nor skill to catch them. With incomes of $100 to $300 per family per year, they could not afford fancy fishing tackle or rods, nor could they buy or operate gill nets. And they could not spear the bass because most Indians do not know how to swim, and, besides, they could not afford the diving equipment. The more I dug around for facts, the more complicated the ecological puzzle became. The intricate "web of life" and dependency of one life form on another was becoming more and more tangled.

By the greatest coincidence, a team of medical anthropologists, Ph.D. candidates at Stanford University, came to Santiago Atitlán. They were studying the villagers' health and discovered a protein deficiency, largely attributable to the decline in fish and crabs. Formerly, most of the people had eaten fish two or three times a week, and some 100 to 125 families had once relied heavily on fishing for income. Now (1965–1968) only 30 to 50 fishermen were engaged in this labor and fish was eaten only a few times a month.

The ecological ramifications of the bass introduction were staggering. Within 5 years the poc population had tumbled from well over 200 birds to 80. The native human population (50,000 Mayans estimated around the lake) was suffering in health and economy. The small fishes, crabs, snails, frogs, and insects had plummeted as the voracious bass burgeoned. Of the eighteen species of fish present in Lake Atitlán in the 1950s, only five were now showing up in the bass intestines. I never found any grebe chicks ingested, though I looked carefully. However, there was no doubt in my mind that bass were preying on waterbird young. But given a lake the scope of Atitlán, a prey population as small as the grebes, and so many predatory bass, it was not surprising that I could not verify this hypothesis.

What could a lone foreign female wildlife ecologist do? I racked my brains that spring of 1965. There seemed no way to rid the huge lake of bass. It would take 1,000 train loads of rotenone to poison them out of Atitlán. Besides, such a dose would exterminate all the remaining native fishes and hence boomerang back on the grebes and the Indians. I finally had to admit that the largemouth bass could not be feasibly controlled. They were there to stay until Nature forced a change. Most likely, in a few years they would eat themselves out of house and home and then crash. Meanwhile, it seemed inevitable that the giant grebes were doomed to follow the passenger pigeons and great auks into oblivion unless I could come up with a solution.

Besides my worry about that, another strange problem had been growing. All during the spring, I had found odd bits of debris on or around my boat. Sometimes it was a circle of stones, or a burned-out candle stub. Other times it was bits of sticks in peculiar patterns, or bird feathers. I figured that Don Emilio's children were playing beside the boat on the beach. Then one morning it became obvious that the signs were not being left by children: a pile of human feces sat right on the bow with burned matches sticking in it. I turned white. It reminded me of stories of pins stuck in dolls and of black magic. Somebody did not like me. These were warning signs.

I could think of no one I'd harmed or insulted. Frightened, I ran to look for Armando. He was painting a car, and as soon as I had babbled out the story, he closed his paint can and accompanied me to the beach. With a strong oath, he picked up the foul mess in the paint rag he carried in his hip pocket and flung it into the bushes. With narrowed eyes, he said, "This is the work of a *bruja*. Someone has asked for a spell to be brought against you."

"But who can it be?" I wailed.

"I don't know. You must think hard," counseled Armando. "Think of anyone you might have spoken to unkindly, or not paid enough money to, or something like that. Could it be one of the fishermen you interviewed? Or one who sold you a bass?"

I shook my head slowly.

"Don't worry," he said. "I will take you to a very good shaman who lives up in the hills behind Sololá. Jesús will tell us what to do." He patted my shoulder reassuringly. "Tell me anything else that happens, but don't tell another soul."

A chill crept up my back. The whole thing was bizarre. It certainly sounded like black magic, but I could not believe in that. Yet, having no alternative, I decided to fight fire with fire. For the next few days I slept fitfully and jumped at the smallest noise. Nothing more showed up at the boat or beach.

Then one cloudy afternoon as I was reading on Doña Rosa's porch, Armando came for me in his Land Rover. "Let's go," he said seriously. "I got word to Jesús by telegraph and runner. He's expecting us. We'll get to the bottom of this."

For two hours we wound our way higher and higher into the pine-clad mountains north of the lake. The air became colder and my breath shorter. Unlike the sharp, powerful young volcanoes rimming the southern edge of the lake, these hills were old and rounded, of completely different geological origin. We must have been close to 9,000 feet up when Armando nosed the Land Rover onto a narrow dirt track and headed down into a deep valley. Dust billowed up under the floor boards and I tried not to look out at the sheer dropoff beside us. We reached the valley floor about sunset. A colonial church dominated the landscape like a huge mother hen. Scattered out around the valley and the slopes like chicks were small Indian huts. No matter which way they went, every inhabitant had to pass right by the church door to enter or leave this *aldea* (tiny town). We parked in front of the steps. Armando pulled out a cigarette and said soothingly, "He will be here soon." As the sun set, golden shafts slipped through banks of threatening rainclouds and gilded the church and the pine forests. A few Indian men plodded by, bent and weary, bound for home after a hard day in the fields. Then one man came striding toward us, tall, erect, confident. Bronze skin was taut over high cheekbones and a narrow aquiline nose. The firmly chiseled mouth and deep-set black eyes gave an impression of Mayan royalty. More than the sheer perfection of features was the look of calmness and kindness. I'd never seen such bearing in my life. Here was a man with power and compassion.

Armando introduced me to the shaman, who bowed ever so slightly, then beckoned us up a footpath leading to two adobe huts. Puffing at that altitude, I followed the men, stumbling in the fading light. The Indian stopped briefly at the first hut, then led us into the second. He produced three tiny straight-backed chairs and invited us to sit down. I stared about the gloomy room. A statue of the Virgin Mary and the Christ Child stood on a small table surrounded by candles and fake flowers. Strings of herbs hung from the rafters. Hand-carved wooden masks were nailed to the walls. The whole room seemed to be a mixture of Catholicism and paganism. The shaman said nothing as he tied a red cotton square of heavy cloth with black tassels around his head. He looked more regal than ever. Now he produced three cloth bags. He lit one candle and placed it in the center of the third chair. Lighting it, he crossed himself, then lighted others, and offered prayers to the Virgin Mary. I was bemused. How could all this ritual help me?

Coming back to us, the shaman knelt by the empty chair and fixed me with his penetrating eyes. "What is your trouble?"

Awkwardly I described what I'd found around my boat. Armando helped out with his colorful, flowing Spanish. The shaman listened gravely. He began to recite the Lord's Prayer, mixed up with Indian and Latin words. Nothing else broke the silence in that tiny room. He switched into a strange language, probably Cakchiquel (another Mayan dialect), and continued his prayerlike recitation, swaying slightly. It was a moving experience. Gradually a curious sensation of peace stole through my body. I also had the sense of a force in that room—something vibrant and harmonious. My scientific training was making me coolly observe, classify, analyze the entire ceremony; at the same time, my emotional being was thrilling to whatever was happening around us. I slipped into a trancelike lethargy, barely moving. Jesús opened the three bags which contained polished stones of many colors. He began mixing the pebbles and dividing them into three piles. As he kneaded the stones with strong brown hands, he chanted an Indian invocation. Three times he formed three piles of stones. Then he shoved them all into one pile, blew out the candle, and sat back on his heels. Except for the flickering lights beside the Virgin, we were in deep shadow.

A long silence passed before he spoke softly. "There is a workman who does not like you. He works for you, but you do not pay him enough money. He wants more. Also he does not understand the strange objects you carry back and forth to your boat. He is afraid of them and thinks they are black magic. However, he is not dangerous. He will not harm you. He only wants to scare you away from there. You must act as if nothing has happened. Go on with your work. Pay him nothing and ignore him. It will pass."

Another long silence. My trance was deepening. Then Jesús suddenly stood up and started chatting with Armando. The atmosphere changed immediately. The force was gone. I glanced at my watch. An hour had flown by, and it was pitch-dark. Armando put a few cigarettes, coins, and fresh candles on the ceremonial chair and got up. "Come, Anita," he murmured quietly.

I was still mystified, as we bounced back out of the valley, but Armando neatly cleared up the problem. "It's Doña Rosa's house-boy," he said. "He's the only person who could possibly expect payment for anything. He probably feels you should give him money for cleaning your room and bringing in firewood. He doesn't realize that you pay rent to Doña Rosa. And, of course, she probably doesn't give him anything over and above his salary for the extra work he does in your room."

"How much does he earn a month?" I asked.

"About thirty-five dollars."

I gasped and immediately offered to pay him more separately.

"Remember what Jesús told you!" cautioned Armando. "I'll speak to Doña Rosa. Don't do anything. You can't interfere with the way she runs her home."

The black magic stopped, although I'm sure the houseboy never got a raise. Once again I could put all my energies to trying to understand Lake Atitlán's complicated ecosystem and to devise a way to save the grebes. However, the rainy season was here in earnest. I couldn't do much on the lake, so I decided to return to the United States. I wanted to make some contacts toward getting additional grants from conservation organizations (and finalize my divorce). Also, I figured that with all the information I was gather-ing, I might possibly apply for a Ph.D. program in wildlife ecology at Cornell University and use the Guatemalan research as my thesis topic. Most important, my little log cabin in the Adirondacks beckoned. The one or two months I had planned to be away had stretched into seven. It was nearly June, time to go home, take stock, and plan for Operation Protection of the Poc.

With real regrets, I said good-bye to Doña Rosa, Don Emilio and his children, Roberto and his mother—all the people, dogs, kids, I'd come to know and love. Armando drove me to the airport.

"You'll come back, Anita?" he asked, his twinkling blue eyes sad and a little misty for once.

"Of course, Armando, of course," I promised, grasping his calloused, capable hands in mine. "I can't thank you enough for all you've done. It's just that I have to go back and do a lot of things to straighten out my life. But you've helped me find some new goals here in Guatemala. Yes, I'll be back."

A Christmas Tree and Poison Pills

By November 1965 I had returned to Lake Atitlán. The time away had been profitable. I received new grants from the World Wildlife Fund, Smithsonian Institution, and National Geographic Society, and with my divorce final I was receiving small but regular alimony payments. I had been accepted and enrolled in a doctoral program at Cornell, remaining *in absentia* the first year. My new graduate committee of professors seemed enthusiastic about my research and suggested many useful approaches and techniques. *National Geographic* magazine had shown an interest in a story, provided I could provide some good photographs. Armed with these welcome and helpful expressions of interest, I felt ready to tackle the conservation campaign.

What a happy day when I gazed again at the immense sapphire lake with its backdrop of volcanoes; when I received bear hugs of welcome from Armando and his father; when I saw my boat freshly painted and another red-and-white one beside it. I promptly announced the good news about the grants.

"Now I'll go to the Guatemalan government and try to get matching funds so we can really start Operation Protection Poc. We may not be able to whip the bass problem, but we can control and manage the other things that grebes need to survive," I cried joyfully.

Armando drove me to Guatemala City to meet the Minister of Agriculture, an active agronomist. Since he had a vacation home on Lake Atitlán, he would surely be interested in helping to save the grebes. In my halting Spanish, I glowingly described the perky birds, their courtship, the zebra-striped chicks. Then I explained the problems of poaching, sport hunting, reed cutting, and competition and predation from the introduced bass. In my enthusiasm, I inserted a few of Don Emilio's swear words.

"*La lobina negra es muy hodida*" ("The black bass is very ———"), I exclaimed. I still don't know the exact translation, but the word certainly had a galvanizing effect. The elegant Minister stared at me in astonishment and, turning red, roared with laughter. I was so flustered that it took a while to find courage to continue. Shyly now, I explained the idea of Operation Protection Poc, including the need for matching funds from the government and official help in the form of a game warden, a patrol boat, gas, and oil.

"After all," I heard myself saying artfully, "this rare bird is found only in this beautiful country. Guatemalans should be proud of it. People will come from all over the world to see and photograph the unique species, and that will bring in more money from tourism."

Unwittingly, I had hit on the two points most persuasive to the Latin mentality—national pride and economics. Any more esoteric arguments about aesthetics, genetics, morality, and ecology would have been wasted.

The Minister of Agriculture picked up the phone, called his Division of Fauna, and ordered the people there to hire a vigilante and provide a boat for his use. He would base himself at Santiago

Atitlán. Armando and I exchanged triumphant glances. As far as we knew, this was the first official conservation enforcement officer to be appointed in Guatemala.

"The Division will send up fifty gallons of gas a month," added the Minister, making a note on his pad.

Now Armando sagely suggested that the Minister appoint Roberto, me, and himself as honorary wardens. "One of us is always on or near the lake," he explained, "and we all have boats. We could help your warden at no extra cost."

"Splendid," said the Minister. "I'll see to official papers for you three."

"Why don't I buy uniforms and design an emblem?" I offered. "We'll have more authority that way, and it's good publicity." I guessed that if no game wardens had ever been appointed, the government would have no uniforms.

"Excellent idea," agreed the Minister, jotting down more notes.

"Is there any way that reed cutting could be controlled?" I ventured. "At least during the nesting season?"

"I'm not sure," answered the Minister. "It might be rather involved, but I'll have the Division of Fauna call a meeting of Indian reed cutters, and you can all try to come to some agreement. Possibly we can then work it into a law."

Armando and I left his office giddy with victory. I couldn't imagine ever getting such ready results with an important official in the United States. I was becoming aware that being a blond female scientist from a foreign country helped more than it hindered. I was not considered a threat, whereas a male conservationist from abroad, unless most diplomatic, might have raised subconscious feelings of competition or inadequacy on the part of his less experienced local colleagues. Indeed, I had occasion to meet a few foreign scientists during my stay and was generally disturbed by their condescending airs. For my part, I tried to be humble and always treated the Guatemalan officials with the greatest respect and courtesy. Thus I usually got what I asked for.

Before we left Guatemala City, we also paid a visit to Jorge Ibarra, Director of the Museum of Natural History. This ardent conservationist was at that time virtually a lone voice crying out for preservation of natural resources. We invited him to come to Lake

Atitlán and talk to the schoolchildren in each of the twelve villages on the lake. They had never even heard the word conservation, let alone known about our poc campaign. We hoped that the children would then tell their parents about our work. This way the greatest number of people could be reached. Mr. Ibarra was most enthusiastic and made three conservation education trips to the lake over the next two years.

The native Indians have habitually viewed animals as sources of food or labor, with the exception of the quetzal, a Central American bird which is Guatemala's national symbol. This bird has been honored and revered in Mayan culture and art for centuries. However, the quetzal is not uniquely Guatemalan, whereas the giant grebe is. If Mr. Ibarra could present the Indians with the idea that the poc was a unique tourist attraction and a worthy motif for their arts and crafts—both extra sources of income in their impoverished lives—our conservation efforts might succeed among these illiterate people.

Meanwhile, the new warden moved to Santiago Atitlán with a small aluminum boat a 1 motor. While we were waiting for our uniforms and emblems to arrive from the United States before we made official visits to the villages, I spent some time acquainting him with the lake, its dangers, and the grebes themselves. Then I went to Roberto's finca to tell him the good news. Roberto was surprised and excited by his honorary appointment and our success with the Minister. He was eager to participate in the upcoming reed cutters' meeting. Being a fine farmer, he seemed to feel that reeds and cattails should be harvested and cared for in the same way that he managed his coffee crop. Indeed, at this meeting, Roberto showed himself something of a statesman. I adamantly proposed that all aquatic vegetation be protected so as to preserve the grebes' only habitat in this time of crisis. The cutters vehemently opposed this plan. To a man, they declared it would cause economic hardship and spoil their cottage industry. For three days, brightly clad Indians, city-suited government personnel, Armando, Roberto, and I stubbornly debated.

Finally, Roberto devised the solution that was eventually accepted. The whole experience taught me a lot about the art of compromise and about balancing wildlife and human values.

The proposal was that reed cutting be curtailed annually between May 1 and August 15, in order to protect grebe families. No eggs or nests could be taken or molested at any time. The rest of the year was left open for cutting; however, every man must cut only half his plot at one time. That way, we would be assured of always having some waterbird habitat standing. This compromise satisfied everyone, especially since few reeds could be cut during the prohibited period, anyway, as it was part of the rainy season. This astute plan became a Presidential law in 1968.

Meanwhile, the Christmas season was approaching. I was happy and busy. Operation Protection Poc was getting into full swing. I divided the days among patrol work en route to the Bay of Santiago Atitlán, observations, making copious notes for my thesis, and photographing the wily pocs. Only this last task was failing, because of my insufficient expertise and equipment. I wrote to *National Geographic* magazine asking for advice and a good telephoto lens.

The day before Christmas a strong norte blew up, so I decided to stay home. The game warden would be on patrol over the holidays. Doña Rosa and I decorated her house and prepared special dishes for the guests she would receive after midnight mass. Highland Guatemala was at its loveliest. Poinsettias bloomed in brilliant red and cream. Calla lilies, which practically grew wild, stood statuesquely in the swales. The sky was the deepest, purest blue I'd ever seen, with fleecy white clouds sailing by on the north wind. No rain fell here during the height of the dry season. Panajachel's 400-year-old church had been strewn with fragrant pine needles, and banks of lilies and poinsettias adorned the silver and gold altar. A childlike sense of excitement filled me.

"Ah, if we only had a *pinabeta* (balsam fir) for a Christmas tree," sighed Doña Rosa as she sat down to survey her handiwork late that afternoon.

"Can't I get you one in the market?" I offered.

"I doubt it. They come from high, high up in the mountains."

"I'll bet Armando would know where to find one," I teased, as he appeared in the doorway laden with gifts.

Always anxious to help, he immediately volunteered to look for a tree. "Come on, Anita," he coaxed. "Come help me. Get Doña Rosa's ax, while I find some rope."

Moments later we were in his Land Rover heading toward the

mountains. Twilight was falling when we reached the first fir forests at about 9,000 feet. The norte was blowing harder up here and a deep roaring filled our ears as the wind soughed through the branches. It was bitterly cold, and I shivered as we got out of the jeep. A thousand stars seemed strung on the black branches and an almost-full moon was rising above the mountain tops. Armando grabbed the ax, the big flashlight, and the extra jacket he always carried. "Here, Anita, put this on," he said gently, holding out the coat.

We started walking into the forest, probing the beam from tree to tree. I followed Armando blindly, having no sense of direction save for the cold wind in my face.

"Here's a beauty," he exclaimed, shining the light on a symmetrical fir. He chopped it down neatly and quickly, then together we dragged it back to the jeep and tied it to the roof top. Once our shoulders met, and I felt a deep tremor run through my body—half cold, half yearning for this good-natured, active man who'd been such a great help and field companion over the past year.

Back in the jeep, I told myself to stop acting like a romantic teenager. I was probably imagining things. In fact, I had wondered if Armando liked Doña Rosa, because he spent a lot of time at her house. For sure, I said to myself, he wouldn't be interested in me, fifteen years his junior.

Doña Rosa was delighted with her tree. Dexterously, she propped it up by the fireplace and decorated it. By 11:45 P.M. it was finished and we walked to the church. The pungent scent of copal incense filled the air as Indian elders swung their smoking pots back and forth on the front steps. Fireworks burst in the starry sky, illuminating the entire village. Solemn Indian women and men dressed in their best, with babies on their backs and youngsters in hand, shuffled barefoot into the pews.

Inside, a hundred candles bathed the old stone building in a mellow glow. The priest, a handsome, silvery-haired, burly Basque, stood reverently beside the altar. He wore immaculate robes with hand-embroidered white lace. The service began. Throughout it, babies cried, firecrackers popped, Indians chanted ancient pagan words on the front steps while the priest droned ancient Latin ones inside. It was a dazzling experience.

When the last chant and prayer were over, Doña Rosa, Armando, and I filed solemnly down the aisle, jammed among Indians, ladinos, tourists, and retired folk. I glanced at Armando's face. It was unusually reflective and content. As I looked, his strong hand took mine for an instant and squeezed it tenderly. He turned his head a fraction and smiled. Suddenly, I knew that the wave of love I'd felt in the fir forest had been mutual.

Doña Rosa's home sparkled with festivity. Dozens of friends dropped in, bringing gifts. We ate, drank, and talked till 4 A.M. It was the jolliest Christmas Eve I had ever spent. When the last guest had gone and we'd cleared up the dishes and wrapping paper, the pink flush of Christmas Day was already in the sky. Doña Rosa had fallen asleep on the sofa and was snoring gently, the victim of too many *ron popos* (rum eggnogs). Armando and I looked at each other and then he gathered me passionately into his arms. At first I held back. Following my divorce, I had vowed never to fall in love again. Yet a longing for companionship and affection had secretly stayed alive. Now it welled up so strongly that I was overcome. On Christmas Day dawn in Guatemala, I allowed myself to be loved again.

The norte blew for two more days giving Armando and me time to talk and get to know each other as we had not done before. We spent the days on Don Emilio's beach, working on the boats, sunbathing, and chatting with the old man. Our outward demeanor was as it had always been—discreet, respectful, attentive—but inwardly we were a whirl of emotions. Needs long suppressed boiled to the surface. Yet my professional commitment to the work and my new career was equally strong. I wasn't sure how to combine them, or what would happen in the long run. All day I kept looking longingly across the wind-blown lake, wishing Armando and I could be out in the boat. As if reading my mind, he suddenly sat up on the sand and said, "Come on, Anita, let's go out and check up a little. We won't go over to the south side—it's too rough. Maybe we'll meet the game warden patrolling and give him a hand." I jumped up gladly and helped him ready the boat. We waved goodbye to Don Emilio, who shook his finger at us angrily. He never dared scold his son because he knew Armando could take care of himself in any situation. For two hours we cruised slowly along the western shoreline, reveling in the bright-blue, blustery day, our freedom, our new-born affection. Then, Armando made a sudden turn in front of the village of San Juan de la Laguna. He stared intently into a reed bed. Gunning the motor, he headed the boat straight for it and crashed into the reeds. As we careened through the thick vegetation, I saw what had caught his eye. The game warden's boat was tied up snugly, and he was inside fast asleep.

"*Hodida!*" muttered Armando, his face flushed with anger. "*Qué pasa, hombre?*" he shouted rudely. The poor fellow almost jumped overboard in fright.

"Ah, Don Armando, *qué tal?*" he gasped.

It was all too evident. The man was afraid of the norte and had decided to hide out rather than work. Shamefaced, he confided that he barely knew how to swim and had never experienced wind and waters like these. I suddenly felt sorry for him, recalling my own fears those first days with the chocomil. But not so Armando. He was furious at both the warden and the officials who had hired him. "Imagine sending such a coward to Atitlán for this job," he fumed.

That warden's job was short-lived. Not only did he shirk his duties except on the calmest mornings, but we soon heard he was selling his unused government gas and oil for an extra profit in the villages. Such shenanigans appalled me, but Armando merely shrugged and said, "*Tipico* (typical)."

Then came another setback. Four of us—Armando, Roberto, the chief of the Division of Fauna, and I—set out in our spanking-new khaki-green outfits with yellow-and-black arm patches to speak to the mayor and secretary in each of the surrounding villages. We were planning to explain the laws against killing waterbirds and cutting reeds and ask that a pregon be sent out to relay this news. Only in this way could we expect to inform and get compliance from the Indians. And I very much wanted to involve these local inhabitants in Operation Poc for their own benefit.

But at our first stop, the tiny fishing hamlet of Santa Catarina, we were met with stares of horror. To my chagrin, I learned that the color I'd chosen for our uniforms was exactly that worn by insurgent guerrillas who were terrorizing local inhabitants in the Sierra de las Minas mountains. Word of their activities had spread through Guatemala like wildfire, and the illiterate Indians imagined the guerrillas had now come to Lake Atitlán.

After carefully explaining our positions and posting poc conservation signs on the mayor's office walls and the schoolhouse, we rushed back to Panajachel. Armando saved the day. He had us buy wide, colorful Indian sashes and new sombreros, and pin our emblems on our shirt fronts in plain view. Surely guerrillas would not wear these things. Then we started out again somewhat more confidently—and we were never arrested or shot at.

Still another unexpected event occurred. A cable from *National Geographic* announced the arrival of a photographer who would try to get pictures of the pocs for the magazine. I was elated. Even if all my attempts had failed, David G. Allen, son of Dr. Arthur A. Allen, and like his father an expert bird photographer, would certainly succeed.

Armando and I dropped everything else to assist David. And succeed he did! Painstakingly, David obtained superb photographs of grebes—males, females, chicks, nests, and various displays, plus reed cutters and our patrol work. My story and David's pictures eventually appeared in both National Geographic Society's *School Bulletin* (now called *World*) and *Audubon* magazine, though not in *National Geographic* magazine itself. As it turned out, that opportunity was pre-empted by another Guatemalan bird—the legendary quetzal. On David's last day in Guatemala, we accompanied him on his good-bye round of thanks. We were sitting in Jorge Ibarra's museum office when the phone rang. A clipped British voice informed Mr. Ibarra that he had just found a pair of quetzals nesting within yards of a jeep trail on his large finca. Mr. Ibarra was ecstatic. In all his years as Guatemala's leading naturalist, he had never seen a live quetzal, much less a breeding pair. He whispered the good news to us as he wrote down directions.

"Ask him if he'd mind having a photographer come to his place?" asked David shrewdly.

"Not at all," Jorge replied after a moment. "You are cordially invited."

David's last words to me as he boarded the plane in Guatemala City were: "Don't be surprised, Anne, if we come back here sometime to work on the quetzal."

"Oh, David," I said, smiling, "you're a dreamer. Besides I have all I can do with my grebes."

Then I hurried back to the lake to pick up where I'd left off. A new census showed that the number of grebes was still depressed. Bass continued to flourish. I decided that if the wild grebe population was doomed to disappear, we could at least keep a small nucleus alive in a refuge. A sanctuary would save a genetic pool for science. Then we might still manage to release birds back into the lake sometime in the future, if conditions improved.

I began discussions with the Ministry about constructing a small wildlife reserve and visitors' center. Armando had suggested we use a tiny bay on the south shore, called Xecamuc. Here, colonial Spanish priests had raised fish two to three centuries before. A low rock wall had once separated the lake from the hatchery. Now it lay in ruins underwater, but, he pointed out, it would provide a ready-made foundation for the refuge border.

To satisfy my scientific curiosity and natural thriftiness, however, I visited every other lake in Guatemala in hopes that we might find an alternative place to transfer grebes for safekeeping. Unfortunately, none we explored had Atitlán's unique set of characteristics, nor were many of them free of potentially damaging bass or human disturbance. I already knew the difficulties involved in transplanting wild animals and of establishing a viable breeding population in a new habitat. Usually 95 attempts out of 100 fail. It became obvious that only the grebes' natural home would serve them as a sanctuary.

With financial help from the government, we hired local workmen to rebuild the wall, leaving a 12-foot screened opening for fresh-water exchange with the main lake. Next we edged the shoreline with fencing and put a large sign, GIANT GREBE REFUGE, on the rocks facing the lake. On a small knoll above the bay, I worked with Armando and Roberto to design and build a rustic visitors' center. Inside we displayed photographs (courtesy of *National Geographic*), primitive Indian paintings and hand-woven rugs depicting grebes, a pair of binoculars, a large guest book.

Meanwhile, I was impressed by the interest Roberto was showing in our project. He showed up almost every day in his old wooden boat, helping to supervise the Indian masons and laborers, most of whom he knew personally. He had a good grasp of construction and carpentry. Suddenly an idea struck me. Why not ask Roberto to be the new official year-round warden? He had lived most of his adult life on the lake and did not fear the nortes and chocomils. He drove to Santiago daily for mail and supplies, and he knew the Mayor and the Secretary. Armando agreed that it was a fine choice.

One day, very tactfully, I proposed the idea to Roberto and his mother. I was almost afraid of insulting him. Here in Guatemala, as in other Central American nations, a game warden earned only about $100 a month. Government boats and motors were not always reliable. The shipments of gas and oil sometimes came late or not at all. There were no fringe benefits. At that time, developing countries were simply not ready for large-scale conservation efforts. I mentally compared what I was offering Roberto with what a conservation officer would receive in New York State. The latter's salary would begin at roughly $8000–$10,000 per year, and his equipment would include a boat and motor, a snowmobile, patrol car or jeep, uniforms, boots, and a revolver. His fringe benefits would include retirement and medical benefits and vacation pay. I feared that Roberto would never accept the job and Operation Protection Poc would have to make do with misfits, or that it would lack adequate enforcement altogether.

Roberto and his mother listened impassively. They exchanged a flurry of rapid Spanish, too fast for me to grasp. Then Roberto accepted the idea with a big smile. His mother was proud. Her son would be important. The job was prestigious. I immediately wrote to the Minister, requesting that he hire Roberto. In the same mail, I sent a grant application to World Wildlife Fund for a safe fiberglass boat and a 50-horsepower engine to use in patrol work. Within a few weeks, Roberto had his official appointment; within a few months, he was cruising Lake Atitlán in a brand-new motorboat.

Everything was moving ahead so well that a problem seemed inevitable. When it did occur, it happened in the most outlandish fashion imaginable.

Once the refuge and visitors' center were finished, the next step was to remove existing bass from the little bay before stocking it with small native fishes for the captive grebes. Through my professors at Cornell, I learned that the Wisconsin Alumni Research Foundation was testing a new fish toxicant called antimycin and needed a tropical body of water to try out its effectiveness in warm, eutrophic waters. I wrote the Foundation at once, requesting that they carry out their experiment in the grebe refuge. The test could be carefully controlled here and might solve our problems of eliminating the bass. A technician was flown down with 20 pounds of the "miracle" chemical. Supposedly, antimycin affected only cold-blooded vertebrates by interfering with the respiratory mechanism in the gills; mammals, birds, and humans would not be harmed. In warm waters, the chemical lost its effectiveness within 48 hours, a decided advantage over rotenone which sometimes lasted for weeks or months. That meant we could safely restock the refuge in a week's time. Nevertheless, antimycin was still experimental. Therefore, we made a strict decision to let no one touch or eat any fish poisoned at the refuge. In addition, we hung a stout length of heavy canvas across the screened opening of the reserve to prevent any contamination in the main lake.

Division of Fauna personnel were invited, and together we broadcast the harmless-looking white powder over the 2 acres of water in the refuge. Indian canoers waited to collect every stunned fish that floated to the surface so we could measure, weigh, identify, and record the data. This way, the Foundation could find out which species and what sizes succumbed first to the poison, and I could obtain a clear idea of the composition of Atitlán's resident fish population.

Within an hour, the first bass started floating to the surface, gasping. Then came mojarras, crappies, guapotes, and a few small cyprinids. Every fish was collected and laid out on shore. We worked for three days, then wrapped up all the fish and buried them.

We made no effort to hide the fact that we were "poisoning" the refuge (actually "reclaiming" is a better term), but the Spanish word for poison—*veneno*—is a scary one. The Indian canoers talked. Rumors spread.

By sheerest coincidence, a die-off of crappies had been going on for the past few weeks. Dead fish were washing up on shore with yellow goo covering their gills—probably a slime-mold infection. Now the die-off worsened. Piles of crappies decayed among the reeds and rocks. Inevitably, the dead crappies were linked to our experiment with antimycin.

One morning, Armando burst into my room crying, "Look at

this!" ¿LAGO ATITLÁN ENVENADO? (LAKE ATITLÁN POISONED?), read the headlines of Guatemala City's leading newspaper.

I shuddered. The story went on to say that fish were dying and it raised some ugly implications. But fortunately, it also left room for doubt and mentioned Operation Protection Poc and the big bass. Given the Latin flair for emotionalism, however, I could see how this story might balloon into real trouble.

"Don't go out today!" ordered Armando. "Some of the Indian fishermen are already grumbling in the streets this morning about the gringa and her 'poison pills.' They are upset and carrying their machetes."

I spent an uneasy day indoors, wrestling with this odd problem. Once again, nothing in my textbooks had prepared me for such an event. Eventually I reasoned that, again, the only way to fight fire was with fire. First I asked Armando to accompany me to the Governor of Sololá, under whose jurisdiction Lake Atitlán lay. He had been a constant source of support. We explained exactly what had happened and the unfortunate twist of events. He immediately sent out telegrams to the secretaries of all the nineteen villages within Atitlán's watershed, advising them that fish and water were safe to eat and drink—no poison had been put in the main body of the lake. Then we journeyed to Guatemala City and gave interviews to the major papers. Both the Division of Fauna and Mr. Ibarra backed me up and explained the procedures and goals of our work. Suddenly I was a celebrity, albeit a notorious one in some people's minds. As I walked down the busy city streets, several people came up and asked, "Aren't you *Doña Ana de los Pocs?*" ("Lady Anne of the Pocs?")

June came, bringing the rains. Luckily, the crappie die-off stopped, and so did the furor over the poisoning. Still, my spirits dropped. In a few weeks I would have to return to Cornell and begin course work. My idyllic scientific sojourn in Guatemala was coming to an end. How could I leave here and part from Armando? Yet how could I not leave to pursue the degree I had decided on?

In the end, fate made the decision easy. Don Emilio was ailing and Armando was called up into the hills to help him with the farm work. He was gone for weeks. Good thing. I might never have boarded that plane if I'd had to say good-bye to him at the airport. As it was, I cried my eyes out all the way back to New York State.

A Rainbow over the Refuge

My return to academic life that fall was traumatic. After a year of field work in Guatemala's glorious climate and countryside, I did not take easily to campus life. I had little patience with academic regulations, graduate student games, stacks of credits. What I wanted was sound pragmatic advice, knowledge, and references to help accomplish what I'd set out to do. My professors—many of them men my own age and some even younger—insisted on course work which I felt had no practical application. How could General Physiology 504 or Russian 101 possibly help save an endangered species or promote conservation in Central America? I began to seriously question the value of a Ph.D.

Spring semester started, and my mood darkened. I remember bursting into tears in my committee chairman's office, declaring I would quit the program. This kind man canceled appointments and spent the next hour reassuring me. "You *must* go on," he insisted. "That degree will open doors and be your credit card for years to come. You'll move on to more and better conservation campaigns with the credential of a Ph.D."

I shook my head doubtfully.

"Then why not take a leave of absence now?" he suggested sagely. "Go back to Guatemala and gather more information for your thesis. After all, you have up to seven years to complete everything."

This sensible advice did the trick. I dried my tears and thanked the professor. It was a critical point, for without his understanding I would have dropped the degree then and there. After persuading the rest of the committee of my need to leave, I flew back to Guatemala.

How "right" it felt once again to speed across that mighty blue lake at dawn in my little boat; to huddle for hours in the whispering reeds watching grebes; and to be with Armando again. Yet the whole ecological picture seemed sharper and the conservation goals were better defined in my mind, thanks to that semester at the university.

In one of my courses, International Conservation, we had explored the idea of "selling" conservation to the public. Ironic as it was, I could now see the value of that ill-timed newspaper publicity about the poisoned fish. At least it had let Guatemalans know about their rare and endangered birds and about Operation Protection Poc, while introducing the concept of wildlife conservation to them. Seeing how vital it was to have public support for our program, I now began giving newspaper interviews and even a few lectures to promote our campaign. One idea which particularly appealed was Sir Peter Scott's scheme of using postage stamps to convey a conservation message. Almost everyone in the world gets mail. What better way to broadcast an appeal than with an attractive stamp?

I obtained an audience with the head of the National Postal Service through the aid of my good friend the Minister of Agriculture. In my naïve way, I was learning that the best way to get things done, at least in a Latin country, is to go right to the top and ask for what you want. Yet, at the other extreme, grass-roots support was crucial as well. If we hadn't tried to work with both Ministers and Indians, Operation Protection Poc might never have succeeded.

The National Postal Service Director agreed on a poc stamp; in fact, not one, but three. *National Geographic* kindly sent duplicates of David's slides and a Guatemalan artist rendered faithful copies. To my delight, the stamps—4-cent, 9-cent, and 21-cent airmail—were eventually printed in full color. There was also a first-day commemorative cover featuring the grebes and Lake Atitlán; it read, "Let us conserve the Grebe or Poc." The stamps turned out to be the most attractive ever issued to date in Guatemala. Within two and a half years, the series was sold out and the postal service had grossed $123,000.

How I wished that the money had been available to Operation Protection Poc, but it went back into a general government fund. Meanwhile, the Ministry of Agriculture continued to support the construction of the visitors' center, laborers, and a full-time refuge guardian, to pay for the game warden, plus his gas and oil, and was talking about putting a rough road into the refuge and making other improvements. The Division of Fauna trucked up 6,000 small fingerlings of native fishes and stocked them in the sanctuary.

But, the best event of all that spring of 1968 was the clear indication that the bass population had peaked and was dropping. Catches and sizes decreased. The largest fish being caught were only 4 to 6 pounds. Many were stunted. Bluegills, which we had stocked in the refuge, were multiplying around the lake and providing a good buffer food for bass, as well as easily caught panfish for the Indians. A few small native fishes, crabs, and other aquatic life were in evidence once again. This natural trend of introduction, explosion, peaking, crash, and decline is a usual pattern among introduced species, but no one had known if and when this phenomenon would occur in a lake the size of Atitlán.

Yet I was still apprehensive. We needed the grebe refuge and a captive population of breeding birds to assure the species' survival. But how to catch them?

It wasn't easy. In fact, catching grebes proved to be the most difficult part of Operation Protection Poc. Those diving birds were absolutely uncanny in their ability to outwit our schemes and ploys. We spent hours chasing grebes with motorboats, but they always slipped away. We tried baiting them with decoys, mirrors, and special traps, but they detected them in time. I donned scuba gear and approached them stealthily underwater, planning to grab their legs, but the air bubbles gave me away. Then we waded and crawled through countless reed beds where mated birds lived, hoping to drive them into nets encircling the reeds. They calmly executed their accordion dive and periscope-surveyed us until we gave up. I shook my head at Armando and Roberto in frustration.

"Let's ask the Indians to help," I ventured. "They know the lake and birds intimately."

Armando arranged for thirty Indian canoeists to meet us one

morning at dawn and spend the day trying to catch live grebes in the Bay of Santiago Atitlán. All returned that afternoon empty-handed. I paid them 50 cents each and asked them to try again. Next day—same results. And the next. So I lost confidence in this tactic.

Roberto offered to erect a special spring trap over the poc nests in front of his farm. But since the birds were nest building, it would take the most delicate maneuvering not to scare them away for good. We decided against this.

In desperation, I wrote two letters: one to my major professor, wildlife ecologist Dr. Dan Q. Thompson; the other to the Director of the Bronx Zoo, Dr. William Conway. "What would *you* do to catch grebes?" I asked.

Dr. Thompson's answer came back promptly, describing the technique of night-lighting. An airboat or light motorboat goes out at night with an extremely bright light mounted on the bow. Waterfowl of all kinds are literally "hypnotized" and can be scooped up in a large net with a long pole. This technique is used on national wildlife refuges where large numbers of ducks and geese are banded.

Generous friends brought up a portable generator and superbright light bulb from the city. Armando and I rigged it on the boat, and then for three nights we cruised the shoreline, nets at the ready. In all those 70 miles we saw only one lone male grebe outside the reeds. He was not mesmerized at all but merely dived in toward shore and disappeared. We did see hundreds of coots, gallinules, ducks, frogs, grackles, and fishes. They froze until we passed, their eyes glowing various colors. Once when we stopped to refuel, I heard a great horned owl hooting and a chuck-will's-widow crying plaintively. This experience gave me a whole new insight into the night life of Atitlán.

It evidently gave the Indians something to think about, too. Soon rumors were spreading about a monster roaming the shores of the lake, one which would eat up anyone chancing to be out alone. Armando and I roared with laughter when we heard this. Yet in more serious moments, I sometimes compared myself to the largemouth bass. Their introduction into Atitlán's ecosystem certainly had caused unexpected repercussions and had deranged the entire food chain. My coming to the lake, as well-meaning and simple as it was at first, had had far-reaching effects too. In an effort to save the country's wildlife, I had, at worst, frightened some people with "poison pills" and "man-eating monsters." At best, my activities probably enriched the folklore of the Mayans.

Our lack of success in catching grebes was becoming embarrassing. Operation Protection Poc had spent a total of $10,000 so far, counting labor and supplies—much of it for the sanctuary. We had built, reclaimed, and restocked this bay, and made it habitable for grebes. But there were no grebes in it!

The second response to my letters of inquiry was a long time coming. It arrived in a bulky, battered envelope, postmarked Cochabamba, Bolivia, of all places. The writer was Charles Cordier, an expert animal trapper who worked part-time for the Bronx Zoo. Dr. Conway had forwarded my request to him. I read his instructions: Make several hundred small snares with slip knots (he enclosed two samples) from 14-pound-test monofilament line—a line that is almost invisible yet strong enough to hold the birds. Tie these snares on a long line between poles right at the edge of the reed beds. When the birds swim in and out, they'll lasso themselves.

We had nothing to lose. Anything was worth a try. I spent three days of patient knot-tying. Armando went out to cut bamboo poles long enough to reach the lake bottom. He, Roberto, and I erected a dozen of them in the water near the Lion's Rocks.

Early next morning, one Indian and I boated over. We painstakingly rigged up 500 snares on the line between the poles. As soon as everything was in place, we tied up in the reeds nearby and sat down to wait. I became touchy with impatience. I was sure it wouldn't work. However, thirty-five minutes after the snares were placed, the first grebe was lassoed. We sped toward the bird and scooped it up before it could harm itself. Then, holding the poc triumphantly, we dashed back to the refuge and gently released it. From size and coloration I judged it to be a young female.

We hurried back to the same spot. If we were lucky, we'd catch her mate, too. But the chocomil had begun. We were thwarted until next morning. By then I had to unravel and reset most of the 500 snares as a result of wind and wave disturbance. By noon, however, we had the male. Within a week, we had two mated pairs and one lone male in the Xecamuc reserve. My job was done.

At this point, I felt I should relinquish most of my responsibilities in the project to the Guatemalan government. Our four-point program was running smoothly. Enforcement was being handled competently by Roberto. Conservation education had been achieved with the sporadic visits of Jorge Ibarra, our newspaper coverage, and my lectures. The Indians were producing some crafts with the grebe motif. The first bird-watching groups had come to the refuge. During the more than four-year span of work, I had gradually developed a philosophy about conservation. Simply stated, it was to help others help themselves. I didn't want to be the kind of foreign scientist that comes into a place for a short time as "the great white father," unable to speak the language, unaware of local customs and manners, throwing his or her weight around. Neither did I believe in staying on to babysit a project. I just wanted to be a catalyst. So, psychologically, it was time for me to leave Operation Protection Poc in the hands of those whose obligation it really was.

Therefore, I decided to give the refuge an inauguration in the best Latin style and tradition. Invitations were sent out, a case of champagne was brought in, and the visitors' center was strewn with pine needles. On June 15, 1968, the Ministry of Agriculture officially declared this small reserve its first national wildlife refuge. The Governor of Sololá delivered a stirring speech, as did the heads of the Division of Natural Resources and INGUAT, the National Tourist Board. Then we raised the blue-and-white flag of Guatemala above the center. At the close, a Catholic priest said a prayer for the success of this conservation venture. Almost as if in answer, the rainclouds parted and a thin watery rainbow arched over the south shore. As we watched, one end seemed to touch against the slopes of Volcano Atitlán, the other to dip down into the very waters of the refuge!

Cornell University requirements called for one year of residency to qualify for a doctorate. So far, I'd been away more than I'd been there so had not complied. If I really wanted that degree, I would have to go back and earn it. Before leaving Guatemala, however, I needed to make a new census. To my great relief, the new count showed 130 birds, an increase of 62 percent since the pocs' lowest point. It looked as if the ecosystem might be mending itself and edging toward a new, more stable balance. While the lake would probably never again (thanks to the bass) have its full complement of grebes and native fishes, it might at least maintain smaller but viable populations of all these animals.

I also needed an estimate of the lake's carrying capacity for grebes—that is, to know how many birds could actually live there, given the present conditions. This figure would provide a basic checkpoint against which to relate all future numbers and trends and was significant to my thesis. Reeds and cattails were the all-important factors because they formed the only existing habitat. Armando and I again circled the entire lake, measuring the length and breadth of every reed and cattail bed. He cleverly devised a way of correlating boat speed with the horizontal distance traveled. To our surprise, only 15 miles of the total shoreline was vegetated. The rest was rocks, cliffs, and a few little beaches. Also, there were now ninety-two vacation homes. By figuring the average width of a grebe's territory (300 feet), I then calculated how many birds could live in the existing shoreline vegetation: 280.

Once I had this estimate, I really felt smug. Not only did it corroborate Griscom's and Wetmore's numbers of 200 or more birds living here 50 years ago, but it verified Don Emilio's vague guess of 300 to 400 birds 70 years ago. Of course, this carrying capacity depended on the assumption that the lake level would not change, thereby altering the amount of vegetation. I doubted that it could, since Atitlán has no surface outlets and only two insignificant surface inlets. Underground springs and rainwater fill it up, and subterranean channels under the great volcanoes filter out to the Pacific slopes and drain it. A most unusual hydrology!

For the moment at least, half the possible population of pocs was alive and well. I could truly feel that my modest cooperative conservation program had reversed the birds' trend toward extinction, and that Operation Protection Poc had paid off in part. More than this, I hoped that the grebes' recent brush with martyrdom, so like the near-annihilation of egrets in North America half a century ago, may have sounded an alert in Guatemala for the need to preserve its wildlife and guard against unwise derangements of any ecosystem.

Then, the day before I had to fly back to the United States, a terrifying event broke my euphoria. I was taking the refuge guardian and his two children to Santiago Atitlán by boat with a load of unused lumber and tools. Boards and bags were piled up in the boat and a late-afternoon rainstorm was blowing in my face. We were all hunched down under plastic sheets trying to keep dry. From time to time I looked up and out over the lake to make sure no other boats were near. But in that downpour, I saw no one.

Abruptly, I felt a heart-stopping jolt. A long gash appeared in the bow just above the waterline. We were too far from the Lion's Rocks to have hit them. Jumping up, I saw an Indian canoe and its paddler topple over next to us. The dugout had been coming dead-on toward us, and I had missed seeing its knifelike silhouette against the gray lake and clouds. One horrifying thought exploded in my mind: neither the guardian, nor his children, nor the canoeist knew how to swim!

Acting purely on instinct, I shoved the motor gear into reverse and backed toward the submerged Indian. At the same time, I ripped off my jacket and flung it at the guardian, shouting to stuff it in the gushing hole. Wide-eyed with fright, he managed to do so. I reached the submerged Indian and grabbed his shoulders. Flipping the motor into neutral, I hauled him in over the transom. His bronze skin was ashen with terror. We made a quick swipe for his paddle and *morral*, but his other tools had already sunk. Now if we could just get to the dock without being inundated, we would be all right. I kept the motor at half-speed and ordered everyone to the back of the boat. That would keep the hole as far as possible above the water. Gradually the shore crept nearer and I began to breathe a little easier.

But as I stared at the dock, I saw something which turned my blood cold. The entire village of Santiago Atitlán seemed to have rushed down to the lakeshore. The speed with which the news had telegraphed itself across the town was incredible. The strongest, sturdiest men were crowded on the dock, carrying their machetes. Women and girls were running to the beach, rebozos and long hair flying behind them. I could sense the angry mood even across the water. Not one friendly face watched me approach. I was literally between two dangers: turn around and risk drowning, or beach my boat and face the mob. I didn't know how violent these usually gentle people might become, but they seemed the lesser of two evils.

I tried to appear calm as I touched shore and matter-of-factly shut off the engine. Carefully I helped the Indian boy out and immediately told him we were going straight to the Catholic clinic for an examination. His parents rushed up, berating me. Hundreds of people surrounded me and an angry murmur buzzed behind. I tried not to think of the machetes. Grabbing my equipment in one hand and holding the boy with the other, I slowly began walking up those cobblestone streets toward the church. The green-eyed Secretary and his aguaciles arrived. A Spanish policeman ordered me to come to his office.

"Not until I'm sure this boy is all right," I said grimly. Again, murmurs rippled out as I defied authority. At the clinic, the nurse was waiting. She made a thorough examination and found nothing more than a bump on the head and a bad scare. She administered a tranquilizer with a hypodermic, which pleased the entire family. Mayans have great faith in *los injecciones* (injections). She laid the lad down to rest and told me to check back in an hour or two.

As I made my way toward the office, a sudden hunch prompted me to step inside the telegraph office and send a quick message to Armando. Maybe he'd receive it and come to rescue me, maybe he wouldn't. Two hours passed, during which the policemen interrogated me. I shivered from tension and wet clothes. The Secretary wrote down every detail of the accident in his slanted, feathery script. Both men were astonished when I openly admitted my fault and offered to pay all expenses. Secretly, I was panic-stricken because I'd heard that Guatemalan law assumes everyone guilty until proved innocent. I might be thrown into jail to await trial and not be able to return to the university.

It was suppertime, and the crowds outside were lessening. I kept wondering if Armando would come. The moment the policeman and the Secretary finished, I went back to the clinic and found the boy sleeping soundly and well. Only then did I hurry to the Mayor's office and ask for an audience. I wanted to settle up at once. I sensed that if the matter waited overnight, the boy's parents might mushroom it to gigantic proportions and demand a large settlement. I needed to act fairly, yet avoid exorbitant financial demands.

The Mayor agreed and began writing out a list of items lost or damaged, with their estimated costs.

1 dugout canoe, repairs	$25.00
1 hoe	5.00
1 machete	3.50
1 bottle with coffee	.15
1 pair sandals	1.50
1 plastic tarp	1.00
3 tortillas	.06
Total	$36.21

He then left to confirm this with the boy in the clinic. I hoped the parents wouldn't start improvising things: perhaps an extra shirt, a transistor radio, pots or pans, an ax, even a dog! In their penny economy, as in our super-rich society, one always tries to take advantage of the "fall guy" or the insurance company.

By 9 o'clock the boy was awake, the list completed, and a meeting called. Suddenly, Armando arrived, breathless. He took one look at me and let out a great sigh of relief. I resisted an overpowering urge to run into his strong arms in front of the whole roomful of people. Instead, I quickly whispered what had happened. He squeezed my shoulder approvingly and slipped some money into my pocket. The nurse informed the Mayor that her patient was in good health and that she would keep an eye on him for a few more days, just in case. I agreed to pay any and all medical costs. A canoe builder gave his estimate for repairs and I paid him. The Secretary presented a bill for the lost items. Again I took care of it. The boy's mother kept complaining and whining from the back of the room, "It's not enough, it's not enough." I told the Mayor I was leaving three days' wages for the boy in case he needed to rest before going back to work. The audience murmured at this sudden windfall, and the mother fell silent.

Armando said a few words to the Secretary, who nodded agreeably. Then he came back to me and whispered, "I've asked for a document stating you did all these things and that the boy is okay. Otherwise, someone might try to instigate some further charges in the future. The boy has his protection, now you need yours."

When the papers were ready, I signed several copies, with Armando and the Secretary as witnesses. He gave one to the boy, the Mayor, the nurse, and me. I was free to go.

A few curiosity seekers still hung around the streets and dock, muttering as we passed. Armando stuffed more old rags into the hole and tied my boat behind his for towing. Finally we were moving slowly across the chilly surface of Lake Atitlán under the blackest sky I'd ever seen. Only then did I throw myself against Armando's chest and start sobbing. The path to conservation and education was far rockier than I'd ever imagined.

"Mama Quetzal"

Though again time crawled, that last stretch at the university was in many ways the refinement and culmination of four-and-a-half years of field and course work. It was the weaving together of data, statistics, hypotheses, and intuitions into a whole tapestry. I'd started out as a neophyte, picking up a thread here, a thread there. At first I did not see the whole design. Through trial and error, and lots of luck, I had learned to probe for interrelationships among the animals, plants, people, land, and water. Then, slowly, I began to reweave the torn tapestry and create a new pattern.

Even though one dreary day dragged into another at the library, reviewing literature, documenting data, the writing of my thesis seemed as much a form of art as a scientific treatise. With it, I hoped to offer an understanding of the complex ecology of one ecosystem, Lake Atitlán, of the serious consequences of an unwise introduction of carnivorous fish to a relict population of waterbirds, of the food habits, customs, and dependency on natural resources by the native inhabitants, and of the critical need to save endangered wildlife in Central America. Most of all, I wanted to instill an awareness of the policies and attitudes involved in conservation in a Latin country.

Shortly after I finished the thesis, a phone call came from David Allen, who had photographed the grebes. "How would you like to go back to Guatemala and write a story on the quetzal?" he asked. "*National Geographic* is interested. No one has ever published a story with color photographs of this bird. Remember that conversation we overheard in Mr. Ibarra's office? The editors want us to follow up on that. I'll take the pictures and you do the research and writing."

"Yes, of course I would," was my immediate reply. And after he hung up, I added to myself, "Bless you, David."

Two weeks later we were climbing, out of breath and riddled by mosquitoes, up the slopes of Volcano Atitlán. A barefoot Indian guide led the way. David followed, blue work shirt crisscrossed with cameras and khaki pants' pockets bulging with film. I huffed and puffed behind him, out of shape from a year of sedentary student life. Five more Indians walked in single file, carrying tents, cooking gear, sleeping bags, blinds, ropes, and more photographic equipment. Armando brought up the rear with walkie-talkie radios and a revolver on his hip.

Following instructions of the enthusiastic *fincero* (farm owner) on whose property we would work, we had driven four long hours from Guatemala City, down and around the great central volcanic chain which separates the highlands from the Pacific lowlands. Then we had chugged and skidded in Armando's Land Rover up the southern slopes of Volcano Atitlán to about 5,000 feet elevation. From there we had to trudge on foot up a tortuous trail.

Mist was settling over the cloud forest, turning the mountainside into an eerie world. Huge leaves fell occasionally from the trees that towered above us. In the absolute stillness, each leaf made a crashing noise like a herd of peccaries coming after us. This home of the quetzal was a green and grandiose world. Oaks, wild figs, Spanish cedars, and many other tropical species rose 150 feet, laced with lianas and adorned with air plants. Treacherous canyons sliced their way between the folds of the 11,600-foot volcano. We could hear water roaring in their depths, but because of the porous volcanic soils not a spring, creek, pond, or swamp stood anywhere above 5,000 feet on the mountain slopes.

The whole situation was ironic, I mused to myself while I climbed. If a horizontal tunnel about 15 miles long could have been dug right through the mass of volcanoes Atitlán and Tolimán we would have come out just above the town of Santiago Atitlán and my beloved lake. No contrast could have been greater, short of a desert island. Instead of sun and shining water, we were enveloped in clouds and towering trees. Awesome rains drenched the forest almost daily except during the two to three months of dry season. It was this period we were trying to take advantage of. Yet every noon, as regular as the chocomil that swept across Lake Atitlán, a cap of clouds descended over the mountain, mantling and muffling the forest. This phenomenon gave it the name "cloud forest." All the moisture nourishes the living foliage to greater fecundity and encourages the dead wood to decay faster. Every drop is absorbed either by plants or by the porous igneous soil. Instead of my perky, water-loving, black-and-white grebes, we were now after emerald-and-ruby–colored trogons who flew in iridescent, streamer-tailed splendor through the lofty canopy.

Our British-Guatemalan host, the man who had called Mr. Ibarra when we were in his office, informed us that the quetzals were still using the same section of his forest. They were beginning their courtship but no one had yet found a nest. The farm owner generously put six of his laborers at our disposal to help make camp and carry equipment. Flat places were few on that precipitous mountainside. I was relieved when we finally stopped in a gloomy but level clearing and the Indians began cutting away the undergrowth. Within an hour, they had magically prepared a campsite complete with *champa* (thatch roofed cooking shelter), a campfire, and a tall stack of firewood. David, Armando, and I were busy setting up our tents and stowing away the precious field equipment and cameras. Humidity and rain would be among our biggest problems. Even as we worked, each one of us was constantly scanning the leafy roof to look for a flash of green and red.

The quetzal is considered by many ornithologists to be one of the most beautiful birds in the world. No larger than a dove, it flys like "an arc of green fire in the sun, an emerald meteor in the mist, a cold viridian flame in rain," as I was to write in an article for *National Geographic*. It takes its name from the Aztec word, *quetzalli* (tail feather), which has come to mean "beautiful" or "precious." The Indians have called the bird quetzal for centuries and revere it as much as Mayan jade or Aztec gold.

As long as 1,000 years ago Indians live-trapped quetzals, plucked out their prize plumes, and released the birds unharmed. (The four long tail coverts grew safely back after the next molt.) The plumes were reserved for royalty and priesthood alone. Any common person who dared to use them was punished. If he killed a bird, he faced the death penalty. In those days both Mayans and Aztecs worshipped a feathered serpent—called Kulkulcan by the Mayans, Quetzalcoatl by the Aztecs—which is depicted in hundreds of glyphs on stelae, stone carvings, and temple stones as a fanged rattlesnake covered with quetzal feathers.

Even today, tradition stands strong. The quetzal is Guatemala's heraldic emblem, and, as noted, the unit of currency bears its name. It also appears on the country's flag, coat of arms, stamps, paper and silver money, arts and crafts, and road signs.

The name of the second largest city is Quetzaltenango—"place of the quetzal." It was near there that the Spanish conquistador Pedro de Alvarado confronted Tecuman, the great Mayan chieftain, in battle. Legend relates that Alvarado mortally wounded the Indian leader. As he lay dying, a giant quetzal fluttered down from the sky and fell dead on his chest. Thus, say the Indians stoically, did their race lose its freedom to the Spaniards. The graceful quetzal is considered the symbol of liberty even today. The popular belief persists that the bird cannot live in captivity. (I believed this myself until I saw two perfectly healthy quetzals in the Bronx Zoo aviary. They have now been there for several years but have never bred.)

Early the next day we began our quest for the quetzal. To my surprise, the March morning dawned clear and sunny, yet cool enough for a sweater. The cloud forest resembled an emerald-and-gold cathedral. A riotous choir of birds greeted us. Toucans tooted, wrens trilled, euphonias sang, woodpeckers drilled, guans gabbled, and redstarts whistled. But nowhere did I hear a quetzal singing. Forearmed by my experience with the grebes, I had obtained a tape recording of the male quetzal's territorial call from Cornell University's Laboratory of Ornithology. It was a melodious two-toned whistle and I played it over and over expectantly. Nothing answered. We paired off to cover more ground. I chose Pablo, a slim Indian boy from the Cuchumatanes Mountains. Barefooted and keen-eyed, he could slip through the forest virtually unheard and unseen. The only giveaways were the faded red T-shirt and silvery sombrero he wore every day of his stay with us. Altogether we made up three teams, staying in touch by walkie-talkie. About noon, Pablo and I heard a faint two-toned whistle high in the canopy. Freezing in our tracks, we scanned the treetops with binoculars. Finally I saw our quarry, perfectly camouflaged, about 90 feet above our heads. How would we ever make observations, let alone take pictures, at that distance?

For a week we rose early and trekked about the cloud forest without seeing courting quetzals or finding a nest. David was growing impatient. He checked and doublechecked his strobe lights, electric cords, lenses, film, blinds, rope ladder, and climbing spurs.

"Find me a nest! Find me a nest!" he chanted every evening when we assembled for our simple meal of tortillas, black beans, tough beefsteak grilled on the fire, and Guatemalan coffee.

"We've only got a couple of months. The money won't last forever," he worried. "The rains are coming. Our work will be much harder then. I must have a nest to work with. That's the only place I can be sure of photographing birds close up with any regularity when they come to incubate and feed the young."

The morning Pablo and I found our first quetzal nest it happened so quietly that I was almost stupefied. Pablo simply stopped and pointed to a tree about 20 feet ahead. He turned and gave me a piercing look from his lively dark eyes fringed by coarse black lashes. He didn't speak, just motioned over my shoulder at some bunches of bromeliads growing around the top of a dead tree stump. In the dim churchlike light, I could see nothing unusual. A gentle breeze swung the leaf blades. Two of them seemed more fragile, greener, limper. Pablo smiled. Feathery plumes hanging out of the nest hole! A live quetzal!

The male was snuggled down inside the nest hole with only his two longest tail coverts curving up and out of the entrance. No wonder the generic part of the quetzal's scientific name, *Pharomachrus*, was chosen: It means "long mantle" in Greek, and this aptly describes the yard-long plumage which only the males have.

Now our work began in earnest. David commanded everyone to exercise the utmost caution so as not to frighten away the birds. During their early stages of courting and nest building, they can easily be spooked. Only after they are incubating their eggs and watching chicks does a truly strong tie exist between parents and their nest sites. Then they'll tolerate much more disturbance and movement around them. The nest hole we had found was situated about 28 feet off the ground on the upper side of a dead tree. In order to get close-ups, David had to be no farther than 30 feet from the hole and level with it. He decided to erect a 25-foot tower and place his blind, cameras, tripods, and lights atop it. Our Indian workmen were invaluable now. They could shinny up trees and carry heavy loads which left the rest of us staggering. No laborer was taller than my 5 feet, 4 inches or weighed much more than I do, but each had incredible strength and endurance.

To camouflage our tower, aluminum ladders, wires, and batteries, David asked Armando to spray-paint everything green. The mosquitoes were biting Armando furiously one morning. Snatching up a nearby can of insect repellent and applying several bursts around his head, he found to his chagrin that the label read, "emerald green." Thus he earned the nickname "Señor green ears."

After days of work, the tower and photo equipment were ready. David began his daily routine of creeping up to the tower with two boys, easing into his blind, settling down for an 8-to-10-hour day, and then sending the boys back. Birds can't count. As long as they see a few people come and go, they will not suspect that one has stayed behind. I was gaining tremendous respect for the superb know-how, patience, and alertness of this wildlife photographer. All we knew of David throughout the day was a thin trickle of smoke from his cigarettes emerging at the top of his blind, or the occasional staccato messages he whispered over his radio set. David had already calculated that during this incubation period, the birds would only present themselves to his cameras a scant 100 seconds in every 10-hour day! Later, after the chicks hatched and began demanding food from their parents, David's chances for getting pictures would increase greatly.

Normally the female bird incubates the eggs all night and is relieved by the male early each morning. She flies off to feed and preen, then returns for a midday stint. He comes back again during the afternoon to brood and allow her another break until dusk. It was during this brief nest-exchange ceremony that David had to snap his pictures. The bird taking over would usually make two or three false attempts to enter the nest without going in. I called this display "bowing in." The incoming bird was announced only by a light thump as it alighted on the nest tree or by the faintest swish of wings.

Armando named the quetzal couple "the *Caballeros*" (elegant gentlemen), because they were so dashingly handsome. The male was shimmering green on his head, back, and wing coverts, with black wing primaries and secondaries. His little crest reminded me of a Roman gladiator's. It stood straight up above two chocolate-brown eyes and bright yellow beak. Also like a gladiator's cape thrown nonchalantly over his back was the male's curling shoulder cape of gilded green feathers. He clung to the tree with yoked toes—two forward and two back. Neither bills nor feet are strong enough to dig anything but the softest, most rotten wood. Four elongate plumes hung below his tail—his shining train to impress females. The male's most glamorous attribute, to my way of thinking, was the carmine-red breast and belly and the darker red undertail coverts. The female by contrast was a "plain Jane" lacking the crest and train of the male. Her breast is mostly gray with only a touch of red near her black-and-white-barred tail.

While David perched in his blind, Pablo and I roamed over hundreds of acres of rugged cloud forest, searching for new nest trees, identifying fauna and flora, and observing quetzal's feeding and courting behavior. The birds seldom, if ever, come to the ground. They obtain water from rain trapped in leaves and air plants and from dew. They eat grubs, snails, insects, and wild fruits, such as avocados and figs, which are often snatched in flight. We found nine more nest sites in dead stubs of trees and located three more pairs of birds who appeared to be incubating eggs or brooding young. None was as convenient and low as our Caballeros.

It was fortunate we had those back-up birds because one morning David astonished us by tersely stating on the walkie-talkie set that the Caballeros had abandoned their nest! Quickly Armando set up ladders and examined the nest tree. Empty! I combed the ground for signs. We found only two breast feathers from the mother.

"An owl did it," Armando guessed. "Remember one hooted last night."

"Yesterday an ornate hawk-eagle swooped by," said David gloomily.

"I've seen a few gray squirrels and a kinkajou," I offered sadly. "It could be any one of those predators."

"What do we do now?" asked the ever-buoyant Armando.

"Try another nesting pair," answered David. "What have you got for me, Anne?"

Laboriously we moved all the equipment and tower to a mossy snag, 50 feet tall, standing lone and wobbly in a little canyon. On the far side, we found a flat area just big enough to take the tower. To cross over with our gear, we had to straddle and slide along a huge fallen tree trunk. It took another week of cautious labor to set up everything, including a perching tree. This was a *Cecropia* about 50 feet high, which required ten men to drag it near to the nest tree and "plant" it. David's hope was that the birds would stop on one of its branches enroute to their nest hole and he could get better pictures by focusing on this perching tree.

Within 5 minutes after the fake tree was set up, a gorgeous male alighted on its lowest branch and gave a low nasal version of the territorial call. I immediately named him "the Organ Grinder" because his voice was so harsh and ragged compared to other quetzals. He treated us to some rare displays over the next few days. Once at dawn I glimpsed his giddy flight display. He spiraled up into the sky, singing exuberantly, hovered a moment above the cloud forest canopy, and then dived back down into the trees where his bewitched and, he hoped, excited female was waiting.

Another morning I saw him fly up to the nest hole with only one long tail plume. He seemed as healthy as ever. At once Pablo and I scrambled down into the canyon and began searching for the lost plume. We found it shortly and I climbed back out of the ravine with the feather waving saucily from my sombrero. Armando broke into laughter and immediately took out his tape measure.

"Forty-eight inches long!" He whistled. "Look at the colors change just like light on a soap bubble." He waved the feather gently in the sunlight and it caught every shade in the spectrum from yellow-green lime to turquoise and ultramarine, with occasional casts of gold and copper.

Since the tail plumes are purely for sexual attraction, the

Organ Grinder was probably not hampered or unbalanced by its loss. He only looked cockeyed. Apparently, plumes often come loose from the wear and tear of nest building, entering and leaving the small 4-inch nest hole, and the chores of incubation and feeding young. The Organ Grinder, the Caballeros, and other quetzal pairs we watched proved that the birds do not make two doors to their nests, contrary to popular belief which says that they do so to protect their flowing trains.

I was so enchanted with the feather that I packed it up and mailed it to Dr. L. Durrell, professor emeritus at Colorado State University, who worked with electron microscopes. "Tell me what makes its many colors," I wrote, knowing he loved this sort of challenge. My friend studied the feather at 10,000-times magnification and wrote back cryptically, "The quetzal isn't green, it's brown!"

His report explained: "Attempts to extract a pigment from the green feather failed. But a chemical test for melanin (brown color) is positive. The feather barbules are composed of granules in orderly rows spaced at approximately 5,400 angstroms apart. As the wavelength of green light is in this range, the physical phenomenon of interference makes light striking the barbules break down and reflect back green."

This phenomenon was first noted in 1960 by an ornithologist studying hummingbird feathers and has been found to be quite common in bird feathers. All in all, I decided the plumage of the quetzal was superbly suited for camouflage under rainy conditions in the cloud forest. Then the feathers show little iridescence and blend in remarkably well with wet, shiny, green vegetation. In fact, without Pablo, I would have missed seeing birds countless times. Very often they'll sit for hours quite motionless, high in the canopy, only occasionally looking from side to side in a slow, suspicious manner. Also, they seldom show their red breasts if they feel uneasy.

Over these weeks I had grown quite fond of Pablo, for his willingness to work, his broad grin over perfect white teeth, his shyness. We rarely spoke, yet we seemed to be on the same wavelength in our work. When he didn't show up one morning at 5:30 A.M., I grew concerned. After work, I asked Armando to drive me down to the finca to find him. I had imagined the boyish Pablo to be about eighteen years old and living with his parents. To my surprise, the lad had a wife, two babies, and was at least twenty-five. I found him lying on a reed mat on a cement floor in the big *galería* (large open dormitory), where the coffee pickers and their families usually lived. He was deathly pale. In poorest Spanish, his wife explained he had cut his foot with a machete chopping firewood the night before and had almost bled to death. The nearest clinic was a bumpy hour's trip down the mountain and there was no one to drive him. So he was lying in blood-soaked rags, waiting for nature to heal him. I was ready to admonish the administrator of the farm and to drive him to medical help myself, but David and Armando impressed on me that we were in a delicate position as guests there.

"You can't interfere without jeopardizing our work," they cautioned me.

Inwardly I fumed, but I dared not say anything. However, I took Pablo meat, vitamin pills, and fresh bandages in order to speed his recovery.

We soon had new troubles to think about. The rains had started and with them heavy thunderstorms. One night, as we were eating, an earthquake set the forest jiggling and swaying. We pondered pessimistically what these elemental forces might do to that delicate, rotted nest stub. Yet each dawn as we approached it apprehensively, there would be the Organ Grinder, safe in his snag, his long plume waving gently in the breeze. What's more we now saw that he and his wife were changing places more often and bringing morsels of food into the nest hole. Clearly their chicks had hatched. We were lured into a false sense of security.

One noon, the nest tree, slowly, silently, majestically, toppled over. No rain, no wind, no quake. It just fell, probably because of an accumulated absorption of rainwater. We had already suffered through three afternoons when 4 inches fell in a few hours. It was like living inside an all-green shower stall.

David almost choked on his sandwich, while Armando and I were rooted to the ground. Then we sprang into action. We careened down the canyon, pawed through the debris, and found first one chick and then the other. Both were alive but the larger baby had a cut across its backbone, the smaller, a hemorrhage beginning on his head. Armando cradled them in his strong hands, breathing warmth over the baby chicks. From the forest, I heard the plaintive chatter of the female—"*waac-a-waac-a-waac.*" Luckily both adults had been out feeding when the tree fell.

We hurried to the jeep, drove down to the finca, and set up a nest box in the kitchen of the farmhouse. We asked little boys to go out and catch bugs, worms, fruits. I hard-boiled eggs and mashed avocado with the yolks. No one was exactly sure what to feed the chicks, but we decided that a varied diet would provide most of the nutrients and vitamins they require. I assumed the job of feeding the baby birds with a forceps for three days, thus earning the name of "Mama quetzal." No mother ever had uglier offspring. The chicks had grotesquely bulging bellies, heavy legs, gaping wide beaks, and tightly shut eyes. Their bodies were half naked. Pinkish, almost transparent skin alternated with rows of fuzzy black and brown feathers. It seemed impossible that such miserable-looking creatures could ever grow up to be splendid trogons.

After three days both chicks were dead. I felt dismal, having become attached to the noisy little beggars. And we had lost a priceless opportunity to record and photograph quetzal growth literally in our laps.

This disaster necessitated serious decisions. None of the other quetzal pairs here was at the stage of breeding at which we could expect to have chicks to photograph. We could not afford to wait through the 28-day incubation period and/or the 4-to-6-week period of raising chicks until they would be outside the nest and visible to cameras. It was already May, and our time and money were about gone. We decided, therefore, to break camp and travel up to the Cuchumatanes Mountains to another location where we had heard quetzals were plentiful. With luck, we might find a pair in just the right place and at just the right time to obtain more pictures. Barring this chance, David felt we only had a 50-50 chance of having *National Geographic* publish our article and photographs.

A Quetzal Reserve

The road to the Cuchumatanes Mountains took us above 9,000-feet elevation into a different world. We drove through fragrant forests of white pines, oaks, liquidambars, and firs. Their branches were weighted down with masses of air plants, golden-green mosses, fragile orchids, and the spidery gray tangles of old-man's beard.

As we bumped over a crest, Armando suddenly jammed on the brakes. Ahead we could see a smear of smoke and orange flames dancing on the hillside. Even worse, from this vantage point we noticed nine other forest fires blazing across the landscape.

We stopped beside two soot-stained Indians who carried axes and machetes. Smoke drifted through the jeep, trees were crashing and sending up billions of sparks, and birds were shrieking. We all piled out. I confronted one Indian with outrage.

"Why are you cutting and burning this forest?" I demanded.

"To plant our corn and beans," he answered simply "We have to eat."

"But why not leave some trees standing to renew the forest and give you firewood? Why not protect the birds and animals?"

"It is the custom this way."

What more could I say? It was the universal answer of hungry, illiterate humans. Not only had our hopes of more quetzal pictures been ruined, but thousands of acres of wildland and hundreds of species of wildlife were being wiped out. Soon a few blackened stumps would stand witness among the green cornstalks. A few years from now, erosion from the heavy rains and soil compaction from the strong sun would render this land unfit for man or beast. By that time, the Indians would have moved their fields to fresh areas of forest and repeated the process of slash-and-burn agriculture.

This ancient method of farming is still practiced throughout tropical America, Africa, and Asia. As long as the human population stays small, the trees and soils can some day regenerate themselves. But where human numbers are increasing, as they are in most of the world, there is relentless pressure to seek more farm and range land. It is driving people up steep mountain slopes and into swamps and deserts where they have no business living, and where the ecological impacts are usually disastrous.

Moreover, flames from slash-and-burn agriculture often escape and become wildfires which burn until weather or topography puts them out. This has been the pattern for centuries. Most developing countries have no fire-fighting services, such as fire towers, observers, patrol planes, or smoke-jumpers. Happening upon the scene in the Cuchumatanes abruptly made me realize the scope and severity of this traditional type of agriculture.

David took the loss hard. He had no other place to go for his pictures. In an effort to cheer him up and save our expedition, we spent two days combing the mountains for other nesting birds. What we found only saddened us more. A sturdy Indian in San Mateo Ixtatán village eagerly offered us a dried quetzal skin for $2.00! Proudly, he showed off the blow gun and clay pellets with which he hunted the birds. I asked him how he could possibly hit such a small creature with this weapon. He shrugged off his heavy black wool jacket, raised the long tube, and unerringly hit a yellow pine cone 50 feet away. I wondered if he had any inkling that Guatemalan law, which has protected the national bird since 1875, prohibits killing, trapping, exporting birds dead or alive, and molesting their nests. Probably not, for he told us he sold quetzals to whatever truck driver, traveler, or animal collector happened into this remote area, and that hunting quetzals was common both here and across the border into Mexico.

Retracing our way to Volcano Atitlán, we saw large tracts of virgin cloud forest being cut for firewood, charcoal, shingles, lumber, or to make way for the planting of coffee, quinine, tea, and other cash crops. In most cases, the forest was clear-cut—that is, all the trees in a stand were leveled—which invites erosion and imposes a long-range threat to the entire watershed, water supply, and water quality of people living below. One Sunday afternoon, we also saw three men looking for wild honey. One bragged about having cut thirty-five trees in one year, most of them 100 feet tall with diameters at breast height (dbh) of 4 to 8 feet.

"How do you know you'll find honey in a tree after chopping it down?" I asked.

"We see bees flying in and out," he replied casually. "Sometimes there's no honey, but usually there's a quart or two. We earn thirty-five to seventy-five cents a quart for honey in the market."

"Those big trees do a lot of damage to the forest when they fall down, don't they?" I pressed the woodcutter.

"I don't know. What difference does it make? There are hundreds of trees."

"It makes a huge difference if there happens to be a quetzal nesting there," I muttered.

It was clear to us now that human activity through habitat destruction was the chief direct threat to the birds. The second serious limiting factor was the fragility and scarcity of nest trees.

Back at the finca, we soberly collected our equipment, paid the workmen, and said good-bye to the owner. He was as disturbed as we by the bad luck which had plagued us and by our stories of mountain forest eradication in Guatemala.

"Come back again if you need to," he offered warmly. "This property will stay as it is. I'll always protect our cloud forest. We love our quetzals. We may even make a kind of bird sanctuary up here."

The last person to see us off was Pablo. He ran alongside the jeep, gesturing. Glad to see that he had apparently recovered from his accident, I smiled broadly and threw him a good-bye kiss. His mouth opened, but no words came out.

"That boy is going to miss you," remarked David.

"That boy's in love," corrected Armando with a dark look backward in the driving mirror.

David and I returned to the United States and somehow salvaged our story. It appeared in *National Geographic* in January 1969. I also wrote two scientific papers, "Biology and Conservation of the Quetzal," and "Behavior and Feather Structure of the Quetzal." With these publications in hand, I started to think how I might use them. Could they serve as a plea and leverage to obtain grants and establish a quetzal reserve? As far as I knew, not one such protected area existed anywhere from southern Mexico to western Panama—the birds' full range of 1,000 miles. Yet, as we'd definitely seen, the species was rare and endangered.

If it had been possible to make a grebe reserve at Lake Atitlán, why not one for quetzals in the cloud forests of Volcano Atitlán? I wrote several exploratory letters and was gratified by the responses. The plantation owner was all in favor and ready to donate 1,000 acres for a sanctuary. Money was promised by World Wildlife Fund, USA, and the Cleveland County Bird Club in Norman, Oklahoma. The main stumbling block was for me to get leave from the university; upon completion of my degree, I had accepted a teaching position as assistant professor. My finances after the years of graduate school and field work were so limited that I had to take a job. (Furthermore, my alimony payments had stopped.)

Nevertheless, I found time during spring vacation to return to Volcano Atitlán, meet with the landowners, and lay our plans. They graciously offered me a small guesthouse and the same six laborers as before. These generous arrangements made a world of difference in saving time and energy. The boys were excited to see Armando and me again. Pablo stared at me feverishly but said nothing. (I had long since forgotten his odd behavior of the year before, but Armando hadn't—I noticed a subtle change in the way he spoke to Pablo.)

Our first task was to make a census of birds and recheck all the nest trees where we had worked before. It was an ideal time, for courting season was underway. Every morning the silvery two-toned whistles of males echoed from the treetops, helping me estimate the size of quetzal territories. I figured out that during the reproductive season each pair defends a territory of 1,000-foot radius around its nest tree. This tree varies in height from 12 feet to almost 150 feet. The home range is roughly 15 to 25 acres per pair. All told, there were about twenty-two quetzals on the proposed refuge and maybe ten nest sites.

Next we had to mark the boundaries. With machetes, the boys and I lightly blazed two 3-foot swaths at about 5,000- and 8,000-feet elevations over rugged terrain. Both the eastern and western boundaries were naturally delineated by very deep canyons running up the volcano. I painted and lettered two large signs reading QUETZAL SANCTUARY and the boys erected these at the southern corners.

Meanwhile, Armando was overseeing another phase of the project: making artificial nest boxes. I reasoned that one management technique which might help the quetzal population was to provide safe homes on live trees. If wood ducks, martins, and bluebirds can use artificial nests, why not quetzals? These boxes were roughly the size of a wood-duck house. Each one had a layer of sawdust in the bottom, a rubber (inner tube) roof cap, and a little ladder inside so the chicks could climb out when ready to fledge. Pablo was indispensable at this point, as he could climb like a monkey. He installed almost all of the sixteen nest boxes about 20 feet high on living trees. We were careful to place the boxes where there were no nearby branches, vines, or lianas to provide access for predators, and we wrapped tin flashing around the trunks of the nest trees so no animal could climb up either. I doubted that any quetzals would use the nest boxes during this breeding season, but I hoped they might accept a few the following year.

All in all, I was pleased by how smoothly and quickly work went. It was plain to see how I had profited from my mistakes and experiences with Operation Protection Poc.

One Saturday afternoon after the boys had stopped work, I got a hankering to camp alone up in the cloud forest. The April moon was full and dry season almost at an end. I asked Armando to drive me up to the site of our old expedition camp and help me set up a tent. This done, he seemed loath to leave. He tied his dog, Jessie, a strong German shepherd, to a tree.

"Go on," I chided him gently, "nothing's going to happen. It'll be like old times."

He shook his head disapprovingly but left. I settled down by the campfire to listen to the evening sounds and soak in the atmosphere. A soft mist began filtering through the forest and gradually thickened. The light turned a somber gray. Tree trunks looked black; leaves, pewter. It became a monochromatic, mysterious world. The only sounds were the campfire's crackling and an occasional large leaf dropping to the jungle floor. Then Jessie began to growl, low, deep-throated, and menacingly. I stared into the forest. Nothing. I grabbed my flashlight and heaped more wood on the fire. I remembered the machete lying inside my little orange mountain tent. When I crawled in to get it, I realized that I felt much safer inside. I settled myself in the center and tried to figure out what was upsetting the dog. A mountain lion? They were very rare on the volcano, and not dangerous. Perhaps a coyote? The only other large animals were peccaries, deer, foxes, margay cats, and kinkajous. I thought I heard a slight shuffling nearby. Jessie's growls increased. The firelight threw shadows on the thin tent walls and I wondered if my silhouette was visible. Finally, I lay down flat, clutching the machete, and waited. After an hour, the dog quieted, and I sensed that the danger had passed. I crept out, rekindled the fire, and cooked my supper.

Later as I lay trying to sleep, I cursed myself for insisting on this mini-outing. Because of the mist there was no moonlight to admire. No intriguing noises broke the night's deathlike hush. Suddenly, from far down the volcano, drums, rattles, bells, and shouts reverberated. What could it be? The sounds grew louder. Should I run and hide? Or stay? Now I was really scared.

To my utter relief, I heard a new sound—a jeep rattling up the dirt track. It could be only one person—Armando! He leaped out of the Land Rover and grabbed my shoulders. "Are you all right?" he demanded. "I had a feeling that something was wrong."

I told him about the strange events and asked him to listen to the clatter and banging below us.

"There just was an eclipse of the moon," he explained. "Those superstitious Indians believe that something is eating up the moon. They run outside and make lots of noise to 'save it.' "

Even as he spoke, a pale, watery shaft of moonlight slipped through the fog and threw a glow on my tent. The clouds were lifting and a breeze began. The forest was coming back to life.

"But the other noises earlier," said Armando, "I don't like that. Jessie's got a good nose—someone was up here."

"Maybe it was some of the boys having fun," I suggested.

"I doubt it. They respect you too much," murmured Armando, fingering his revolver. As he turned to spark up the fire, I'd never seen him look so grim. He pulled a small flask from his jacket. "*Aguardiente*—white lightning," he explained. "You're nervous as a cat. Take a big swallow and relax, Anita. I'm staying here with you tonight."

Gratefully I obeyed. The raw liquor hit my stomach like a blow. A warm flush spread over my body. Bright blue-white moonbeams streamed reassuringly into the cloud forest. Above the sheltering canopy of trees a clear ebony sky stretched into space. Maybe the quetzals were sleeping that night, but Armando and I didn't.

The next week I devoted to the last and most enjoyable phase of setting up the reserve. I spent two days giving a modicum of training to the six workmen. Three would be paid as private game-wardens to patrol the sanctuary on weekends. The other three would act as honorary ones, filling in when needed and acting as guides for visitors. Since the farm did not have easy public access and the reserve was to be opened only to scientists, photographers, conservationists, and educators, we were not too concerned about enforcement. Then I lectured to the schoolchildren on the farm, explaining why the quetzal was unique and why we were trying to save it and its cloud-forest habitat. I used David's slides, a projector, and a portable generator. Again, as in Lake Atitlán, I hoped the children would carry our conservation message home to their parents. The little tykes sat absolutely spellbound, never having seen colored pictures on a wall. It occurred to me then what a marvelous teaching technique this would be—to travel about Central and South America with a van and a portable generator, giving conservation lectures in remote areas.

My final duty was to meet with the landowners and help them form an association for legal registration of their reserve. We hoped that the Ministry of Finance would thereby declare the land tax-exempt. The owners were taking 1,000 acres out of possible cultivation and donating the land for a conservation area, so it seemed right that they receive some compensation from the government. We chose the name Asociación Atitlán para la Protección del Quetzal (Atitlán Association for the Protection of the Quetzal) for this nonprofit, private organization.

On our last day at the finca, we came in late from the volcano. I walked into my bedroom and stopped abruptly. Someone was in the bed! In the dim light, I couldn't make out who, but it seemed like a fat person. I screamed. Armando ran up and stared into the room.

"Get back!" he whispered, pulling me into the kitchen. "Stay here!" He pulled out his revolver and grabbed a flashlight. Then he slid sideways against the wall toward the room. I froze in horror. I saw the bright beam play onto the bed and Armando take aim. Half a minute of rigid silence passed. Then his body relaxed and the gun dropped. He motioned me to his side. Together we walked up and stood looking down—at a dummy!

Someone had stolen into my room while I was away and cleverly put together a caricature of me. It was authentic from the beat-up sombrero to the worn hiking boots. Only one thing was wrong with the likeness—the dummy was pregnant!

The whole creation had to be the work of a sick mind. And it had to be someone who knew me well, knew my clothing, knew our schedule. It had to be one of the six boys we worked with. Stunned, I mentally ran over the list. We both spoke the name at once—Pablo! Armando broke into a harsh tirade.

"It was Pablo who tried to sneak up to your tent the night of the eclipse, I'm sure. It is Pablo who made this dummy because he's so heartsick for you. It has to be."

I hated to agree, but the evidence pointed that way. The entire situation made me feel sad for the Indian lad. "I'll speak to him in the morning," I began. "The poor fellow—"

"No, you won't!" stormed Armando, shoving the revolver back in his belt. "I'll handle it!" And with that he ran out into the night. I never knew what happened.

We left early next morning. On the trip from Volcano Atitlán back to Lake Atitlán, I did a lot of thinking. In a few days I had to return to the university and it would be months before I could see Armando again. If we were to be together, it would have to be in Guatemala at the lake where Armando had his roots, a position of good standing, and where his sharp native intelligence fit so well.

A decision was forming deep inside me, as dramatic as driving from the dim cloud forest to the sparkling lake, as symbolic as growing from graduate school to my first professional job. This time I didn't cry when I returned to the university.

From Atitlán to Anegada

During all the academic duties of my second year of teaching—committee meetings, graduate-student interviews, staff sessions, classes, grading exams, and writing papers—I yearned to be back in the field. The experience and satisfaction of setting up the grebe and the quetzal reserves had made me eager to spread my wings farther as a fledgling ecologist. Gradually I was turning away from academia.

What an intoxicating day it was when a colleague wrote from the Caribbean Research Institute of the College of the Virgin Islands, asking me to participate in an ecological survey of Anegada Island in the British West Indies. Anegada! The very name, lyrical and wild, conjured up visions of white sand beaches, coconut palms, blue-blue seas, coral reefs, and sun as penetrating as an acetylene torch. I knew Anegada lay equally positioned between the Greater and Lesser Antilles, yet it bears no resemblance at all to its mountainous sister isles in the American and British Virgin Islands or to Puerto Rico. It actually looks more like flat Anguilla and Barbuda, about 75 miles away.

The Institute was trying to assemble a team of scientists to visit Anegada and gather the basic biological information needed before a large development corporation from England which had leased 6,000 of the island's 9,592 acres could move ahead with its plans to build a large retirement community and tourist resort. The Institute was very keen to do a baseline study prior to major construction, so as to find out what to protect and manage. Also it hoped to use Anegada as an ecological reference point in relation to other more highly developed Caribbean islands. The island's value as an indicator of ecological change caused by modern development would be unquestionable. A quick review of the literature at the university library showed me that only five or six scientists had ever worked there, among them my friend Dr. Alexander

Wetmore of the giant grebes. None had ever attempted to specifically enumerate or describe the major habitat types of this island or list all the birds and mammals. Its main claim to zoological fame was the presence of a huge, rare, endemic lizard—the Anegada ground iguana, *Cyclura pinguis*. At once I was captivated by the chance to add new scientific information and be a "mini-pioneer" in the conservation of this remote island.

I wrote and agreed to come during our long Christmas vacation. The trip was to be financed by a grant of the Division of Research at Cornell University, with all the equipment and logistics of travel to be taken care of by the Institute. I could begin now to reap the benefits of having a Ph.D. My kindly professor had been right; already, grant money was far easier to obtain and people seemed to have more confidence in my ability. Strange how one piece of paper could make such a difference in doing conservation work. . . .

When I stepped out of the plane in St. Thomas on a January morning, the blazing sun nearly blinded my winter-weak eyes. I blinked like an owl and reached for sunglasses. The tangy sea breeze began clearing my sinuses. How good it felt to be back in the tropics. However, none of the other team members had arrived. Each had listed different dates of availability. Instead of tackling Anegada in a concerted effort, we would be doing piecemeal studies over the next several months, using two marine biologists, a botanist, a herpetologist, a marine archaeologist, and possibly a park planner. The pieces of this ecological picture would be a long time coming together.

Nevertheless, I was here, ready to go, and the hours were ticking relentlessly away toward a reluctant return to the classroom. A young student assistant had been located, his camping gear assembled, and our supplies piled on the dock by midafternoon. The captain of the college boat, however, was not eager to start out late in the day on this 4-hour run. The reefs around the north and east of Anegada are treacherous and extensive. Most ships give the island a wide berth. Over 200 wrecks are charted for Horseshoe Reef alone, and channels are poorly marked. Moreover, the 7- by 3-mile low island barely presents any profile to the navigator. Dusk was falling when the lavender smudge that was Anegada first showed up on the horizon. The sea was alive with phosphorescence, sparkling and winking in our wake. The captain steered toward the only channel and jetty on the entire shoreline. Behind it, a few hundred yards away, lay "The Settlement," Anegada's one hamlet.

When we finally docked on the leeward shore and began unloading, thousands of mosquitoes swarmed over us. We worked faster and faster to avoid the ravenous insects. Soon a jumbled heap of scientific gear, sleeping bags, tents, backpacks, and food lay on shore. The captain hurried us off his boat. He was anxious to get back to St. Thomas before midnight.

"Be back for you next Saturday," he promised, then eased cautiously away from the rotting wharf.

Jim, my student assistant, and I were left alone on shore with the topsy-turvy mess of gear. "Let's straighten this out," I said irritably, as the boat dwindled in size out on the moonlit sea. "We've got to find some repellent and put up our tents. We may as well camp right here tonight."

Now the sandfleas from nearby mangroves discovered us. Maddening! Within half an hour we had managed to organize things and get a small smudge burning with driftwood and dry seaweed to drive the bugs away. Jim started to crawl into his tent then backed out, moaning, "Oh, no, there's no netting. It's rotted out." I couldn't believe it. In the hurry, someone had grabbed the wrong tent for this kind of job.

"Well, you can sleep in mine," I offered, glad now that I had insisted on bringing my own field gear. (This was only one of many times when I've had to share my shelter with needy colleagues.) "How about a cup of cocoa?" I said comfortingly to my young, distraught helper. "Then, we'll go to sleep."

"Okay. Where's the water?" he asked, unearthing a pan.

Then it hit me. Water! The one and most important thing we needed was water. No one had thought to ship a goodly supply for our week's work. Without at least 2 gallons apiece per day, we could not survive field conditions on the semi-desert island. I remembered reading that Anegada has no fresh surface water at all. Inhabitants get their meager supply from sinkholes and depressions in the limestone where a few fresh-water seeps and rainwater collect. We didn't want to drink from those.

"We'll have to go to The Settlement first thing in the morning," I decided. "There are supposed to be three hundred blacks living there. Maybe we can buy some water. Otherwise . . ." I let my words drift off. This was *not* the right way to begin a field expedition. We were here with nothing to drink, over 100 pounds of equipment to move, and one topographic map. After the onslaught of insects we'd experienced, we realized that we must move across to the windward shore and camp on the beach. The sea breeze would blow bugs away and cool us in the heat of the day. We could base out of there as well as anywhere. For the survey, I'd planned to do trapping and netting of small mammals and birds at the five major ecosystems on the island: beach scrub and dunes, freshwater sinks and seeps, salt-water lagoons, dense bush of the interior, and The Settlement.

Shortly after dawn, we walked into the town. We followed a well-worn path and were soon on "Main Street." This one-track lane was lined with tiny wooden shacks, weatherbeaten to pewtergray. Each one had a cistern with pipes leading to the rusty sheet-iron roof. I didn't see how people could ever collect and keep sufficient rainwater to survive all year since Anegada receives only about 30 to 40 inches annually and that mostly in rainy season.

On all sides of us, old tin cans, faded cardboard boxes, plastic bottles, broken glass, discarded metal drums, and nondescript rubbish lay profusely. Apparently, the residents of The Settlement just threw refuse on the ground and let the antiseptic sun, air, roving dogs, and rats perform their cleansing acts. Not a tree in sight. The bald white limestone was as hard as cement. One small shop was open. Other than this, the place was deserted.

Then I noticed a very old man rocking on a shady porch. His clothes, his beard, and his fedora were all various shades of gray, blending with the silvery boards behind him. If it were not for his fringe of snow-white crinkly hair and the creak of his rocker, we might have gone right by him.

"Hello, sir," I called companionably, stopping and looking at him.

The creaking stopped and a pair of beady bright eyes bored into mine.

"Hello, missus," came back a high-pitched voice. "Did you just come in by boat?"

"No, we arrived last evening," I replied in a loud voice, not sure how well this old gnome could hear. "We came from St. Thomas and are here for a week to study the animals."

"That so?" he asked politely. "Well, come right up here on this shady porch and tell me about it, missus."

I gave Jim a look of relief and we walked over to the old Negro and shook hands.

"Mr. Wallace Vanderpool, your servant," he said deferentially, almost bowing.

I caught myself wondering if he was a descendant of slaves and where he came from. This black man was probably no older than Don Emilio, but he lacked the proud carriage and vitality of the Basque. Rather, he seemed fragile and stooped. Only his eyes hinted at an underlying spunkiness.

Sitting on the railing of the porch, Jim and I told Mr. Vanderpool who we were and what we planned to do. He rocked rhythmically and seemed interested. Then he jumped nimbly to his feet. "I'll just get you some lemonade, missus," he exclaimed. "You must be right thirsty."

Jim and I both thanked him, but I secretly had visions of greenish liquid probably full of rust specks, tiny lizards, and amoebas. To our surprise, the three chipped jelly glasses he carried out looked clear and lemony. Their contents tasted even better. He must keep his cistern strained and scrubbed, I decided. Thanking him for the treat, I asked Mr. Vanderpool if we might find some place to buy water during our stay. On many Caribbean islands, it's as dear as soda pop or gasoline.

"Why, right here," he said pertly. "You just come and get all you want, missus."

"But you won't have enough to last you till rainy season," I protested.

"Well, Miss Anne," he explained, "I have a big cool cistern half full, a well in the yard, and a couple of sinkholes in my crop field. I use the sinkholes to water my plants, the well for cooking and washing, and the cistern to drink. Now, how's an old man like me going to use up all that water? I don't work out in the sun much any more."

Gratefully we agreed on a price for the water. Mr. Vanderpool said he would provide jugs. Jim volunteered to walk in from our camp every day to pick it up at dusk.

"Would anyone have a jeep?" I asked dubiously. "We also have a lot of gear to get up to the north side of Windlass Bight."

"Of course, we do. Andrew, my next-door neighbor, can take you over—*and* bring the water," he added cannily. "Since the development company came over here, most of the men have given up lobster and conch fishing and have gone to work building roads. They make a lot more money. A few have even brought jeeps and cars over here." He shook his head sadly. "I hate to see and hear the change. Used to be all we heard was the wind and waves and birds, day in, day out. Lots of good food from the sea, too," he added. "Now, it's candy and crackers and sody pop and canned spaghetti." He spat distastefully over the railing. "I miss those fresh groupers and conch chowders, missus."

I perked up my ears. It sounded like Santiago Atitlán all over again. An introduction—be it largemouth bass or a construction company—could change a whole society's health and diet and way of life. I wondered if a protein deficiency might be showing up here, too.

"Are the people still healthy?" I asked.

"Oh, I don't know, missus," he answered plaintively. "I know *I* don't have the get up and go I used to, but then I don't go to sea no more. The boats are all moldering by the dock. You must have seen 'em, Miss Anne. The sea is good for a man. It makes him strong. So does its food, them shellfish." He grinned impishly.

"Oh, there's been a lot of changes here," he mused and lapsed into reminiscences.

Clearly, Mr. Vanderpool didn't have any medical information. Besides, the company had been here less than a year. Perhaps it was too soon for physical changes in the islanders' blood, teeth, and bones to show up.

"How far is it to Windlass Bight?" I asked, to bring him back to the present. "We want to camp over there."

" 'Bout a league," answered Mr. Vanderpool.

"How far is that?"

"Well, I'm not sure," replied the old Negro. "Maybe five or ten miles. We don't use miles here. Leagues is left over from the English pirate days."

"Jim, what do you say we take our lunch and walk over there? Andrew can bring our gear when he gets home from work, if Mr.

Vanderpool will be good enough to arrange it. That way we can start exploring the island and save some time."

Jim looked at me dumbstruck. I knew precisely what he was thinking. To leave a pile of valuable equipment unattended in St. Thomas or St. Croix would be foolhardy. It would be gone in ten minutes. Yet I had an intuitive feeling already that this man was deeply honest and the island still untouched by racial strife and deceit.

"It's all right," I said quietly to Jim. "I know Mr. Vanderpool will watch out for us."

We reached the great white beach of Windlass Bight at noon and took shelter under an overturned rowboat near the dunes. My thermometer read 92 degrees F and the sand was blazing hot. Beyond the beach a sheltered shallow lagoon of purest Caribbean blue ran out almost half a mile to the great toothlike reef which separated the island from the Puerto Rican trench. On the horizon, the water was an angry blue, as angry as Lake Atitlán had been in the chocomil. Here the 5-mile depths of the trench suddenly came up against this land barrier. It was a tremendous change in relief—28,000 feet to about 8 feet—and the sea balked at the sudden restraint after its free fetch of over 4,000 miles from Europe. It threw itself ceaselessly against the long coral strands.

We rested through the midday heat, bathing, sunning, and sleeping. At 4 P.M. the heat dropped, so Jim and I headed to the three southwestern lagoons shown on the map. I was eager to scout out the area and run our first trap line. It was almost sunset when we broke through a fringe of mangroves and gazed out on a brick-red body of water. Three Bahama ducks were preening nearby and a great blue heron stood statuesquely in the shadows. A mangrove cuckoo called sweetly from the underbrush. Then the sharp rattling call of a belted kingfisher surprised us as he flashed by. Seconds later, a small black bird streaked over the salt lagoon close to the surface with a neat *"zit-t-t-t-t"* sound and doubled back into the bushes.

"What was that?" wondered Jim aloud.

I rapidly ran through Bond's *Birds of the West Indies* in my mind. But I could come up with nothing that small, that black, and that fast. Then it struck me—a bat! "There must be bats on this island, Jim. But where in the world would they roost? There are no caves here."

"Unless they fly down into the sinkholes?" he countered.

"Oh my word, can you imagine that! We'll have to find out if they do. But first of all we have to identify them. Let's put up the mist nets here," I said excitedly.

As if in jest, several more bats suddenly appeared, scouting for insects. It was an odd but strangely lovely scene—the dark-green band of mangroves edging the peaceful lagoon which turned almost scarlet under the setting sun. At least a hundred agile little black bombers crisscrossing the water with their *zit, zit, zit* sound. Then in the distance we heard the noise of an old jeep missing on at least one cylinder. We hurried back to Windlass Bight and found Andrew waiting for us. All our camp gear was neatly piled well above the high-tide mark and assorted jugs and bottles, holding 10 gallons of water, stood in a row. Andrew was an affable, tall, enormously powerful black, who had worked his way up to fore-man on the construction crew.

"I be here at dis time every day all week, missus," he promised. "And don' you worry none, 'bout de water." Then he left before it was dark, since he had no headlights on his jeep.

Jim and I set up a cozy camp. Everything was intact. Jim attached a plastic tarp to the back of his tent to keep out any vagrant mosquitoes, while the front was left open to the wind which blew continuously and was the best repellent possible. We cooked a hot camp supper that night, with cups of tea to quench our thirst. Then we fell into our sleeping bags. Far out across the moonlit tranquil lagoon the Atlantic thundered on Anegada's great reef, lulling us deeper and deeper into sleep.

The results of our week's field work were surprising. We learned that the only native mammal on Anegada is the fruit-eating bat (*Artibeus jamaicensis*). The bats did indeed roost by day in sinkholes. In fact, Jim climbed down into one with a young local boy to verify this. Undoubtedly, a few other indigenous mammals once inhabited Anegada, such as agoutis, wild guinea pigs, certain insectivores, and rice rats. However, over the centuries, they were either wiped out by exotic introductions which arrived by sea or ship or were trapped out for food. By interviewing Mr. Vanderpool (I was reminded of my talks with Don Emilio), I heard that over the centuries Anegada had been visited by Carib Indians, bucca-neers, Spanish sailors, a few colonists, slavers, and traders. Accompanying these sporadic visitors had been black rats, house mice, house cats, and some domestic livestock. All of these have become feral—that is, they roam about in a wild state. The feral creatures—cattle, sheep, goats, donkeys, cats—have vied with native wildlife and eventually taken over, just as the bass did at Lake Atitlán. Lacking natural predators, they increased. Their grazing, browsing, and preying decimated the fauna and flora of the entire island. They themselves became pitifully scrawny.

So, too, colonists and sailors harmed the little island. The land was cleared and burned off for farming; the trees used for firewood, charcoal, lumber, and ships' timbers. Such treatment soon reduced the vegetation to a few scraggly trees, thorny shrubs, weedy plants, and cacti eking out an existence upon the eroded limestone. The only places where residents can farm on Anegada today are in the pockets and depressions of limestone where enough nutritive soil to support crops still lies.

Jim and I encountered trees only in the area behind Windlass Bight and Loblolly Bay. This dry forest stood no more than 25 feet high and contained West Indian birch, strangler fig, lignum vitae, and mahogany. The bush, as it is called, is the chief habitat of the Anegada ground iguana. Other Caribbean islands—Hispaniola, Grand Cayman, Cuba, Exuma, Andros and Turks islands—have their own species of iguanas, but none is as large or as threatened as the Anegada one.

Our exploration of the bush enabled me to suggest boundaries for a fenced preserve for these endemic lizards. It was a far cry from reeds and grebes, but the principle was the same: Save the habitat in order to save the species. This time, I was hoping to keep a different animal alive, in the face of a proposed international airport, golf courses, industrial sites, retirement homes, tourist hotels, a generating plant, and a sod farm!

The other sanctuary I proposed was a large waterbird refuge at Red and Flamingo ponds. Although we saw no flamingos during the survey, Mr. Vanderpool recounted how the great ruby-pink birds used to be seen here by the hundreds and sometimes nested. Gradually, however, they decreased as a result of poaching and egg stealing by the natives. He had seen none since 1968. "Fillymingo," he explained, "is considered a great delicacy in the islands."

"Do you eat their eggs sunny side up or scrambled?" I quipped, thinking he was joking.

"Oh, fried," he replied seriously. "Fried fillymingo eggs is mighty tasty, Miss Anne."

This information helped explain the vast decline from hundreds of thousands to roughly 20,000 flamingos over the past hundred-odd years in the Caribbean area. Today the birds nest successfully only on Inagua (Bahamas), Bonaire (Netherland Antilles), and the Yucatán peninsula (Mexico). In these three places, flamingo reserves have been established and low-flying aircraft prohibited from passing over the areas in order not to frighten and stampede nesting adults and young.

At the end of the week, Jim and I said good-bye to Mr. Vanderpool and Andrew, promising to see them again in about three months. I planned to return to Anegada in April for more birding and mist-netting in order to pick up migrants not seen in wintertime.

My second visit started off like clockwork, except that no other team member was available and I had no assistant. But this didn't worry me. I felt quite at home on the island. Windlass Bight would be my base again as I resampled the five ecosystems. As long as water could be delivered, I'd manage alone. Andrew assured me of his dependability and helped me set up camp on the beach. Yet when it came time, he seemed reluctant to leave me there 5 miles from the nearest person. I assured him that my log cabin in the United States was the same distance from my closest permanent neighbor in winter and that I'd be fine.

The days slipped by as smoothly as the clear lapis-lazuli waters of the lagoon ebbed in and flowed out with the tides. Each morning I awoke in the cool dawn, took a quick dip in the sea, and even shivered as I dried myself before my little campfire. I birded till nine, then checked the mist nets and released any trapped birds. By eleven the heat was mounting, so I returned to my beach and upturned rowboat, sat underneath the boat in the shade and breeze, and wrote up my field notes. This spring visit was paying off. I had already observed twelve species I had not seen in January. Three birds were outstanding finds—a piping plover never before recorded in the entire Virgin Island group at any time of year; a marbled godwit which had been seen only occasionally in winter in the West Indies; and a cattle egret, a recent immigrant from Africa. Another interesting discovery was a metal band that Mr. Vanderpool had obtained from a hunter during the winter of 1970. He gave it to me, wonderingly. Later, I checked it out with the Migratory Bird Population Station in Laurel, Maryland. It had been placed on an adult drake blue-winged teal in Maine!

Late afternoon found me setting off again to check out some new corner of the island. Andrew delivered my water at dusk and stayed to chat by the campfire until he could barely see his way back to The Settlement. After supper, I'd sit a while on the powdered sugar beach or skinny-dip in the tepid lagoon. I recall floating on my back, watching the moon rise, my body gleaming and silvery as a fish. Far off to the north, the ocean thundered restlessly and I thought of all the dark shapes out there hunting along the reef by night, just as the furry bats were zooming across the lagoon behind me. But here in the peaceful shallows no danger lurked. I rolled over like a seal and paddled back toward the tent and campfire. Later, snug in my sleeping bag, I listened to a lone mockingbird singing his heart out to the moon. Spring's mating urge was upon him.

By the end of that tranquil week, I had counted 55 species of birds—28 of them first records for Anegada Island. Then, on the last evening, a jarring element inserted itself. Andrew arrived early with his jeep and announced that "de plant doctuh" had come and was camped near the shell mounds near the east end of Anegada. He'd been there three days, but no one had seen hide nor hair of him. Andrew, out looking for his strayed cow, had happened upon him.

"Mon, dat doctuh, he got de fancy food and tent and eveyting," exclaimed Andrew, "but de site is no good. No, missus. No one go down dere much and de bugs is bad."

"I should go visit him now and see what he's doing," I said. "Otherwise the boat will come tomorrow or latest next day and it'll be too late. We might be able to share some information."

"Well, you gonna break de camp here anyway. Let's go dere now," Andrew offered.

An hour later we were in the jeep bouncing over pocked limestone, with the land growing poorer and less vegetated as we headed southeast. I noted stripes of International Orange on the rocky ground. Ahead, a huge heap of weathered conch shells rose like a monolith. Beside it, close to a salt pond, stood an elegant green stand-up tent with its fly stretched out like an awning. Around it were a folding table, and chairs, an ice chest, a huge lantern, plant presses, and boxes of canned goods. Peeking into the tent, I could see several half-empty tins on the floor. Small land crabs had apparently smelled the food and eaten their way up through the canvas floor to feast on them. They now scuttled back into their holes like sneaky thieves. What a mess! No one was there. Andrew waited uncertainly. It was growing dark and he longed to traverse the winding track home while he could still see. Yet he was most concerned that "de plant doctuh" had not come back.

"It not good to be out in de bush so late," he warned.

I searched about for a note, map, some clue as to where the botanist might have gone. Nothing. Then we both heard the sound of clumsy footsteps stumbling toward us. A thin, disheveled, elderly man appeared, limping badly. Andrew and I rushed over to help him, but instead of a greeting or thanks, we received a glower.

"Who are you?" he demanded suspiciously, looking from one to the other of us and all around his tent. I introduced Andrew and myself and explained I had just come over from my own campsite to discuss our joint research for the Institute before I left Anegada.

"Can't do it," was his abrupt reply as he hobbled toward his chair and threw down a heavy knapsack. "Got to press and identify these specimens. I'm finding dozens of species never recorded here before."

"Are you painting those orange lines on the limestone?" I asked curiously.

"Yes," was his curt reply.

"Why?"

"Gridlines," he answered, throwing a machete carelessly on the ground. It rang cruelly as the blade nicked itself on the stone. Then the botanist sat down and slowly began to ease off his brand-new-looking boots.

"You have some terrible blisters," I sympathized, leaning forward.

Again he glared at me. I stepped back. Painfully he pulled off his socks and revealed two fluid-filled circles the size of silver dollars on his heels.

"What possessed you to bring new boots out here to do your field work?" I asked good-naturedly.

He gave me a strained look and made no answer.

"Let me boil up some water, prick those blisters, and drain them properly," I offered. "They should be bandaged, too. Is your gas stove working?"

"No, it's *not*," he spat. "Leave me alone. I'll be all right."

Andrew and I looked at each other in amazement. Such behavior was hard to fathom. I decided to try once more.

"Look," I said gently, "you'll never be able to finish your field work with feet like this. You need medical attention, some soft slippers, and a good meal. Let us help you."

"I don't have any slippers," he answered peevishly, "and I forgot the gas for the stove. I've been eating cold canned goods." Then to our astonishment, he burst into tears.

Suddenly I realized the man was close to heat exhaustion, or a sunstroke such as I had had in Guatemala, and was almost incoherent. Andrew took over. He ambled up to the botanist, lifted him bodily, and carried him carefully to the jeep, ignoring the pronounced flinch and the grimace the white man made at him. "We gonna take you to de Settlement, mon. You is in no shape to travel de bush, Mistah Doctuh."

Next morning, a very dejected botanist accompanied me on the boat back to St. Thomas. He took nothing with him but the plant press and his half-filled knapsack. Whether he ever went back to Anegada for his things I don't know.

Reports eventually came in from other scientists as they completed their parts of the survey. To my initial recommendations I added two more. One was to set up several pristine dune-beach parks along the windward shore. We worried that the development company might bulldoze the three lines of barrier dunes flat in order to increase the extent of its shoreline property and its value. The ecological backlash of this real-estate maneuver would be the loss of the natural stability and protection afforded by the dunes against hurricanes, high seas, and beach erosion. Furthermore, such parks could serve as prime water-recreation areas. Anegada's beaches are practically unparalleled in the West Indies.

The second recommendation was to make an historical monument, encompassing the old conch-shell mounds and adjacent salt flats at the eastern tip of Anegada. These undoubtedly are both pre-Columbian middens (kitchen refuse piles left by early Indians) and post-Columbian mounds. A search through the discarded shells might yield valuable information about the early fauna and the archaeology of this uniquely positioned island.

In general, our reports advised against lavish developmental changes which would attempt to make Anegada look "civilized," greener, or more attractive by north-temperate-zone standards. Such amenities as golf courses, a sod farm, a nursery filled with exotic plants (and insects), grass lawns, and flower gardens did not belong on this remarkably uncontaminated island. As far as we could learn, Anegada was one of the few places in the entire Caribbean which had so far escaped chemical fertilizers, pesticides, phosphates, fluorinated hydrocarbons, weed killers, electricity, and (until the last few years) even gas-driven engines. As such, it was an unusual find and a reference point for environmental "purity." Moreover, Anegada had an abundance of those two most precious ingredients for tourism—sun and sea. It could stand on its merits as it was.

I never saw a final report from our "team," or an environmental-impact statement. I don't know who read our individual reports. No one asked any of us to return to the island. However, through the grapevine of colleagues, I heard that the development company abandoned its project in 1973 but the government of the British Virgin Islands might continue tourist development. Five years later, I heard that this, too, had been given up but plans were afoot to set up an industry to quarry sand on the island. The Anegada community successfully vetoed this on the grounds that the excavations would make the land more vulnerable to flooding and the enterprise would generate no jobs for residents since they are not trained to run heavy mining equipment. Then there was talk of using the island for military target practice and drilling for offshore oil. These projects also fell by the wayside.

And so today, as far as I know, Anegada is still drowsing in the sun. Its people have returned largely to fishing and conching by the old-time methods, exporting some of their catch to the Virgin Islands and Puerto Rico. Flamingo Pond has officially been turned into a preservation area, and iguanas still scuttle through the bush.

I learned two important lessons from this assignment. The first was that teamwork is essential. In handling ecological surveys, there have to be coordination, good timing, cross-fertilization, and commitment. Second, I realized the need for careful preparation and adequate field gear. A successful expedition and conservation campaign can stand or fall on an old tent or a new pair of boots.

Benjamin and Barú

Grebes—quetzals—iguanas. Atitlán—Anegada. I was more and more drawn to independent field work. In June 1971, I made a crucial decision—I would go free-lance: I had saved enough money to survive for a year. I would use my rustic Adirondack cabin as an office and base of operations, thereby cutting down overhead. And, I hoped, I had made enough contacts in the last five years to assure me assignments as an ecological consultant and writer-photographer. I reasoned that, with most professionals tied down to academic or institutional schedules, a person who was free and flexible might hold an edge in obtaining worthwhile short-term environmental and conservation jobs.

Yet at the end of the second week without a pay check waiting, I knew this was the psychological turning point. No big institution, no sugar daddy, no independent source of income was backing me up. From now on, I needed a lot of faith, for I was strictly on my own. The realization was both exhilarating and frightening.

I got by for the first half-year on a few small writing jobs and day consultancies. Then, on a blustery day in January 1972, the first big field assignment came. I had trudged over the frozen lake on snowshoes to pick up my mail and found, to my surprise, a cable from Switzerland. With cold-numbed fingers I tore it open. The International Union for Conservation of Nature and Natural Resources (IUCN) was requesting me to go to Panama for a month to conduct an ecological survey of its first national park, Volcano Barú. Moreover, they wanted me to hire a photographer to accompany the team and document the entire expedition for future reports, records, articles, and brochures. I let out a whoop of exultation which echoed across the hoar-frosted hills and startled a few nuthatches and snowshoe hares. Here was my opportunity to earn good money, learn new techniques, meet foreign professionals, travel into different ecosystems, and contribute to Panama's newborn national park program.

The incongruity—not to mention the size—of the project didn't really hit me until I was halfway home. How was I going to pack all my tropical field gear—tents, mist nets, traps, weather instruments, cook sets, canteens, sleeping bags, cameras, film, tapes, notebooks, and the rest of it—out of the cabin and carry it a mile and a half down the ice-bound lake to my truck and the nearest road? Where would I find a photographer who would be ready on such short notice to spend a month climbing around an over-11,000-foot peak in Panama? My jubilance was so great, however, that I simply glossed over these logistic problems and sang the rest of the way home.

Fortunately, friends loaned me a snowmobile, so, despite blizzards and deep drifts, I was able to drag two toboggan loads of equipment to my truck fairly easily. I wrote to a list of free-lance photographers. Direct communication was a problem: The closest phone was 5 miles away. The man I finally engaged arrived at my cabin one afternoon on snowshoes, swiftly made out a contract for us both to sign, and headed off again into the teeth of a snowstorm. I decided that if Clyde Smith could conduct his business that well in Adirondack winter, he'd do okay on a Central American volcano. And he did.

Clyde and I flew into Panama City together with about 300 pounds of gear. We were met by government officials from the Ministry of Agriculture and two of our Panamanian teammates: Dario Tovar, chief of Panama's budding National Parks Service, and Javier Ortega, a young forester who was our driver.

Mr. Tovar explained that the survey had been requested by the former Minister of Agriculture, Carlos Landau. This far-sighted gentleman was convinced that a national park not only would bring in tourist dollars but could also preserve the unusual mountain flora and fauna of western Panama and protect the mountain watershed against erosion, flooding, silting, and other degradation downstream. His belief was affirmed by a United Nations Food and Agriculture Organization (FAO) study which pointed out that Panama could profitably develop six national parks, making Barú its number one attraction, with quetzals as a main feature.

The next day the four of us traveled along the Pan American Highway to Davíd, Panama's second largest city, near the Pacific Ocean. Until now I had not been aware that the Panamanian isthmus curves in an east-west direction and that its western highlands are the market basket for the entire country. Temperate-zone food and flower crops thrive here—cauliflower, potatoes, green beans, and carnations. I found it hard to believe, too, that frost frequently dusts the top of the continental divide. Off across a wide stretch of cattle pasture, we got our first glimpse of Volcano Barú. It certainly didn't look like the highest point in the country (11,410 feet), but more like a large, lazy hill with a few irregular lumps on its sides—rather as if a cook had carelessly frosted a cake with a blunt knife. Little did we realize, looking up from sea level, how grandiose its geological formations are.

We began our first week of reconnaissance around the eastern base of Barú, climbing as high as 7,500 feet, and working out of the pretty little resort town of Boquete. Each day we visited key areas proposed for park development and possible visitors' centers. One such site was beside the Rio Bajo Chiquero. The river literally sprang out of the volcano side, cascaded down a wall of sheer rock in a lacy water veil, turned into a tumbling, gurgling stream, and hurried away toward the Pacific. I tried a dip in the freshet and found it crystal-clear, toe-tingling, and almost too cold for comfort. As I dried myself, the liquid warbling of American dippers (water ouzels) in the streambed made me think of the Rocky Mountains.

Another beautiful spot lay 1,000 feet above the stream valley in a magnificent primary forest of magnolias and oaks. Some trees stood 100 feet tall and had trunks 4 feet in diameter. As we stepped to a lookout at the forest edge, Panama's famous *bajareque* (misty sprinkle), was lying above Boquete. This phenomenon occurs when light rain is skimmed off the tops of heavy cloud banks held against the Atlantic slopes and then is blown over the continental divide by strong trade winds. Gently it falls out miles away on the Pacific slopes and valleys from seemingly cloudless skies. Shafts of late afternoon light played hide-and-seek with the bajareque as we watched, forming single rainbows, double rainbows, triple rainbows.

Each day some new dignitary came to visit us in Boquete. I was delighted by the interest of these officials and the logistical support we were being given. It was a far different beginning from that of my early days in Guatemala. As far as I was concerned, though, the most valuable person we met in Boquete was Benjamin Cuevas Montezuma, the government's only guardian for this huge proposed park. I took one look at the sturdy Guaymi Indian who was to guide us up the volcano and I was impressed. His muscular shoulders were to prove invaluable for carrying our scientific equipment, food, and most precious water up to the summit. His keen eyes and nose were far better than mine at finding hidden animal trails, signs, and scents. And his wonderful stoic nature was to help us all endure the hardships that lay ahead.

Early the next week, we began phase two of our survey with explorations on the western slopes of Barú. The vegetation and landscape were much drier, starker, and sparser than they were around Boquete. A great lava discharge from Barú's fiery past had strewn rocks and rubble over much of the ground. Looking up, I saw an intimidating sight. The volcano's summit loomed above us, looking more craggy and steep than it had from any other angle thus far. Gazing at the mountaintop, I whispered nervously to Clyde, "I doubt if we'll ever make it to the top with all our gear, don't you?"

He shot back a worried frown and nodded. Yet secretly I sensed we were both eager to begin the climb and get to know that lofty peak. But before we could tackle the summit, we had a week of field reconnaissance at lower elevations. One of the exciting aspects of our team cooperation was working closely with the Panamanian technicians. As Javier identified tropical trees, he showed me new species. Dario explained the country's natural-resources program in detail. I reciprocated by teaching them how to make soil measurements, take weather readings, trap and net wildlife, and make a forest profile. At that time (1972) this type of team approach and photographic documentation was most innovative, and Panama was one of the first Central American countries to consider parks.

The regional forester came to lead us up a rough jeep road to the 7,500-foot contour where the park's proposed boundary lay. We planned to set up camp there and make a new study site. As we leveled off in a small valley, the sight we beheld made me cringe and Dario curse. There, backed right up to the park's border and probably intruding upon it, was brand-new pastureland. Not a tree had been spared. Downed timber lay scattered every which way waiting to go up in flames or down in rot. Cows were already grazing on new patches of grass. When we stopped to get out of the jeep, we heard the steady chop-chop-chop on nearby hillsides and the crash of a falling tree. It was the Cuchumatanes Mountains in Guatemala all over again! Disgruntled, we held a quick discussion. Stay? Or turn back and search for another study site?

Suddenly I heard the *"waac-a-waac-a-waac"* alarm note of a female quetzal. Amazed, I quickly hiked partway up a hill still clothed with untouched cloud forest and played my old quetzal recording. Immediately, a male bird responded with his territorial whistle. An hour of observation convinced me that we had stumbled onto a group of the birds. I hurried down and persuaded my team members to stay and make our field headquarters at the edge of the pasture and forest.

After a week in this area I had estimated a population of about twenty quetzals. All were engaged in early courtship. Almost every morning I saw bunches of three to eight birds chasing one another, calling seductively, flirting. Once three females and five males performed a provocative "ring around the rosy." The "gents" flew around and around a small sapling with their long green tail plumes fluttering behind, while the "ladies" chattered boisterously from its branches. One cool, misty evening, a lone quetzal alighted only 5 feet above my tent and calmly surveyed me as I oiled my boots. Evidently the birds here had never been bothered by people, and had yet to be scared off by land clearing. Actually, the new openings in the forest enabled me to obtain far better observations of the birds than I could in Volcano Atitlán's dense cloud forest. Clyde was able to obtain a few pictures of the normally shy trogons without all the elaborate equipment David Allen had used. The species was at the southernmost point of its range here. Unlike the birds I had studied in Guatemala—the northern sub-species (*Pharomachrus mocinno mocinno*)—this was the southern sub-species (*P. m. costaricensis*), being somewhat smaller and less brilliant in color.

According to Dr. Alexander Wetmore's *The Birds of the Republic of Panama,* quetzals were quite abundant on the slopes of Barú between 1856 and 1902. Since then, however, their distribution has been greatly reduced as a result of increased human activity. Even though the birds are not subject to as many pressures as in Guatemala—not being the national bird or part of Panama's historical and anthropological traditions—they are still disappearing fast throughout the southern range because of the destruction of cloud forest and collecting for zoos and aviaries. I learned that quetzals were being sold by a German firm in San José, Costa Rica, for roughly $250 a pair with air shipment guaranteed to deliver the birds alive. Dr. Wetmore had written that the birds still occurred around Barú at elevations of 7,000 to 9,000 feet; however, we found them only in the remaining swaths of virgin cloud forest on the eastern and western sides; the Pacific slope was under intensive cultivation and grazing as high as 8,000 feet.

It was dry season in Panama—not too hot, not too cool—so our work was pleasant. Javier and I took several environmental measurements: air and soil temperatures, soil samples, small-mammal census, humidity, wind velocity, and a forest profile. Benjamin showed me the ancient, deep trails of tapirs and the rootings of peccaries. But to our concern, the wind blew stronger every day. One night, as it was buffeting our camp at 40 miles an hour, Clyde discovered a small forest fire. Sparks had blown down from one of the woodchoppers' campfires into a mass of dry fallen treetops. Flames were already racing up the ravine toward our campsite when he alerted everyone. We charged in with shovels, machetes, sticks, and a few pitiful pails of water scooped from a tiny creek. If we hadn't put out the fire at once, it could have destroyed our campsite and equipment and probably penetrated the cloud forest. We slept uneasily after that.

I was awakened at dawn by the sound of a tree cracking. It fell on the tent where Dario and Javier were sleeping but fortunately missed both of them. My own little pop tent blew over during breakfast. Benjamin squinted up at Barú's cloud-streaming peak and said quietly, "The wind is very strong up there. We cannot climb tomorrow as planned. It could be one hundred miles per hour and we'd be blown right off."

Dario looked disappointed. He had hoped to scale the summit with us, have a look around, then return to his office in the capital. Clyde and I were frustrated, yet we agreed it would be foolhardy to force this third and most important phase of the survey. Instead, we packed up our tents and drove to Davíd to see Dario off. It was a good chance to renew our supplies and have clothes laundered. While Benjamin was helping me push a cart around a super-market, choosing light-weight foods for our stay on the summit, he said shyly, "I know how much you love the quetzals. Sometime I would like to take you into the Guaymi reservation where I was born and introduce you to the chief. He has a special hat filled with quetzal feathers. He wears it once a year for a corn harvest celebration."

I stared at Benjamin in surprise. Quetzal plumes! Indian chief! Ceremonial headdress! It sounded like one of my Guatemalan adventures. How different the world is, I thought, away from academia. How very unscientific! I felt suddenly excited and re-energized.

"Is it far from Davíd?" I asked.

"Only an hour by car or bus, then eight hours by horse. I know a place to rent horses, too. We could get there in one day," he replied.

Just then I saw the headlines on a newspaper by the checkout counter: WINDS HIT 65 MPH AT DAVÍD AIRPORT. It was a norte just like those at Lake Atitlán, only this one was apparently stronger and longer-lasting than most. I knew from experience that we'd have to wait another two to three days until it blew itself out. We actually had an enforced "vacation" ahead of us. The thought struck Benjamin and me simultaneously. "Why not go now?" I cried.

We finished shopping in a hurry and went to find Clyde and Javier. Over a fragrant lunch of *arroz con pollo* (chicken and rice) and cold Panamanian beer, we made plans. Everyone was excited except Javier—he had never ridden a horse before. I was eager to witness a native custom involving quetzals and to photograph and describe it. This side expedition would be money well spent if it expanded our knowledge of the area and customs around the national park.

Next morning found us speeding along the Pan-American Highway to our "jumping off" place. Benjamin directed Javier through a ramshackle hamlet to a farm which had four cadaverous horses. After a short bargaining session, we swung into our saddles, equipment tied fore and aft, and urged the gaunt creatures to walk. Our way wound through dry and dusty range land, third-growth tropical woodland, across a shallow river, and up into scrubby-looking hills. The land seemed poor and the cattle were as thin as our mounts. In midafternoon, Clyde's horse simply lay down and refused to get up. Six hours of carrying his 200-pound frame plus camping gear was more than she could manage. We unbuckled the saddle and packs and left her behind to rest. Clyde walked. By 4 o'clock we began passing stilt huts that looked like Seminole *chikees* in the Florida Everglades. Just before sunset, we reached a large hut where a friend of Benjamin's lived. "We'll camp here," he told us, "and go on early in the morning. The chief lives about half an hour from here in a large group of huts, but we must water the horses here and let them rest."

While Clyde and Javier set up the tents, Benjamin and I led the horses to the watering place. I followed him confidently through a cool green forest and up a small gully to a spring hole. The pool was no bigger than a wash basin, cupped with mossy stones, and clear as champagne. It was the only water source within 2 miles. As I watched this dependable, diffident man fill our canteens and pots and coax the horses to drink, I realized again how very fortunate I was to have such a guide and companion.

That night I stayed awake a long time, staring out my tent flap toward the Pacific. Tomorrow I would meet a real Indian chief and see a secret ritual. How lucky could I be! It sure beat teaching Introductory Wildlife Conservation to 500 students or sitting through interminable committee meetings! Far off along the coast, a few tiny lights winked back. They seemed to signal "You're right. You're right."

My midnight imaginings of the Indian ceremony were pallid compared to the actual event. Benjamin had us up at dawn, getting ready for the visit. He sluiced water over his strong torso and donned a brand-new light-green *guayabara* (shirt). He stroked fragrant pomade on his glistening black hair. Clearly this was a big moment in his life. I teased him lightly. "Why, Benjamin, you look as if you're going to a wedding."

He flashed a rare smile and said, "It is the first time gringos have come to my home."

Not until then had I realized how little known and how untouched these Indians are. This is one of three groups—the San Blas, Chocos, and Guaymi—and it occupies the westernmost highlands. The total population is between 30,000 and 40,000. Few Guaymis speak Spanish and fewer still want to be integrated into Spanish Panamanian society.

We reached the cluster of huts around 8 A.M. and found a few families sitting on the raised wooden floors. They looked out at us with huge, luminous sloe eyes. Two women dressed in long colorful patchwork gowns were pounding wheat in a log mortar with heavy pestles. The rhythmic beat resounded through the clearing. Old men were weaving thin strips of palm fronds to be used later in making Panama hats, while other women were fashioning beautiful beaded necklaces called *chaquiras*. When we arrived all of them stopped what they were doing and stared at my blond pigtails.

A wizened elderly man came forward and introduced himself with great dignity. He was the chief indeed, but hardly as I expected. He wore a very old, mildewed tuxedo jacket in our honor. His son-in-law, next to be introduced, wore a pink metal hard hat and Western-style shirt and pants. Clyde and I glanced at each other and barely suppressed our giggles. Obviously the men had dressed up in their finest. The wife of the chief now extended her tiny clawlike hand and grinned a toothless greeting. After these formal introductions, no one knew what to do next.

Clyde saved the day. He shyly offered a small flask of rum to the chief. Ceremoniously, the elder uncapped it, took a swig, and passed it to his wife. She downed a healthy gulp and passed it back. Three times they shared the potent liquor. Then they offered it to the hard-hatted son-in-law. Other Indians began edging closer. Their mood was quickly mellowing. Benjamin whispered something to the old man, who went into his hut and came out with a long, hollowed-out bamboo pole. Gently easing a plug from each end, he began pulling out one, two, three—twenty quetzal plumes! With greatest care, he stuffed them into the band of an old sombrero covered with sequins. Finally a headdress of shimmering, 2-foot-long emerald feathers stood above the gaudy crown and trembled in the breeze. The chief placed the spectacle on his head reverently.

Now he spoke to his wife and son-in-law, who scurried into the huts. The son-in-law came back with charcoal, an ancient red lipstick, and some white claylike material. Deftly the old man began applying a geometrical pattern to his face. Then, wonder of wonders, he started painting mine. Benjamin stepped to my side and said softly, "You may feel honored, Anna. My people decorate their faces only for special occasions, and you are a special guest. The chief is putting on a design which fits you alone. Here comes his wife with a dress. She would be pleased if you would wear it when you dance with them."

Dance! Who said anything about dancing? I'd come to see a quetzal ceremony. Suddenly it looked as if I was to be part of it! The son-in-law started playing a flute, while another man began blowing into a conch shell. A small drum was added to these instruments.

Now Benjamin brought a long, polished pole and handed it graciously to the chief. "Although this is not the right day to celebrate, he will show you a bit of the *balseria*. It's an old, old game we play every spring to celebrate the corn harvest. Only the strongest, most agile men can avoid being tripped up by the balsa stick and they stay on their feet for hours, even if they've been drinking *chibcha* (a fermented corn liquor). The champions of the balseria usually become chiefs or respected elders," he explained to us. "Watch!"

At that, the old man swung the pole at Benjamin's muscular legs. He leaped nimbly out of the way, then pranced about like a prizefighter waiting for the next thrust. The chief feinted and swung again, almost but not quite catching him off guard. I could see that if Benjamin had chosen to stay on the reservation, he probably would have been a leader, given his strength, endurance, even temperament, and loyal nature.

After a while, the tempo of the music increased, and the young girls, women, and men formed a conga line. With much good-humored laughter, they urged me into the line. I quickly caught the beat and mastered the steps. The old chief dropped the pole and went to the head of the line. He pulled us along in a shuffling, weaving dance, his quetzal headdress waving woozily. A more ludicrous sight would be hard to imagine. Here I was, at 10 o'clock in the morning, supposedly conducting a serious ecological survey, in a tight, bright granny gown, with my face painted, dancing in a remote corner of Panama.

Benjamin was noticeably morose on our way down from the reservation. Reining my horse close to his, I gave him a questioning smile. Turning to me, he said simply, "My wife died near here." A tear glittered in one corner of his eye.

I was shocked. "Was it long ago?" I asked softly.

"About four years. She was bitten by a snake while gathering wild fruits."

"Was there no way to save her?" I gasped, my heart going out to this bereaved man.

"No. It was much too far to the clinic, and we had no horses," he replied stoically. "She died quickly."

We lapsed into silence, letting our tired mounts pick their way through the scrubby woods. Then Benjamin spoke abruptly. "I left the reservation after that and went to work picking coffee around Boquete, as many of my people do. The best beans grow on the slopes of Barú. Instead of coming back here after the harvest, I stayed out. It was too lonesome even with my own people. I began to work for the Department of Natural Resources cutting trails up the volcano and guiding officials. Then there was talk of a park and I was made a guardian. This is the first time I've been home since I left."

"Wouldn't you rather live on the reservation now?" I inquired. "It seems like such a pleasant life."

"No," he said gloomily. "There are too many dangers facing us here."

"What do you mean?"

"In the eastern part of the reservation, Panamanian mining engineers have discovered the largest copper deposits in the world. They are building a huge plant and digging a mine on our land. My people tell me that the government will build a school for the Guaymi children and teach them Spanish. They will show the men how to operate heavy machinery. The government wants to mix us up with the Panamanians and make us disappear. No one is proud of the Guaymis. Soon we will lose our customs, our clothes, our language, our beliefs.

"Also, between here and the volcano, they are building a large reservoir and hydroelectric plant. Again they will use the Guaymis as cheap labor. Gradually my people will drift away from their homeland and their traditions."

"But surely other Guaymis feel as you do," I protested. "They won't let that happen."

"Yes, some do," agreed Benjamin, "especially the ones who worship Mama Chi."

"Who?"

"Mama Chi. It's a new religion that started about fifteen years ago. A Guaymi woman had a vision in which she was told to start a new cult. Worshipers of Mama Chi do not drink chibcha, will not take part in the balseria, and try to keep the old ways. Many Guaymis here on the reservation have joined this religion."

I was speechless. The more I traveled abroad, the more I learned of the occult, the extrasensory side of life. The straight, hard lines of science mattered little here. People just did not think or function as I had been trained to do. It was a humbling experience.

A small, new thought began formulating in my mind. Turning in my saddle toward Benjamin, I blurted out, "It sounds like the Guaymis are just as threatened as the quetzals or my grebes in Guatemala!"

He nodded. Never before had I considered that human beings—be they Guaymis, Eskimos, Bushmen, or Amazonian Indians—could fall into the category of rare and endangered species. Yet their homelands were being threatened by technology and industry just as wildlife habitats were. The same kind of repercussions were resulting from the introduction of exotic customs as from that of exotic species. Was cutting the reeds for real-estate development or putting bass in a lake any different from making a copper mine on an Indian reservation or setting up schools for children never before exposed to foreign ideas and language?

Benjamin and I were both silent and morose as we continued down the mountain to our jeep.

A Starry Night

Back at Barú we found that the wind had died and the days were clear and warm. We decided it was time to climb to the summit and camp there for as long as we needed to survey the area. Benjamin led the way with a heavy knapsack full of foodstuffs, while Javier plodded along glumly under a cumbersome pack frame with a plant press tied to it. Clyde darted here and there taking pictures, seemingly oblivious to his 60-pound Kelty pack. I brought up the rear, trying to take notes, identify new birds, handle cameras and binoculars, and cope with my 35-pound pack.

Lunchtime found us at Portrero Muleto, a curious craterlike depression on the eastern slopes at an altitude of 9,500 feet. We clambered down. Steep andesite walls rose on three sides, while ahead we could see toward the summit through a V-shaped cleft. My legs were aching and my back was soaked with sweat as I sank down on the dry, cracked mud and pumice floor of the false crater to eat. Sun-bleached bones of tapirs were scattered among the tussocks of grass. I munched a sandwich and drained my canteen. Looking over at Clyde, I thought of asking him for a few extra swallows, then noticed that his canteen also was empty. Benjamin had insisted that each of us carry a 2-gallon plastic jug to be filled on Barú's upper slopes. But where? We hadn't passed a stream, spring, or seep anywhere since the 7,500-foot contour. I thought longingly of the clear, cold Rio Bajo Chiquero and its countless little waterfalls. All Barú's water was springing out of the porous volcanic soil far below us. How would we survive doing strenuous work at these rarified altitudes without that priceless liquid?

Now Benjamin's knowledge of the area came into play. He led us up a narrow ravine and into a small bamboo glade. A pool no larger than a dishpan lay filled with cool seepage water. Evidence that wildlife came here to drink and bathe from miles around was ample. Dainty tracks of brocket deer embroidered the pool edges. Bird prints of every size crisscrossed the damp earth. The wet mud had been packed down into a wallow for wild peccaries. As we approached, we heard the splashing of a black robin in the "dishpan." With infinite care, Benjamin filled our four jugs and every canteen, and I immediately dropped halazone tablets into each container. This bamboo glade was the last watering place we were to see.

The added weight of our jugs (a pint's a pound, the world around!) plus the ever-higher elevations, made the final part of the climb a torture. Even after we stopped in an elfin woodland draped in golden-green mosses and gilded by the setting sun, I could not find the energy to appreciate it. My groaning muscles were about to signal a halt when Benjamin thoughtfully dropped back to offer encouragement. The 11,410-foot peak was in sight, and he had already found a level camping spot 300 feet below the summit and half a mile away. Supper would be ready by the time I got there. Then he sprinted ahead.

I broke through timberline, tottered up a tundralike slope, and stopped dead in my tracks. A full moon was lifting through a blanket of gray clouds beneath me. In the opposite direction, where the sun had set, luminous shafts of rose and gray were shooting up. Benjamin was crouched over a campfire, boiling rice. Clyde had one tent set up and was erecting another. Only Javier, crumpled up beside his plant press, looked as exhausted as I felt.

At dawn, after a good night's sleep, I scraped the frost off my backpack, donned an Icelandic sweater, and gratefully gulped down a cup of hot Panamanian coffee. Now I was ready to tackle that last stretch. We negotiated a knife-sharp ridge where the mountain fell away on both sides for a thousand feet. Then we climbed hand-over-hand up the rocky summit. From our vantage point, we could see both the dark blue Pacific and the gray-green

Caribbean. What a superb lesson in geology and geography! The Talamanca Range melded into even higher peaks in Costa Rica to our west and fell in lowering humps eastward toward the Panama Canal, 275 miles away. North, we could count at least eight mountains more than 10,000 feet high along the continental divide. (Barú actually stands a little south of this central spine.) Beyond it, toward the Caribbean, the hills were broken, rugged, and heavily forested. This is an area of extremely heavy rainfall. In fact, clouds were thickening above the coastal plain as we watched. Neither roads nor towns exist in that direction, save for foot trails and the village of Boca del Toro. There was free access for wildlife to migrate in dry season between the volcano and other mountains down to the lowland rain forest. This wild corridor was extremely important for animals' survival, since the other three slopes of Barú are already being encroached upon by human development. Fortunately, the park's proposed plans protected this avenue.

From Panama's highest point, we could also look directly south onto Barú's crater complex. "It looks like a huge doughnut," I exclaimed hungrily to Clyde. We could see the very break in the rim from which scalding lava had poured long ago, devastating the western slopes. In some pre-Pleistocene era, geologists say, the volcano grandly blew its ejecta over a 700-square-mile area. But since there are no definite records of its eruption in historic times, we didn't worry about any great blow-ups during our expedition.

The crater complex looked so fascinating that we immediately decided to explore it. The weather was ideal—clear, 70 degrees F, and calm. We threw lunch into one pack, climbing ropes and first-aid kit into another, and scrambled over to the bottom of the doughnut. Scaling its sides looked hazardous. Giant blocks of lava, scorified as moon rock, lay jumbled one upon another. I could teeter some of them by gently pushing with one hand. Deep holes sank into darkness between them. Clyde stared into one of these and suddenly announced that he was going to rope down inside. Benjamin, eyes aglow, volunteered to join him.

I denounced the idea at once as crazy and profitless. "If either of you gets hurt," I protested, "it could prove fatal. We're at least eight hours' fast walk straight down the volcano and another hour and a half by jeep to the hospital in Davíd. That's the closest good medical help."

But Clyde and Benjamin stubbornly insisted. "Who knows what we'll find in there?" asked Clyde excitedly. "I've been to the top of Barú more times than anyone in Panama," exclaimed Benjamin, "but I've never had a chance to go down in it." How could I stop them?

Producing two 50-foot coils of stout line, Clyde tied one end to a pinnacle of rock and eased himself into the bowels of Barú. Benjamin followed close behind. Soon I heard a bellow, "We're down thirty-five feet. There are some weird-looking plants growing down here!"

"Plants!" Javier jumped off a boulder and pressed his face against the hole.

"What do you see?" I asked eagerly.

"Nothing but Clyde's flashlight."

Minutes later, Clyde and Benjamin squeezed back out with some choice specimens. The plants were roughly the size of African violets and covered with short tan hairs. Javier promptly popped them into a plastic bag and sealed it tight. They might be a new species or the first records for the volcano. Then we continued up over the crater rim and looked down. The scene was as bleak, lifeless, cold, and devastated as any I'd ever witnessed. Barú's eruption must have been incredibly powerful. Four small craters lay within the main doughnut-shaped mass. To the southwest, the breach in the main wall showed where the molten lava had poured out. We clambered down inside and scrambled from crater to crater, trying not to scratch ourselves on those cruel rocks. Surprisingly, a pair of large-footed finches appeared from nowhere and hopped after us curiously. A few frail plants struggled from cracks and ledges, kept moist by passing clouds.

The sun paled for a moment and a chill crept into the air. Wisps of clouds trailed through the crater complex. A few minutes later a patch of fog enshrouded us. High noon. Gray scud filled the doughnut hole and I became completely disoriented. There was no sun, no wind, no shadows.

The phenomena of horizontal precipitation and microclimate became sharply evident to me that day. Things I'd read about in ecology books were happening right before my eyes on Barú. Strong orographic convection currents were sucking up the warm Pacific sea water and condensing it above our heads, just as I'd seen from afar over Volcano Atitlán. A considerable quantity of water is caught, condensed, and collected by plant leaves, branches, and epiphytic vegetation from these fogs, mists, and clouds which drift by more or less horizontally in the tropics at high elevations. Such moisture, if only in the form of tiny droplets, can support a miniature community of mosses, ferns, orchids, sub-alpine flowers, and shrubby plants.

During occasional short breaks in the murk we continued exploring. I rested briefly under one shrub whose canopy contours exactly matched the colorful carpet of mosses and lichens I was sitting on. Outside these contours, the ground was as bare and stark as a desert. We also found a dwarf tree clinging to the southwest wall where most clouds rolled into the craters. Its branches were covered with hundreds of small magenta orchids like bright balls on a Christmas tree—the only gay sight in that drab world.

This miracle of horizontal precipitation, interception, and condensation has been studied by Dr. L. R. Holdridge, renowned tropical ecologist. Working in Panama's Talamanca Range, he found that the water derived from condensation in cloud forests makes a great difference in the total yearly runoff downslope. Such high-altitude moisture adds as much as 20 inches annually. This becomes very important to the humans and animals that live below the mountain tops and depend on running water for survival. It is also critical to the regulation of stream flow, erosion control, irrigation projects, potential hydroelectric plants, and large-scale ranching operations.

Toward late afternoon, the clouds lifted and we climbed back out of the crater and headed for camp. To the west, towering thunderheads glowed peach and ivory atop the purple skyline of Costa Rica. Here and there along the rough ridge, a dead bush stood starkly silhouetted against the boiling silver clouds over the Pacific. It was the most dramatic sky we had seen yet.

Back at camp, Javier busied himself with pressing and labeling our finds. Clyde was numbering his film rolls and captioning them. Benjamin was cooking supper over a smoky fire. I sat apart, looking over the coast where the waning moon would soon appear. I was lost in thought about what I'd experienced that day. It now seemed more important than ever to secure this mighty volcano as a national park. Any tampering with its delicate water regime at higher elevations would only lead to troubles below. People would find a decreased stream flow in dry season, more rapid runoff in wet times, excessive leaching of the fragile, unstable soils, silting of streams, and losses of fish and wildlife if the vegetative cover were cut or burned above.

Already I had heard from Panama's Department of Natural Resources (RENARE) and other sources that recent removal of cloud forest on Barú's midslopes had resulted in a bad flood along the Rio Caldera in November 1969. It had washed out homes in Boquete, croplands, bridges, and trees and had widened the channel several hundred feet in places. In the Rio Chiriquí Viejo, another stream springing from the mountainside, the average annual water temperature had risen by 5 degrees F over the past 30 years. At one period, the water had silted to such an extent that introduced rainbow trout had disappeared. Worse than these cases was the estimate that 90 percent of the original native forest below 6,000 feet was gone from Barú.

I shifted uneasily at the prospects. Given the pressing need for more food and fiber to feed and clothe Panama's ever-burgeoning population, a decreased quality of life for humans and wildlife alike would result when agriculture, ranching, and lumbering were practiced in the wrong places.

I caught Benjamin's steady gaze upon me. "*Qué pasa?*" he asked quietly. "Are you tired, Anna? The supper is almost ready. Are you hungry? We have rice, beans, cheese, and coffee," he said, as if to cheer me.

"No, Benjamin, it's not that. I'm just worried about the water," I said abstractedly, not prepared to explain the full ecological regime to him at that moment.

"The water!" he exclaimed, and his face fell. "I was afraid to tell you about that. We are almost out of water."

Perplexed for a moment, I realized that he meant our drinking water. Even though none of us had bathed, laundered, or brushed teeth in the last 24 hours, we were using it up at a terrific rate just for cooking and quenching our thirst. Only 1 gallon of the initial 8 remained.

"Javier and I must go down to Portrero Muleto early tomorrow and bring up more," Benjamin told me seriously.

Although this meant that we could accomplish only half the

work I had planned at the summit, we could not survive without this most vital life-support item. So the next day (and once again after that) the two men had to backpack four full jugs back to the top of Barú. The general lack of water was also evident in the virtual absence of mammal life here. I had seen only droppings of forest rabbits and rootings of coati mundis. No doubt the larger mammals—puma, tapir, peccary, ocelot, deer—moved down to the wetter Caribbean slopes during dry season. Yet, to my surprise, birds were plentiful. I assumed they existed on dew, condensation, and wild fruits, as did the quetzals. My favorites were the volcano hummingbirds, flame-throated warblers, and yellow-thighed finches which flitted brightly through the elfin woodlands. At dusk, if we were quiet, we could hear black-billed nightingale thrushes singing.

I decided that in my park-planning report I would recommend several strategically placed water-catchment basins for wildlife. These would provide water for both animals and people at the top and also serve for fire-fighting in case a campfire got out of control. In addition, I would strongly urge the provision of some sort of garbage pits or other disposal units. I found signs of *Homo sapiens* all over the summit, despite the difficult ascent. Beverage cans, broken rum bottles, and plastic debris littered the trails. There were blackened remains of campfires gone wild, and dozens of names and dates were painted on rocks.

Benjamin told me that roughly 800 to 1,000 people had climbed Barú in 1970–1971. Given that number of people before it was formally declared a national park, I wondered what the use—and abuse—would be like after it opened officially. The current population of Panama was about 1,500,000, excluding the Guaymis, other tribal Indians, and Canal Zone residents. This number is expected to zoom to 3 million or 4 million by the year 2000. Panama is probably the most prosperous country in Central America, has the highest per capita income and gross national productivity, and is a key nation in the banking world. It contains the smallest number of people working in agriculture and ranching and one of the highest urban populations (45 percent). All these statistics portended an active future participation in outdoor recreation in Panama. I figured that the volcano park would become a prime target for local and foreign visitors.

What facilities would be built here, I worried. Would paved roads and plush accommodations like those in the Everglades and Grand Teton national parks be built here? Might a car route be constructed right to the top of Barú? A revolving restaurant be put at the summit? Or a cog railway? Or a golf course beside the sparkling Rio Bajo Chiquero? Not everyone agrees that a national park's chief function is to conserve wildlands, species, ecosystems, and natural beauty. The possibilities made me cringe.

Meanwhile, we had more work to do. After taking weather data and soil samples, running a trapline, and censusing birds, as we'd done at both of our 7,500-foot study sites, Javier and I collected subalpine and elfin woodland plants. The plant press soon was bulging—seventy-two specimens! When Javier groaned at the thought of carrying the heavy weight down the mountain, I reminded him that these were probably the first plants ever collected atop Volcano Barú. They would make a fine addition to the University of Panama herbarium.

On the fifth evening, Benjamin sadly announced that our food and water were nearly gone. All we had for supper was oatmeal and rice, with half a cup of cocoa apiece. For breakfast next day, we would have just oatmeal. Clearly we had to leave. No need to push our luck. Another norte might begin, or an accident befall us if we were in weakened condition. Nonetheless, we had camped longer on top of Barú than any other group ever had to our knowledge.

After our scanty supper, Benjamin said he felt like climbing to the summit, as it was an exceptionally clear night. Would Clyde or I care to join him? Javier was already snoring. Clyde chose to work on his films, but I rallied. When would I ever be on Barú again? The waning moon had not yet risen, so we walked by starlight only. Distant halos of light hung over the hidden towns of Boquete, La Concepción, and David. Benjamin pushed ahead on his steel-springed legs. At last mine gave out and I sat down exhausted. "Go on without me," I urged him. "Do you have a flashlight?"

"Si, Ana."

"Be careful, Benjamin."

Minutes passed. The only sounds were the low hoot of an owl and the occasional clatter of a stone falling from under Benjamin's boots. I pondered on how soon the volcano could be declared a national park so it might take its place alongside the 1,200-odd other parks in the world. And I wondered if it could become a model for other countries where cloud forest and mountain sanctuaries were urgently needed. Certainly, Barú had all the right national park prerequisites: extensive area, outstanding contents, the beginnings of an effective system of protection and eventually management by the highest authority of the country, and authorization of tourism. Or were parks possible at all in Central America?

My friend Dr. Norman Myers, a wildlife ecologist in Africa, has often called conservation "the art of the possible." Perhaps, I thought, it *is* possible here.

Just then a light blazed from the summit—Benjamin's torch! He blinked three times at me, and I answered back with three flashes. My spirit soared up beside him through that black night, for I knew he was standing on the very apex of Panama. He was the king of Panama—highest man in the world for all he knew of Mount Everest, the World Trade Center, and space ships. That night, that mountain, that countryside belonged to Benjamin, a simple uneducated Indian, a lowly government employee, more fully and more deeply than it could ever belong to us specialists with our diplomas, cameras, and plant presses.

Next day we made the descent down dizzying slopes and dangerous scree safely. We arrived in David—11,410 feet to sea level in 8 hours—famished and with splitting headaches. After four aspirins each and a short nap, we were ready to dive into an enormous Chinese dinner. As we gorged ourselves, we discussed plans for the next two days. We had to pack, repair equipment, and sort out our specimens. Then we needed a day in Panama City to visit government offices, make our final report, and say our thanks.

To my surprise, Benjamin asked for his pay and the next day off. He said he had a sick uncle in the David hospital whom he had seen before climbing the volcano, and he now wanted to check up on him. I readily agreed to let him go but asked that he be back on time to see us off. I was much too fond of the Guaymi to leave without saying good-bye. We waited two extra hours for Benjamin. Clyde and Javier were champing to drive off, but I refused. When Benjamin finally showed up, his face seemed strangely altered. Could he have been drinking, I wondered. Or just sleeping after the weeks of hard work? My mind flashed back to the game warden we'd found hiding in the reeds at Lake Atitlán years before.

A moment later I was deeply ashamed of my suspicions, for when Benjamin hugged me good-bye he whispered in my ear, "Anna, my uncle is better. He is going back to the reservation. And I met a girl, a Guaymi girl, under a tree outside the hospital. Her husband abandoned her and she has a little baby."

"Oh, Benjamin," I sighed. "I'm glad for your uncle, but how sad for the girl." Then it dawned on me. "How wonderful! Did you feel affection for each other?"

"Yes. Right away. It happens like that with us Guaymis." He smiled and I saw happiness in his wide black eyes for the first time since I'd met this quiet, sturdy companion. Then he broke away from me and waved farewell.

I left Panama next night believing that Volcano Barú and its cloud forests would be saved. And believing that not only conservation but many other things are possible in this world. Perhaps it's because I am still aware of Benjamin standing under the stars on Barú's summit.

Conservation Made Easy?

My next big consulting job came by mailboat directly to my log cabin on a hot, sunny July day in 1973. This time the cable read: CAN YOU JOIN SURVEY TEAM AS WILDLIFE ECOLOGIST FOR PROPOSED NATIONAL PARK DOMINICAN REPUBLIC AUGUST 1? REPLY AT ONCE.

August 1 was only three days away! Immediately I got to a phone and dialed my colleague, Dr. Edward Towle, director of Island Resources Foundation, who was in the Virgin Islands assembling the survey group. His voice came clearly across the 2,000 miles between the Adirondacks and the Caribbean. He explained that this project would be jointly sponsored by the Dominican Republic government and by part of a huge multinational corporation, Gulf + Western Industries, Inc. The team would be large and would be composed of Dominican sociologists, anthropologists, archaeologists, and botanists and American park planners, marine biologists, and me as wildlife ecologist. Dr. Towle described the proposed park as flat limestone country, consisting of an almost uninhabited island and peninsula in the southwestern corner of the Republic. He assured me that we would have the best of accommodations and transportation in the field, since Gulf + Western was generously supplying all the logistical support.

Until then, I had never heard of this company. Now I learned that it owns vast acreages of sugarcane and ranchland in the Dominican Republic, that Paramount Pictures is one of its subsidiaries, and that it stands among the top corporations in the USA.

"Well," I mused, after hanging up, "this should be interesting. It's a new approach for me to do conservation work for a giant corporation. I wonder how effective we'll be?"

After frantically packing and skimming through my library on Caribbean fauna, I managed to be on a plane to Santo Domingo two days later, arriving at La Romana, a coastal company town near the proposed park, just in time for an evening briefing session. A dozen scientists clustered in a smoke-filled room, poring over maps and making travel plans for the next day. Since the park area had no roads, no towns, and no docking facilities other than a small Navy station on the island, getting into the park site was a major problem.

We were split into three parties. The archaeologist, an historian, and two sociologists would drive around to Boca de Yuma, a tiny fishing village, having the closest approach by road to the proposed park border. From there they would walk south into the park and begin looking for caves where ancient Indian petroglyphs (rock carvings) and paintings were said to exist. They would also check to see whether any scattered squatters might be eking out an existence along the coast. The marine biologists and a park planner would cruise over to *Isla Saona* (the island of Saona) by sport-fishing boat and make their initial reconnaissance of beaches, reefs, bays, and islets. The third group, which included a geographer, botanist, a park interpreter, and me, would survey the entire 100,000-acre tract by helicopter. Our task would be to observe the various ecosystems within the park and note the condition of the forest cover. Helicopter! Guatemala and Panama were never like this. I could see that we were part of a tightly coordinated, efficiently run, well-planned undertaking. It should yield fast and accurate results.

"Remember," cautioned our team leader, "this is not an indepth, complete survey. This time it's a 'broad brush' treatment. We just want to know what's out there. Right now no one knows what birds, mammals, beach resources, trees, archaeological remains, and so on are in the park area. Later on we can concentrate on the details. We have only five days to work, so find out all you can."

With those heady words ringing in my ears, I went to my hotel room and began laying out clothes and equipment for the early-morning flight, my first helicopter ride. I could hardly wait.

A company car whisked us to the La Romana airport right on time. A shiny Ranger sat trimly on the heliopad. A mechanic was finishing up the preflight check and another was topping off the gas tanks. The pilot, a stocky, blond Texan with Vietnam experience, lounged expectantly in a small waiting room.

"Ready?" he asked, rising.

We followed him out to the chopper. I climbed inside first and took a seat beside the right-side window. The others squeezed in. The Ranger carried five people, including the pilot, and had a separate passenger compartment complete with radio-phone, bar, and leather padding. Breathless, I listened to the rotors starting to hum, to turn, to whirl. An infernal racket and quivering shook the chopper. I held my breath. Suddenly, without the slightest jerk or shudder, the helicopter eased into the air, tilting forward and down yet rising swiftly. I watched the air strip diminish beneath us, and then the hazy outline of the peninsula came into focus ahead. It was covered with dry, short, dense woods. The botanist shouted in my ear, "That's probably the largest contiguous tract of subtropical, dry-to-humid, lowland forest left on any Caribbean island. Just look—no one seems to be living there at all!"

We flew down the western side of the peninsula over narrow, immaculate white beaches and aquamarine water. This leeward

side looked limpid, calm, and shallow. At the base of the peninsula, about 12 miles from the upper park border, we reached a
huge bay, Bahia Catalinita. The water shaded to jade and yellow-
green over the turtle-grass flats. Around one islet, Isla Maria, I
saw a cloud of black specks dancing. Tapping the pilot on his
shoulder, I motioned downward. He put the Ranger into a fast
descent—almost too fast. Before I could warn him, we were right
on top of a huge breeding colony of man-o'-war birds. Afraid that
the rotors' downblast would terrify them, I motioned hastily to the
pilot to veer off sideways. There, at a safe distance, we hovered a
few feet above the mangroves and watched those elegant birds soar
and wheel above their nests on slim, 8-foot wings.

The park interpreter caught my eye and yelled, "Great place
for a nature boardwalk and bird-life display."

I nodded enthusiastically. Then, like a giant hummingbird,
we sideslipped off across the bay and approached Isla Saona. It appeared almost flat except for an upward tilting of the northeastern
coastline, which culminated in an outcrop known as Punta Balajú
(Whale Point). There the Caribbean changed to the deep and turbulent Mona Channel, a favorite route of migrating whales. Off to
the east, 40 to 50 miles away, lay Puerto Rico.

The chopper leaned over and I gasped. The seatbelt bit into
my side and belly. Our pilot was treating us to a close inspection of
the old lighthouse on Saona's southeastern tip. In a blur, we circled the rusting light on top. Then we darted off along Saona's
southern coast. Enchanting beaches flashed by. We detoured
around Mano Juan, a Dominican Republic Navy base, so as not to
alarm the 200 sailors there. Then we were flying over lagoons as
red as those on Anegada. I strained to see a flamingo, but nothing
moved on those vast, wind-ruffled surfaces. Again we turned hard
and headed back up the center of the island. Like the mainland
peninsula it was largely forested, with no lakes, ponds, streams, or
swamps.

Now we had come full circle around Saona and were ready to
fly up the eastern, or windward, side of the peninsula. To my astonishment, a totally different scene met our eyes. From a tiny
clearing with five huts and huge conch piles on the southeastern
tip on up to the village of Boca de Yuma at the northeastern end,
the entire coastline was a series of raw, rocky escarpments. The

ocean dashed ceaselessly against cliffs. Grottoes, natural bridges, and blowholes had been carved out by this endless pounding. And where the land had risen in geological times, sea caves and hollows had been left pocking the cliffs. Reaching the park's border, the Ranger climbed steadily up into the sky. From 2,000-feet elevation, the pilot pointed down and yelled back to us, "Notice the fault line that runs across the peninsula here. It's more or less the proposed park boundary. North of it you'll see the beginning of cane fields and ranches that run up into the mountains on the north coast. The whole park, including Saona, will be about 430 square kilometers."

This would truly be a park of impressive size and quality for the Caribbean. Four other areas in the Dominican Republic had already been designated as national parks, but all these were primarily forest reserves and not open to the public. In addition, at this time, no national park service existed for the country. The concept of this park was to provide safeguards for preservation of its natural resources, encourage local public use and tourism, and engage in an active program of education through interpretation and research of this natural patrimony. These aims could have far-reaching consequences for the Republic and provide a model for improving the four existing "parks" as well as developing any new ones in the future.

Already the Ranger was descending and the airport ahead was growing larger. Our flight time had passed like a whirlwind. I felt as if we had been airborne only a few minutes, though my watch told me it had been over 3 hours since we took off. My ears were still ringing after I ducked beneath the revolving rotors and joined my teammates in the waiting room. "Can you imagine any better way to examine an area?" I exclaimed giddily.

"And at what expense!" replied the Dominican botanist soberly. "That Ranger costs a hundred and fifty dollars an hour to operate if it costs a penny. Our little morning exploration probably cost the company a cool five hundred, not counting the fuel."

I was dumbstruck. I had never really thought about how much our survey work would ultimately cost. Now I queried the botanist, "Who is really footing the bill?"

"The Gulf + Western Dominican Foundation is providing funds to inventory and evaluate the park's natural resources and to develop the master plans for it," he explained. The Foundation exists strictly to bring about the best and most imaginative use of Gulf + Western philanthropic funds in all types of human development. This national park isn't the corporation's only interest. I happen to think it's the greatest, though, for our island's four million inhabitants."

Later that day, I happened to stroll past several of the company's huge sugar warehouses. Each was the size of my former high school and each was packed to the roof with fragrant raw sugar. I stood for a moment trying to translate that enormous aromatic tonnage into dollars and to follow the path from here to the supermarkets in the United States where sugar sat in prim bags and boxes on the shelves, and back again to the wilderness of Isla Saona. I knew that a pound of sugar sold for 10 to 15 cents down here in the Caribbean and in New York State for 40 to 50 cents at that time. That was quite a markup. My consulting fee was $100 per day, plus airfare and my housing at the company hotel. Clearly conservation cost a lot more handled this way than the way we'd done it on a shoestring in Guatemala. I finally gave up trying to calculate what it all meant. All that really mattered to me was that the corporation wanted to help make a national park for the Dominican Republic and its people and was willing and able to be its sponsor.

The next three days zipped by. The sport-fishing boat took us for a closer look at the park area. I checked out the man-o'-war-bird colony and dived on a couple of reefs. I bird-watched and explored one end of Saona Island, getting a total of sixty-five bird species. The rest of the fauna was typical of an oceanic island—that is, limited to small mammals like mice and rats, a few reptiles, and insects which had reached the island of Hispaniola on natural rafts. Large mammals could not have arrived by any means save importation by man, as on Anegada. The habitats I saw seemed relatively untouched and not yet destroyed by feral stock. In general this boded well for national park development. Knowing that the population of the Dominican Republic was increasing at the rate of 3 percent per year, it was far wiser to preserve this unique peninsula and island as a park than to let it fall into second-rate cultivation and pastureland. That would ultimately prove deleterious to the entire environment, for the area was too dry and fragile to

Flightless Atitlán grebe, adult male.
Photo by David Allen.

Don Emilio, old Basque resident of Lake Atitlán who became the author's best informant. Here he holds cover of ancient ceramic Mayan ceremonial pot.

Huge specimen of largemouth bass that had been introduced into Lake Atitlán in order to improve sport fishing. Plan backfired when bass began eating small fish and crabs which were main food of grebes and Indian inhabitants.

Author struggles through a cattail bed, searching for nests of Atitlán grebe.
These were usually set in densest parts of reed and cattail beds, hidden from view,
and safe from all but Indian reed cutters.

First known photo of a young Atitlán grebe chick.
The precocious baby could dive, swim, and peep just two hours after hatching.
He is held for a few moments in the author's hat.

Site of Atitlán Grebe Refuge at Lake Atitlán, Guatemala. Author and dog Jessie scan the reed beds for signs of the flightless grebes while Indian workmen clean weeds in bay.

Anne LaBastille explaining new sign at grebe refuge to Indian workmen and guardian. Conservation message was written in three languages to advise foreign and native visitors about this rare bird, found only at Lake Atitlán.

First day cover of grebe conservation stamps tells a conservation story.
These stamps were issued in full color and were greatly prized by stamp collectors.
In three years, the issue ran out and netted the Postal Office more than $123,000.

Author and Indian guide are dwarfed by giant trees in cloud forest on Volcano Atitlán, site of the private quetzal reserve.

Artificial nest boxes were designed by author to try to reduce mortality of nesting quetzals, whose nest trees and stumps often fall down. The boxes were placed in cloud forest in safe locations and eventually accepted and used by a few birds.

*A makeshift camp was set up in Windlass Bight, on the windward side of
Anegada Island in the British Virgins. The author camped here alone for
five days while conducting an ecological survey of the island. The vast
Puerto Rican trench lies a few miles offshore.*

Members of the ecological survey team of proposed Volcano Barú National Park in Panama work on measuring and preserving small mammals trapped in the park. Left to right: author; Dario Tovar, chief, Panama National Park Service; Javier Ortega, forester.

Chieftain of Guaymi Indian tribe in Panama poses with gorgeous quetzal feather headdress. Normally headdress is worn only for special festival associated with corn harvest.

Benjamin Cuevas Montezuma, Guaymi Indian guide in Volcano Barú National Park fills a bag with sulfur found in a deposit near the crater of the volcano at 11,000 feet elevation.

*West coast of the proposed Parque del Este in the Dominican Republic.
Author conducted an ecological survey here,
backpacking 55 miles of coastline.*

Precious drinking water had to be flown in by helicopter to support the three-member surveying team. No fresh water exists along the rugged windward coastline of Parque del Este. Here, author gives donkey carrying water jugs a drink.

Squatter inside proposed park carries wood for his canuco (charcoal-burning pile). Each bag of charcoal weighed 100 pounds and sold for $3—hardly a wise trade-off and use of forest.

Along the coast, piles of discarded conch shells indicate where conch fishermen have stopped to extract the meat. Size of shells from bottom to top show that the conchs are decreasing in size and quantity, due to overfishing.

Felipe Benavides, winner of J. Paul Getty wildlife conservation prize of $50,000 for helping to create the Manú National Park in Peru, one of the largest parks in South America and Amazon basin.

The MS Lindblad Explorer *on a channel of the Amazon River.*
The author spent a month aboard and traveled 2,300 miles downstream.

The muddy Manú River braids and twists into the vast distances of the
Amazon rain forest in Peru.

A calf is carried by dugout canoe on the Amazon River.

A caboclo (*mixed-blood native of the Amazon basin*) *spears a* tucunaré *with his bow and arrow, on a tributary of the Amazon in Brazil.*

The Transamazonica Highway crosses many rivers and streams as it heads west towards Peru. Author drove over 200 miles in pickup truck along a mid-section of the highway.

The Cuibá-Santarém Highway where it leads off north from the Transamazonica Highway. This road was brand new when author traveled it and had not yet been subjected to devastating colonization.

Graphic results of cutting off protective rain forest canopy turning land into pasture.

Black-pepper bushes represent the most incredible trade-off that the author found in Amazonia. Virgin rain forest trees are being cut and burned to grow this short-lived, non-nutritive crop, thereby exposing fragile tropical soils to erosion and compaction. ▶

withstand much exploitation by humans or domestic stock. As a national park, it would meet the recreational needs of the people and could still keep its ecosystems intact.

Our last day at La Romana, we were called in to meet the head of the Gulf + Western Dominican operation, Señor Alvaro Carta, and explain the results of our survey. He would assist the team leader and key people in making decisions about the park, and also serve as our liaison between the government and corporation in many cases. We were late returning from the sea, and I ran to his office without so much as putting on my shoes. I made a cursory examination of the office—no desk, no papers, no briefcases, no smiling secretary in a corner. Rather, it held an assemblage of stunning Cuban mahogany and leather furniture; photographs of tennis and polo players, racehorses, and prize bulls; bridles, bits, stirrups; and burlap sugar sacks tastefully tacked to the walls. What sort of office was this for a corporation head?

Then the door opened, and a compact, lithe, heavily mustached man clad in impeccable khaki pants and a white polo shirt slipped in. I was suddenly embarrassed by my cut-off jeans, bare feet, hunting knife at my belt, and pigtails. I looked like a ragamuffin. To compensate for my appearance, I murmured a greeting in Spanish and then offered the most formal thank you I could muster for Gulf + Western's help and hospitality. To my great surprise, I was the only one of the Americans who spoke that language, though most of the Dominicans knew English. I received a firm handshake and warm glance from Señor Carta in return.

He spent the next hour and a half with us, listening to our descriptions, looking at maps, asking a keen question now and then, and nodding at our plans for future research. He said little and took no notes, yet his dark eyes probed us intently. I gradually realized that a photographic mind was recording every word and detail. No phone rang, no secretary interrupted us. We might have been having an animated afternoon get-together rather than a planning session that involved millions of dollars and a hundred thousand acres of undeveloped land. Then, abruptly, our host stood up, shook hands with each of us, and excused himself. A moment later, his receptionist bustled in to dismiss us.

"Señor Carta has never spent so much time with anyone except the highest executives of the company," she fussed. "He must be very interested in this park and in your survey work." Then as the others filed out, she detained me a moment with a courteous hand on my arm. "Señor Carta was so pleased you spoke Spanish," she said warmly. "He hopes that you can come back to continue your research and especially to be here for the official declaration of the park, if possible. You would be able to explain the master plan to his Dominican colleagues and the government officials. I do hope you can."

Once again, my Spanish had served me well. "Of course," I told her with a smile, "I'd be honored."

As a matter of fact, wild horses could not have kept me away. It wasn't every day that a wildlife ecologist got in on the ground floor of exploring new territory *and* helping to create a new national park. Conservation had never seemed easier.

Dominican Espresso

Back at my Adirondack cabin, I prepared a wildlife report and illustrated it liberally with photographs I had taken during the five days in the field. The other scientists submitted their reports. Counting the survey and planning and mapping work, a total of 60 days had been devoted to the proposed park. Over a year passed before our reports were assembled, produced in a handsome master-plan folio, and distributed to top Dominican government officials, including President Juan Belaguer. In September 1975 he officially declared the area *Parque Nacional del Este* (National Park of the East).

Soon afterward, I was invited to the Dominican Republic to participate in the first planning session. Key people from the government, Gulf + Western Industries, Inc., and the Museum of Dominican Man were participating. I was unimaginably flustered as I stood up to address these august persons: the corporation head for its Dominican operations, a high-level general and admiral of the Dominican Army and Navy, the young chief of the brand-new park service, and the Museum's director. Carefully, in Spanish, I described the general ecology, natural resources, main attractions of the park, and outlined our plans for future study and tourist development. Señor Carta passed bound copies of the master plan and pictures around the table.

When it was over, he shook my hand warmly and thanked me. "I'd like you to do an in-depth survey of the park soon, help lay out the road, pinpoint visitors' centers, and anything else needed. We'll provide whatever you want—helicopter, assistants, boats," he said, matter-of-factly. I was speechless. It was like being asked to play God. I managed to nod agreement. He gave my hand another firm squeeze and added, "Everyone is enthusiastic about the park. We can expect good cooperation from all these various organizations which have an interest in it." And then he was gone.

I reserved three weeks in which to make the survey and returned after Easter the following year. My plan was to cover roughly the same route we had flown over. I'd start at the northeastern corner of the park below Boca de Yuma, and walk the entire perimeter of the peninsula around to Bayahibe, a beautiful beach used by the company's hotels, just above the northwestern corner—a distance of 35 to 40 miles. Much of this was not accessible by motorboat because of the rough seas, high escarpments, and shallow mud flats. Then I would switch over to Isla Saona and walk its southern shoreline from Punta Catuán to Punta Cana and the old lighthouse at the easternmost point—roughly another 15 miles. While backpacking, I planned to observe birds, particularly the spring migrants, run a small mammal trap-line each evening, and make extensive notes and photographs of the different ecosystems. During the last few days I'd work with Gulf + Western engineers on laying out a roadway into the park.

I had asked for two Dominican assistants. One person would carry the extra pack with snap traps, live traps, and bait; the other, an extra tent, food, and water. I would be loaded down as usual with cameras, binoculars, notebooks, field guides, my own tent and sleeping bag. But I wasn't exactly prepared for the type of assistants awaiting me. One man, Luis, was 75 years old, could neither read nor write, and had spent his entire life on Isla Saona.

The second, Ramón, was at least 55 and weighed less than I do. His cadaverous frame and hacking cough were not promising for the rugged trip ahead.

Yet the old adage, "You can't tell a book by its cover," had never proved truer. Luis and Ramón turned out to be the hardiest, sweetest, most considerate field helpers I've ever had or probably ever will again. Luis easily toted his 50-pound pack all day, helped me set traps, made the campfire every evening, imparted fascinating bits of natural history, and apparently could survive on about three cups of water a day. His years on Saona as a hunter and fisherman had made him a stalwart woodsman indeed. As for Ramón, he managed the food pack, cooked all our meals, told us sea stories, and generally maintained a jolly mood. Not for nothing had he been a popular mate on numerous fishing boats around the Dominican Republic. Within the first 24 hours the two black men and I had become fast friends.

One major goal of our field trip was to find, if possible, a very rare and endangered insectivore, the Hispaniola solenodon. This small, secretive, slow, nocturnal mammal is found only in Haiti and the Dominican Republic. It has been almost exterminated as a result of increasing land development, deforestation, hunting by dogs, predation by feral cats and mongoose, and capturing for zoo specimens. The solenodon's range and numbers are completely unknown. I hoped to find a few of the long-snouted, bewhiskered, little creatures in Parque del Este. Perhaps they were surviving in the many caves, sink holes, or hollow trees of the dense forest-bush. Photographs showed it to be not much larger than an opposum, with the same naked tail and clawed feet. I knew that solenodons mainly eat such insects as ants, roaches, and grubs, and also worms, as do its relatives the shrews and tenrecs, but it has also been implicated in feasting on poultry and gorging on vegetable crops. I longed to see one of these unusual mammals at first hand. With this purpose in mind, Luis was carrying several large, collapsible live traps which we would bait with what we hoped would prove delectable tidbits.

The main problem we faced and could not conquer, despite lavish funding and equipment, was water. I knew that the heat would be brutal at midday and we would each require several quarts daily just to maintain our well-being. A Gulf + Western engineer had warned us that we would find no drinking water at all on the peninsula or on Saona, except at the little naval station, where a supply was brought in by boat each week. I couldn't afford to have Luis and Ramón go out every day or two to replenish our water as Benjamin and Javier had done on Volcano Barú. Besides, near the base of the limestone peninsula it would be much too far to walk out—25 miles round trip. Furthermore, no boats would dare to land on that craggy, wave-lashed eastern coast. Our only hope was the Ranger. I found the Texan pilot and presented him with our problem.

"Yeaaah," he drawled affably. "I could drop off ten gallons of water every other day in between my other duties. Generally I'm flying over the cane fields most days, dropping off machinery parts for broken tractors and giving visiting firemen the royal tour." He yawned widely. "Put some X marks on this chart and take a can of bright orange spray paint along to mark the place you want the water left. I'll see you get five two-gallon plastic jugs every other day."

"Oh, great," I replied. "We can probably get by on less, but one of the jugs might leak or break. If you drop them off in the late afternoon we'll be able to use up a lot of the water at the evening meal, washing up, filling our canteens and so on. That way we'll have less to carry the next two days."

"Well, I can't promise for sure *when* I'll get 'em to you," he hedged, "but I won't let you die of thirst, okay? Say, be sure to mark an area about twenty by twenty feet with the spray paint so I know where you are. Now tell me, do you want to be dropped off and picked up, too?"

I nodded. "Come and get us near the man-o'-war birds next Saturday," I said, as I jotted down the date and x-ed the map. "Do you remember the spot from our first trip?"

He said yes, laconically, and I chuckled. Probably after ferrying soldiers and supplies around Vietnam, this would just be a milk—I mean, a water—run. We estimated we would walk 5 to 8 miles a day, which meant he'd have to make three drop-offs during the week. Surely no water had ever been so expensive or as difficult to provide.

Next morning a wide-eyed Luis and Ramón accompanied me to the airport and shakily entered the helicopter. My initial excitement was nothing compared to theirs. These men, who had never been higher off the ground or the sea than a treetop or a flying bridge, must have been close to heart attacks. On our swift flight over to Boca de Yuma, I found more amusement in watching their faces than in scanning the landscape below. As soon as we landed, the pilot unstrapped the three backpacks from his co-pilot's seat and unloaded three jugs of water.

"See you in a couple of days," he said, waving nonchalantly. Then the chopper rose noisily over our heads and clattered away. Luis and Ramón were so rattled and the silence seemed so enormous that we sat down under a tree and ate lunch just to get back to normal. Then we helped one another into our packs, picked up the jugs, and began walking south.

Less than half a mile inside the park we reached the first interesting area. A 30-foot gray-and-white cliff dropped down to the heaving sea. Atop it grew a little woodland whose canopy had been sheared off as neatly as if by a pair of giant garden shears—an example of pruning by the sea wind. A short while later we emerged on a rough, flat, bare coastal shelf of blackened limestone. We followed the merest hint of a trail. Ahead a spout of foaming water abruptly shot up out of the rock.

"Old Carlos's blowhole," announced Luis, grinning from ear to ear. "I've heard of it for years, but I never walked this part of the peninsula before."

The geyser spurted up every few minutes, then fell back into a large grotto in the limestone. Beneath us I could feel the rock shudder and hear a dull booming. Although the hole was a good 200 feet from the ocean, an underground passage evidently allowed breakers to push inland and blow out into the open. Old Carlos was as regular as Old Faithful in Yellowstone Park.

After I photographed the huge blowhole, we trudged on along the exposed coast. Sun and wind beat into our faces. The Mona Channel, restless and blue-gray, heaved to our left, while a perpendicular, 120-foot escarpment rose in tortured patterns to the right. There must be a splendid view from the top, but I could see no way to climb up there. I made a note to recommend that a circular iron staircase be built up the face of the cliff to a lookout on top.

I heard a sudden intake of breath and turned abruptly to see if the two men were all right. But they were quite a distance behind me, adjusting their packs. "Must have been the wind," I thought and walked on. Again, that strange sound. I stopped in my tracks and looked around. No animals. I glanced overhead. No birds. Nothing but scrubby sea plants, sand, and black rock. Then the sucking noise came once more. Easing out of my pack, I began a minute inspection of the ground. Luis and Ramón, who had caught up with me, helped. To our amazement, we found a hole, no bigger than a pencil, going straight down into the rocky pavement. Periodically a long sigh escaped from it. Then I realized the whole of this coastal shelf was undercut and under enormous pressure from wave action. Somehow, air was being forced in and out that tiny blowhole as the sea rose and subsided. Someday, given time for wind and wave action, it might enlarge and become Old Carlos the Second. I made a small orange X mark with the spray paint. We must be able to find this amazing phenomenon later on and use it in an interpretive display to educate the public.

We continued down the coast all day, marveling at the sea grottoes, sea caves, and blowholes we found. The only signs of human habitation were faint tracks, bits of dried donkey dung, and the shorn trunks of thatch palms. Apparently people came here to harvest the huge fanlike leaves of the palms for roofing huts. The poor trees didn't have a chance. Once their leafy heads were topped, the wind and sun discouraged them from living. One rule in the park, I decided, would be "no more harvesting of thatch palms." It would make the scenery much more attractive to have clusters of them standing green and tall.

I was beginning to realize that our trip in the Ranger over the park had been like seeing an impressionist painting. As the team leader had said, "a broad-brush treatment." Now we were doing the fine pointillistic work by going step by step over the area. The two extremes were absolutely necessary to any honest and thorough ecological coverage.

That evening we made camp on a circle of sand surrounded by cruel limestone outcrops not far from a dry wood. We had the ocean breeze to discourage insects and a source of firewood at hand. A thin skein of clouds slid over the sky, turning the sea to gunmetal gray and cooling the air. After the 90-degree heat of midday and our 7-mile hike, I was ready for a bath. But the only place was the sea. How could I manage? To climb down that steep, spray-wet cliff would be foolhardy. No calm bay or beach broke this entire coastline.

Ramón solved the problem. Handing me a plastic pail and a length of light nylon line, he suggested I dip up water from the cliff and take a sponge bath on shore. "That's what we do aboard the fishing boats," he explained, "when we don't feel it's safe to swim in the sea." Putting a few rocks between me and the men, I found a little indentation at the edge of the escarpment and flung down the pail. When it seemed to have filled, I gave a yank to haul it up. But a big wave caught the pail on its outgo and tugged back at me. For a second I teetered on the brink. If I had fallen, I would have been dashed to ribbons on the rocks. Even if I managed to swim out, how long would it take my helpers to discover my plight and how could they pull me up the cliff? We had not brought a strong rope along. Shaking, I grasped a corner of rock, braced myself, and pulled up the pailful of water. The cool salt water on my naked body felt wonderfully refreshing, but the close call had sobered me.

When I returned to the campfire, both men were staring nervously toward the sea. Ramón jumped up and grabbed my arm. "Anna, are you all right? What a fright you gave us! We couldn't see you, yet we didn't want to disturb you bathing. If you'd fallen in and drowned, Luis and I would probably have been convicted of murder."

His dark face looked terrified and I realized that he spoke the truth. No one would believe two simple native working men if a high-paid foreign female consultant in their company suddenly disappeared at a remote place like this!

To ease his mind, I laughed and said lightly, "Oh, I'm sorry, Ramón. I was just enjoying my bath and waiting for the wind to dry me off." From then on though, I vowed to be extra-careful and not get our little team into any trouble. And somehow the incident brought us closer together.

At daybreak I was awakened from a sound sleep by Ramón softly calling, *"Ana, Ana, es el tiempo a despertarte"* ("It's time to wake up").

I sat up in my sleeping bag and groped for the tent zipper. Ramón deftly opened the mosquito netting and handed me a tiny steaming cup of rich Dominican espresso heavily laced with sugar. What a treat! I gave him a sleepy smile and eagerly sipped the fragrant drink. Already Luis had started a fire and rolled up the other tent. Leaving Ramón to fix breakfast and break camp, Luis and I headed back into the woods to check our trapline. Most traps had been baited the evening before with a mix of peanut butter, raisins, and oatmeal. Evidently the land crabs and ants had discovered this delicacy early and had cleaned up. The bait levers of every trap were bare and most had been sprung. We caught only a couple of Norway rats and house mice in our snap traps (just like Anegada) and a gray-and-white feral house cat in one of the live traps. I opened the door and allowed it to streak for cover while Luis recovered the other traps and untied the red flagging we used to mark each site.

After a hearty breakfast, we began our day's trek south. The coastal shelf widened and became sandier, while the escarpment angled back away from the sea and lowered. At 10 A.M., we came upon a rude hut built of every conceivable kind of flotsam and jetsam imaginable—weathered planks, flattened tin cans, plastic sheeting, lengths of frayed line, rusty oil drums. The little yard was swept clean and bare, and a few small fruit trees and beehives clustered behind the house. We approached and called out a greeting.

A gaunt, very black old lady in a ragged patchwork dress peeked out. She looked us over, then, with a toothless grin, threw her warped plywood door open wide and beckoned us in. She lived in a poverty so complete that there was nothing inside but a crude bench and table on a dirt floor, a wicker basket of eggs, and a battered old calendar on the wall. Yet this delightful crone insisted on making us coffee. She poured a dollop of precious water in a pot without a handle, blew on the embers of a tiny wood fire, and set three chipped cups on the table. All these utensils were gifts of the sea. Then she dropped a handful of ground Dominican coffee in a stained square of cheesecloth and brewed us each a cup. It seemed a novel way to make espresso. She sweetened each cup with thick honey, then sat back to watch us drink. The coffee was delicious. Our compliments soon had her beaming and bobbing her head self-consciously. She insisted on showing us her beehives, which earned her enough money to enable her to survive here alone as a squatter. She had absolutely no idea a park was in the offing, or what that might do to her way of life.

I was genuinely sad to leave the old lady. How tedious her life must be, hoping each day for some stray passerby to break the monotony. Her life consisted of sweeping the yard, feeding her chickens, listening to the sea, and watching her hives. She had no husband, no children, no car, no horse, no burro, no dogs, no cats, no radio, no TV, no books, no magazines, no washing machine, no sewing machine, no anything for entertainment. Yet she seemed as ordinary and pleasant as a grandmother in Kansas.

I whispered to Ramón to leave her some of our sugar, coffee, and extra water, for we had more than enough. Then I asked her about the solenodon and showed her a picture of one, so she would not confuse the creature with anything else. She nodded at once and said, "Oh, yes, the little *oso* (bear) comes to steal a chicken every so often. I swept one out of the chicken coop with a broom two nights ago!"

What a statement! If it were true, it meant that solenodons were present in the park, which would make it more valuable. They might even be common and unafraid of people. Nevertheless, I still had to prove their presence by actually trapping and/or photographing one.

Throughout the day, we passed other squatters' huts. From what I could observe, they survived on seafood, honey, treasures found in the flotsam and jetsam, and beachcombing, carrying in that vital commodity, water, from Boca de Yuma. To earn a few dollars for coffee, medicines, and clothes, they harvested palm fronds, kept beehives, or made charcoal. Each person we spoke with was as hospitable, open, and sincere as the old lady. Might there be truth, I wondered, in Thoreau's sage comment: "A man is inversely happy in proportion to the things he possesses."

The one disturbing activity was the charcoal-making. The squatters were girdling and cutting live trees or picking up dead ones to burn in huge circles called *canucos*. Although we had not noticed these from the air, here on the ground it was easy to see that they were eating into the forest like mange spreading across a dog's skin. The piles of wood burned for hours, eventually turning into chunks of charcoal. This was bagged in burlap sacks holding 100 pounds each and packed out by burro to Boca de Yuma. There it sold for $3.00 a bag. This terrible destruction of the peninsula's woodlands for such a pitiful remuneration reminded me of the honey-tree cutters in Guatemala. When people are poor and hungry, they will glean any conceivable resource from their environment and cannot be expected to consider the effects.

On this expedition, I first realized that perhaps conservation can only be a concern of a wealthy society, even though it helps all humans, rich or poor. I also decided that the first thing the government should do, through its Park Service and Museum of Man, was to sponsor the move of these poor squatters out into new homes and accept the economic responsibility of finding them jobs which would offer them a better quality of life. Undoubtedly, some could work for the park, but there might not be enough positions to go around. This was where the Dominican sociologists would come in handy, to ease the transition and integrate these people smoothly into a different life style.

At Punta Titín, we marveled again at the sea's artistry. A natural bridge stood, arched and symmetrical, and another blowhole here brought a spume of water up at least 30 feet from the ocean's surface through the limestone shelf to foam out above into a natural "bathtub." The water was warm and frothy, and I longed to strip and immerse myself.

That afternoon was the time for our first water drop-off. Luis and I found a level stretch of limestone atop Punta Titín and sprayed a giant square in orange paint. Then we sat down on the windswept promontory to wait. An hour went by before I saw the Ranger as a distant speck to the south. It hawked and hovered like some giant dragonfly, searching for us. Gradually it worked its way up the coastline. Now we could hear its clattering. Suddenly the pilot spotted us, the Ranger veered straight toward our point. Minutes later, the tall Texan was handing us five fresh water jugs and glancing around nervously at his makeshift landing site.

"Everything okay?" he asked, ducking as a gust of salt spray wet his face and shirt.

"We're fine," I replied.

"Great. Then see you day after tomorrow," he said, relieved. He slammed the door and roared away, leaving us with the problem of carrying all this water, plus our backpacks, off the rocky point and south. Miraculously, it was solved a short while later when a palm-frond cutter and his mule passed us, heading to the cluster of huts at the peninsula's end. For $2.00 we hired the mule to carry all the jugs and Ramón, who was tiring, to the tiny hamlet of El Algibe. If we set up our base camp there, we could work our way back up the coast or across the base of the peninsula and not have to lug these heavy loads around. That night found us camped a quarter of a mile away from the five wattle-and-thatched huts of El Algibe. We were kept busy fending off hungry pigs, curious children, and land crabs, until we could finish supper and hide our food. Then we paid a visit to the five families who lived there off and on and explained our mission. In their soft drawling Spanish, they welcomed us and described what they knew about the wild-life and the sea's resources. These nomadic fisherpeople were the friendliest humans I had ever met. They brought us fresh conch, cut and marinated in key lime juice, and presented me with a beautiful shell.

The saddest sight, however, in that clean little village perched by the shimmering shallows of Bahia Catalinita was the huge piles of conch shells. Conch is a time-honored and valuable source of protein all through the Caribbean. It also provides shell tools and digging instruments. However, in looking through the piles and measuring the discarded conch shells, newest and oldest, I found that the shell lengths had diminished over the decades from roughly 12 to 18 inches down to 5 to 10 inches. The fishermen themselves confirmed the decrease: conchs were getting harder to find and smaller in size, they complained.

"Why?" I asked.

They shrugged. "Too many people fishing for them. Even the hotels in La Romana want conchs now for fritters and *seviche* (raw seafood marinated in lime juice). There are just not enough conchs to go around."

It was the same story of overpopulation and overuse of natural resources that I heard everywhere I worked.

We could hardly wait for the Ranger to fly in on its appointed day with our water and give these good folks something to talk about for the next ten years. Sure enough, the pilot gave us a nerve-tingling show by swooping right over the huts, then descending slowly and majestically into our midst. Chickens squawked, babies screamed, small boys jumped behind their mothers' legs, and even the aggressive pigs turned tail and fled. Graciously, the Texan let everyone look inside after he'd unloaded our jugs. Then he was gone in a swirl of sand, after promising to deliver more water two days hence at the other corner of the peninsula.

Next morning we set off across the base of the park, skirting belts of mangrove and shallow lagoons, keeping just inside the forest. The bay looked like ideal manatee habitat. Luis assured me that once these grotesque mammals (sometimes called sea cows) had frequented these waters but had largely been wiped out by hunting. Weighing close to 1,500 pounds and being sluggish and slow in movement, manatees are easy prey to hunters in motor-boats or dugout canoes. The cigar-shaped creatures have no natural advantages except their front flippers, their flattened, strong tails, and the bristles about the thick lips for browsing on aquatic vegetation. "I hunted them for years," he confided, "especially during rainy season. They have wonderful meat, and the oil is good for lamps and cooking. They liked to come around Saona and the mainland and drink from underwater 'boils.' They're easy to catch with a dugout when they are in the shallows."

"You mean they drink at fresh-water springs *under* water?" I asked, perplexed, knowing that the air-breathing mammals drink only fresh water.

"Yes, the fresh water bubbles up from the sea floor, oh, twenty, thirty, forty feet from shore in some places on the shallow leeward side. If you're thirsty, you can dive right down and have a drink," explained Luis. "I'll take you and show you how, Anna. I happen to know where some boils are."

Later he showed me how to swim down and hold an empty bottle upside down to fill it. Once again I marveled at that wonderful native intelligence.

Now that we had left the windward coast, the heat was much more oppressive. No breeze stirred the trees, and humidity was high. No tree cutters had penetrated this far into the interior to make their canucos or to skid out valuable mahogany, and this portion of the park was restfully green. Later, however, we ventured out into the broiling afternoon sun to photograph the bordering salt marsh and salt flats. It hit our heads like a hammer blow. We walked laboriously through a stand of uncut thatch palms, taking care not to cut our pants or bare arms on the knife-sharp sawgrass beneath. Heat waves wriggled on the horizon. I felt dizzy for a moment and looked down. Near the ground there curved a delicate spray of lavender orchids, as fancy as any I'd ever worn to a high-school prom.

"Look, Luis!" I called.

"*Los angelitos*" ("the little angels"), exclaimed the old hunter, gently cupping one in his gnarled hand.

As I bent down to take a few pictures of these lovely orchids, I noticed several spent shotgun shells on the ground. Aghast, I called again, "Luis!" I was pointing at the ground just as if I had discovered a murderer in our midst. "Someone's been shooting here."

"Oh, yes," he nodded. "A little farther out on the flats you'll see thousands of shotgun shells."

My eyes widened. "*Thousands! Why?*"

"This is where *las palomas* (the white-crowned pigeons) come to nest every spring. They fly in by the thousands upon thousands to the western end of Saona and to the tip of this peninsula. No one knows where they come from. The trees are so full of pigeons that people can shake a dozen down from any branch. The poor people used to feed the poults to their pigs. Now just the rich people come to shoot them. I'll show you."

Far out on the salt flats shimmering with heat devils, we came upon several shooting stands constructed of shaky mangrove sticks, with palm-frond-thatched roofs. The ground around them was literally covered with shotgun shells—red, blue, green, yellow. It was almost like finding a multicolored carpet out on a desert. I flinched inwardly to think how many thousands of birds had died from these barrages. I took several photos and gathered up shells as evidence. Later I learned from the National Park Service director that this is considered to be the largest breeding colony of white-crowned pigeons in the world. A Dominican law protects the birds from hunters, but no enforcement exists. According to my two assistants, government officials and wealthy individuals were still sneaking in for shoots at the beginning of each nesting season. Clearly, one of the most pressing jobs of the new park would have to be patrol and enforcement work. And that was where the general and the admiral on the park's board could help.

Until the National Park Service could train and send out park rangers, Dominican Army and Navy personnel might be ordered to protect the natural resources of Parque del Este. A novel approach!

Finally, on Saturday afternoon, we were over by the man-o'-war birds, waiting for the Ranger to pick us up, exhausted but enormously content. It had been a wonderful, enlightening week.

"You take a rest now, Ramón," I urged the gaunt man. "And please don't go back to Saona yet, Luis," I cajoled. "Just as soon as I finish helping the company engineers lay out a roadway along this side of the park, we'll be ready to go to your island to explore and trap. I'd like you both to be with me. We may have an ornithologist along to study the flamingo lagoons and see if a population could be built up on the island. He'll need help. And I want to climb up that old lighthouse to see the view. Oh, and I sure would like more of your delicious espresso, Ramón."

Both men's eyes lit up and weary as they were they nodded in enthusiasm. We barely had time to take a catnap under the thatch palms before the Ranger descended on us like some prehistoric bird. Then, aches and pains forgotten, Luis and Ramón jumped up and ran like kids to open the door for their second helicopter ride.

Playing God

For three days, a Gulf + Western engineer and I walked the western edge of the park, from Bayahibe to the man-o'-war birds. We spray-painted a tentative route and marked the most important biological and geological points of interest. If there can be artistry in engineering, then we had an arty road.

Where large trees such as strangler figs or West Indian birches deserved saving, we split the road in two and protected them between lanes. Where an attractive vista overlooked the placid Caribbean, we curved the road close to it, yet not so near as to show from the sea side or create an ugly open parking lot behind. Where limestone sinks filled with fragile ferns and air plants lay like inverted greenhouses, we bent the road away and laid out a walking trail to them for nature lovers. It really was a little like playing God.

We pinpointed the best sites for visitors' centers, bathing beaches, campsites, and a small outdoor amphitheater. We also discussed building a boardwalk and blind out over the salt flats to view the man-o'-war birds. Everything was to be built of native woods, stones, and fibers. My interest and pride in the park was growing by leaps and bounds. Visions flashed constantly in my head of how it would look when finished and of the first Dominicans and tourists enjoying it.

The American park planner and park interpreter were also back at their drawing boards at La Romana. They offered me lengthy philosophical pronouncements about roads.

"They can be the beginning of the end," stated the planner gloomily. "I've seen it happen in South America. Unless you have a strong enforcement staff, rigid rules, and tight park boundaries, a road can be an open invitation to squatters and exploiters to move into hitherto inaccessible and virgin areas. I hope that won't happen here at Parque del Este."

"Roads can be the 'cancer of the tropics,'" agreed the interpreter.

"Oh, come on," I argued optimistically. "This road is going to be so beautiful and the park so well run that nothing bad will happen. Besides, I think the land will be better off with the road than without it. If things just drift on as they are now, there'll be more canucos, more conch fishermen, more hunters sneaking in to rip off the resources. A road can stop all that by allowing adequate police protection."

So it went. Every evening we sat at the hotel, pondering the good or evil of national parks. It really boiled down to a type of planned development for natural resources instead of their rampant exploitation. Paradoxically, by prohibiting short-term abuse of the environment by a few people, you provided a long-term use for the masses with a national park.

Soon it was time to go back into the field, for the ornithologist had arrived. I walked down to the marina to find Ramón and tell him about our plans. I found him looking rested and clean-shaven. We embraced each other happily.

"And Luis? Where's Luis?" I asked eagerly.

"He'll be here right away, Ana. He's been dying to get back to Saona and show you his precious island."

Luis jumped onto the dock, stalwart and stoic as ever, and gave me a big grin. "When do we start?" he asked without preamble.

"Tomorrow. By boat. The bird man is here with tons of stuff. Nets, strainers, chemicals, bottles. Can you both be ready to leave at seven in the morning?"

"Yes," they chorused.

At 10 the next morning we were rolling in the gentle swell off Laguna Flamenco—so named for the former flocks of greater flamingos which frequented the area. The company's sport-fishing boat had been put at our disposal for the week's work. The captain, Luis, Ramón, and I helped load the ornithologist's gear into a dinghy, a Boston whaler, pulled behind us. Then we all went ashore, pushed through a band of mangroves, and stood at the edge of a huge sheet of rust-colored water.

"I'll have to spend most of the day here," announced the ornithologist, "wading in this goop and taking samples of water and mud. Then I'll strain and collect the animals in them—brine flies, tiny shrimp, small fishes, and crustaceans. Flamingos eat those miniature items. I probably won't be able to identify everything in the field, but I'll preserve samples and check them out at home under the microscope. That way we can get an idea of how productive these lagoons are and if they can support flamingos during all or part of the year now. I know that historically the birds stopped here. But what made them cease coming? Humans? Poor habitat?"

Then he tugged on a pair of waist-high waders, donned an old hat, grabbed his dip net, and sloshed competently into the lagoon. Ramón had been assigned to help him that day, but all he had was an old pair of sneakers. Grimacing, he tightened the laces and started to follow the ornithologist.

"Be sure to wear something on your head, Ramón," I cautioned him fondly. "These salt lagoons can reach a hundred and ten degrees under the midday sun, and I'd hate to have you get sunstroke."

He looked back at me gratefully and tied an old handkerchief around his head like a turban. Luis and I watched the two men wade out into that hypersaline water through the reeking mud. We were already perspiring, just standing there, and I was secretly glad not to be involved in that work.

Our job that day was to walk the shore from Laguna Flamenco to Mano Juan, the Navy base. I would gauge the possibility of a backpacking nature trail along the coast, with some small campsites and bathing areas. Later we would pay a visit to the naval officer in charge of the station and make sure he understood our mission. I didn't want a repeat of the Guatemalan experience when we were taken for guerrillas and have the Dominican Navy throw us off the island as spies or insurgents.

At 5 o'clock that evening, Ramón and the ornithologist picked us up at Mano Juan in the Boston whaler and we returned to the big boat. After the day's heat and thirst, it was an indescribable treat to relax on padded seats, sip ice-cold Cokes and beers, and cool off under—of all things—an air conditioner! The captain served us supper. Then we all turned in and slept like babies as the boat rocked gently at anchor. Once again I smiled to myself— Anegada had never been like this.

For four days more we surveyed Isla Saona in this fashion. As dawn suddenly lit the sky with flaming banners of scarlet and cerise, I'd rise from my bunk before the men woke up, slip into a bathing suit, and dive into the sea. As I swam and floated off the bow, they had a chance to get up, dress, urinate off the stern, and wash up without embarrassment. Climbing back on board, I was presented by Ramón with my cup of steaming Dominican espresso. We'd greet each other good morning, eat breakfast, and begin the new day.

The ornithologist was finding that flamingo food was scarce in the lagoons at the end of dry season. These great bodies of water evaporated and shrank, so the birds would go hungry if they stayed on the island. During rainy seasons, he prophesied, Saona would be a fine stopping off place for flamingos.

"They could easily fly here from Grand Inagua in the Bahamas. There are about ten thousand birds nesting there," he said, "and a three-hundred-seventy-five-mile flight is nothing for them. The important point is that no one disturb them *here*. I have a suspicion that the sailors at the base may do a little target practice from time to time on those big pink birds. That kind of activity would certainly discourage them from coming to Saona."

"We don't know for sure if they do shoot," I said, "but we can try to put a control on it. An admiral of the Dominican Navy is on the national park board. We can ask him to put out a directive requesting that Navy personnel at Mano Juan be prohibited from shooting at birdlife." (Once again I was playing God. How easy it was—when you had the right connections!)

On the third day we had worked our way up to *Canto de la Playa* (Song of the Beach). The sand was so white it made me squint, so fine it squeaked under my bare feet, so pristine I felt like Eve. Someone had once planted a thin stand of coconut palms and these rustled alluringly in the breeze. I could already imagine the pleasure tourists would derive stretched out here: winterwhite skin slowly turning golden-brown. Or Dominican children, romping in the mild surf, as they learned about marine biology. As long as Canto de la Playa was accessible only by boat and not developed beyond a few thatched huts, it could keep its rustic simplicity and still be a joy to many people.

On the fourth day we had progressed all the way up to the lighthouse at the southeastern tip of Saona. The ornithologist had walked inland with Luis to check the last lagoon at this end of the island. Ramón, the boat captain, and I decided to climb the ancient lighthouse. Inside, a steel-rung ladder stretched upward into the shadowy heights. The structure must have been at least 80 feet tall and had been abandoned years ago. I hesitated. No one knew how rusted the iron bolts and bars might be. If one pulled loose or broke in two, it meant a straight fall down the shaft to a concrete floor. I was about to say it seemed too dangerous when the captain grabbed a rung and swung himself up to the first level with all the bravado of a rooster. Ramón started slowly up next, more from peer pressure, I suspect, than from any personal sense of adventure. Out of shame I followed. If the men could do it, so could I. At least, both of them were heavier than I. If the captain made it, so would we behind him. But, if he fell, he'd probably sweep us along with him. It was one of the scariest climbs of my life. My hands felt cold as ice and grabbed the iron supports convulsively.

But the view from the top parapet was worth it. As far as we could see, not a single human—only sand and sea and forest, wind and sun and space. To our east the Mona Channel churned in royal blue; while to the west the idyllic curves of white sand edged turquoise-blue shallows. Below us on the beach, I noticed gleaming white bones and decided to investigate these as soon as we were down. But descending was far worse than ascending. The rungs were quite far apart. One had to rely heavily on the iron hand grips while groping with one's bare foot for a rung below. At times, my entire weight hung from one hand. I began to tremble. Ramón must have sensed my fear. Soothingly he talked me down, taking one foot at a time and positioning it above his head. When at last we all stood safely outside in the blazing sun, I broke into a sweat.

The lanky captain threw me an admiring glance. He turned to Ramón and, assuming I couldn't understand him, muttered, "She's got balls!" I mustered all my resolution to keep from laughing.

The white objects on the beach turned out to be turtle shells and bones bleached by the sun. Later Luis told me that local fishermen prowled the beaches during the late spring nesting period. They flipped over the giant green and leatherback female turtles as they were laying eggs, left them helpless, killed them at leisure, retrieved the eggs, and sold the shells unpolished for $25 apiece. Turtles have been exploited for centuries as an exotic food, for leather goods, cosmetics, jewelry, and decorations. Little wonder that there has been such a dramatic decline in sea turtles around the world. Three of the largest species—greens, Pacific olive ridleys, and loggerheads—are now designated as either endangered or threatened under the United States Endangered Species Act. In the Caribbean, greens, Atlantic ridleys, and hawksbills are alarmingly low in numbers. Along the coast of Florida and Georgia, the thousands of greens which used to nest there have plunged to a few dozen. Yet a thriving black market for sea turtles exists, in which a poacher is often paid $200 for one really big specimen. The most distressing record is that of the Atlantic ridley, which as late as 1947 nested in an aggregation of 40,000 but today comes to Mexico in pitiful bands of only 500.

For this reason, Dr. Archie Carr of the University of Florida had started the Caribbean Conservation Association with the express purpose of saving marine turtles. Thanks in part to his influence, Costa Rica has already declared Tortuguero Beach on the Caribbean side and Nancite in Santa Rosa on the Pacific coast as national parks, and Mexico has made at least one turtle-nesting sanctuary on the Gulf of Mexico. The Dominican Republic, too, could help stem the drain once Parque del Este was functioning and such practices were firmly outlawed.

We were just eating lunch when the company helicopter paid us an unexpected visit. It settled down near the lighthouse and a man wearing a white shirt, a tie, and city shoes, and carrying a briefcase, climbed out awkwardly. The pilot guided him under the rotors, then turned to hand me a note. He looked with amusement at Ramón and me, our salty clothes and hair and sneakers full of mud, and me burned dark as cork by the sun.

"Looks like you-all are having yourselves a good time," he jested. "This here is Mr. Brown, another park planner. The park board thought he ought to spend a day with you and see what Saona has to offer. Oh, I'm supposed to wait for an answer to that note."

I shook hands with Mr. Brown, then turned to scan the slip of paper. It was in Señor Carta's bold, fast scrawl. "Can you please show me highlights of park tomorrow 10 A.M. by helicopter. Continuing on to New York City at midday."

My heart thumped. The big boss actually wanted to inspect Parque del Este. I had only 2 hours to compress 100,000 acres, 3 weeks of survey work, and 55 miles of walking into a meaningful package. I reached for my pocket notebook.

"Gladly," I wrote back. "Meet you at lighthouse 10 A.M." Then I told the pilot, "I'll have a route planned out by morning and go over it with you then. Okay?"

"Roger," drawled the Texan. He gestured apologetically at the newcomer and said, with a slight smile, "I'll pick up Brown tomorrow, too. He ought to see the highlights."

The rest of the day I was kept busy trying to guide our visitor around Saona. First I offered to climb up the lighthouse with him so he could get a bird's-eye view of the countryside. He pointed to his shiny shoes defensively. "I'm afraid they'd slip."

"Well, you can do it barefoot. It's much safer that way," I suggested.

"Barefoot? I never go barefoot."

"Oh. Well, I believe the lighthouse can be fixed up to make an excellent educational display. Besides the splendid vista from the top, it could offer interpretation on oceanography, the island's history, shipwrecks, and marine-turtle conservation."

He nodded and took a few notes.

We cruised back to Canto de la Playa and anchored in hip-deep water. Since the tide had gone out and Luis and the bird man had taken the dinghy, we had to slip over the side and wade in. Our guest refused. "I wouldn't want to ruin my pants," he explained.

At that the captain jumped overboard and reached up his arms. "Grab me piggy-back," he offered in Spanish, "and I'll carry you in."

"What did he say?" Mr. Brown asked.

"You don't speak Spanish?" I queried him politely.

"No. No, I don't."

"Well, the captain's offering to carry you ashore."

Gingerly, the park planner eased over the side and straddled the mulatto's strong back. He insisted on bringing his briefcase with him and held it over his head. We sat down under a palm and I began to explain some of my ideas for utilizing the beach in an unobtrusive, rustic fashion. Meanwhile Ramón went off with his machete to cut us some ripe coconuts. Mr. Brown fidgeted uncomfortably on the sand. Already his starched shirt was soaked with perspiration and his face was beginning to burn. When Ramón handed him a coconut, husked and pierced for drinking, he declined. "You can get dysentery from that," he warned me in a whisper.

"Really?" I murmured. "We've all been drinking coconut milk for four days now. I should have the worst case in the Caribbean, but I don't. By the way, Mr. Brown, don't you have a hat? Your nose is getting quite sunburned."

"No. I didn't bring one."

I handed him my smoky, sweat-stained bandanna. He refused it.

"Would you like to walk along the coast a bit and see the proposed hiking and nature trail? I could point out some of the native vegetation."

"I'd better not," he said. "I'm not used to this climate, you know. I might have a heat stroke."

"Where did you say you're from?" I asked.

"Washington. Washington, D.C."

"So what would you like to do?" I asked, a trifle annoyed.

"Oh, just go back to the boat and take a few more notes."

About what? I wondered to myself.

When it was time to pick up Luis and the ornithologist, we moved the big boat down the coast to meet the Boston whaler. They clambered aboard, stinking of muck from the salt lagoon. Mr. Brown visibly shrank. I was only too happy to let the ornithologist take over and sit in the air-conditioned cabin describing his flamingo work. I climbed up to the flying bridge and sat alone for awhile, trying to quell my disgust at the incompetent man below. Imagine sending a park planner to a tropical Latin country without the proper clothing, language, stamina, and attitude. The high cost of his consultancy would produce practically nothing. One could be sure he would write a fancy report that would contribute little to the over-all project. But my displeasure evaporated as evening came on and the sea darkened. I began planning the short tour for Señor Carta next day.

It went like clockwork. Allowing for an hour of air time, we would have an hour to make three ground stops and an aerial reconnaissance. We circled the lighthouse, then landed for a moment at Canto de la Playa, where the sandpipers did a ballet before us. We swung over the flamingo lagoons and dipped down to see the man-o'-war colony. The fisher folk at El Algibe smothered me with hugs and produced a beautiful conch shell for Señor Carta. The Ranger stopped and cut its engines within yards of my secret blowhole. I walked nonchalantly to the small orange X mark and motioned for silence. Puzzled, Señor Carta followed me. (Mr. Brown stayed in the chopper and threw up.) Then the sea's great breath was sucked in and let out of that tiny orifice. Now Señor Carta was on his hands and knees, entranced, ignoring scratches on his boots, the stains on his white pants. The division head for that mighty multinational corporation stuck his finger in the hole like a child playing with a toy. Then out, then in.

"How pleasant it sounds." He smiled quietly. "Ah, Anna, I could stay here all day. No company problems out here. So peaceful." Then looking around, eyes aglow, he said, "Anna, it's going to be a fine park!"

I came back to the Dominican Republic a few months later and spent a week in liaison and planning work with the corporation, park board, museum, and new National Park Service. The roads and buildings were slated to be begun that winter. I was offered a retainership to consult on a monthly basis for the next year or two. I was ecstatic.

Later, back in New York State, I went to the supermarket one day. I hadn't bought sugar for months, the price had been so high. Sometimes it had reached $1.00 a pound. Now, to my surprise, it had dropped back by almost half.

A few days later, I received a note at my log cabin asking me to call Washington, D.C. Unbelieving, I heard one of my teammates from the survey explain that the crash in sugar prices had seriously affected the Dominican operations of Gulf + Western. Parque del Este was to be delayed indefinitely. Señor Carta had been transferred. Everything was in a state of flux.

"But, but, but—" I sputtered. "How can the park just end like this? We did so much, and we did everything right. We had good teamwork, air and ground coverage, a super master plan, photographs, the road routed, research, recommendations, future plans. Gulf + Western was just great in helping us."

"I know, I know," sighed my colleague unhappily. "That's big business for you. You can never be too sure of anything when corporation money is involved, despite good intentions."

"Maybe," I said slowly, as the idea grew, "the only way to make conservation work is by the grass-roots approach."

After I hung up, I sat a long time thinking about all this. Up till now, it had seemed that the ideal formula to accomplish conservation work in record time was through a large corporation. They had the money, the philanthropic bent, the clout, and the high-level contacts to effect speedy change. There was no government red tape to wade through. A researcher had no poverty-stricken days, no lack of equipment, no crippling breakdowns and lengthy repairs to suffer. The corporation merely had to decide on a conservation project, snap its fingers, and the work was off and running.

Yet now I had ample reason to doubt. I couldn't help comparing my Dominican Republic experience with my earlier wildlife and wildland campaigns and consultancies. Each had involved a different approach, in terms of funding, personnel, and time. Each had given different results. For example, the Guatemalan giant grebe campaign had started as a one-woman effort with months and months of hardship, slow work, and little money. It had grown to include both grass-roots and high-government support. The quetzal cloud forest reserve was more of a private group effort—interested landowners and two cooperative conservation groups. Yet it had suffered from limited funds and gear. Anegada was handled on a part-academic, part-private-industry, basis, with a quasi-team approach which never really meshed although we obtained some useful scientific data. The Volcano Barú park was a joint project of government and a large international conservation organization, utilizing outside expertise and local technicians. However, it had dragged slowly along, like most government programs and initially did not have large funds, adequate equipment, or manpower available. Of them all the Dominican park had seemed most likely to succeed, given the coordinated teamwork, high priority by both government and a huge corporation, and ample funds.

Which way was best? Was there a formula to success in this field? Was it normal that some should win and others lose? Perhaps all methods are feasible. Perhaps conservation accomplishments depend ultimately on enthusiasm, cooperation, and competency—plus good timing and luck.

Gandhi and Grimwood

A wildlife ecologist does not learn only from university courses and field work. I gradually discovered that conferences and associated field trips play an equally important role in polishing one's professional skills. Conferences can be crucially important for maintaining a sense of solidarity among scientists, allowing the exchange of up-to-date information, rekindling enthusiasm, and strengthening concern about the steadily mounting threats of industrialization

and technology. Meetings can give one an almost religious conviction that our small ecological community is bettering the over-all
quality of life.

Moreover, by holding conferences in various countries, governments and private conservation organizations are often gal-
vanized into a realization of environmental problems and persuaded to take a stand on them.

The first, and most important, international conference I attended as a fledgling professional was the Tenth General Assembly
and Eleventh Technical Meeting of IUCN in New Delhi, India, in
1969. The thought of flying halfway around the world and mingling
with prestigious scientists was both impelling and frightening. Yet,
I had to "break the ice" into my own professional circle.

New Delhi hit me as a swirl of dust, majestic palaces, strange
Mogul towers, silks and saris, throngs of skinny humans, smoky
sunsets, car horns, cups of fragrant tea, and incense. The conference itself was imposing. Names I had long admired, even idol-
ized, became associated with real faces. During registration I met
as diverse a group as is imaginable—a white-bearded Russian zoo-
logist, a tanned Australian forester, a tiny eighty-year-old Indian
ornithologist. However, one thing bothered me: Male conferees
kept asking me whose wife I was, or what was I doing here, as if I
couldn't possibly have a professional reason for attending. Even
the "Dr." before my name didn't help. In fact, a few gentlemen
just ignored it and talked about trivialities. This subtle form of
male chauvinism was getting me down until I saw Mrs. Indira
Gandhi.

She was invited to give the inaugural speech at our opening
session. We met briefly in a hallway and stared at each other for a
few seconds, woman to woman. Her wheat-colored sari with
threads of gold matched her eyes. They were tawny brown, totally
fearless, and demanding of respect. Never before had I met a
woman with power in a high position. And until then, I had been
bothered by the conflict between following my career drives and
maintaining my tomboyish demeanor or bowing to more traditional
conceptions of feminine roles and appearance. Yet, seeing Mrs.
Gandhi, a resolute woman, as proud and graceful as a tigress, I
suddenly gained courage. From then on I mingled more easily
with the conferees, quelled feelings of shyness, and began acting
like a professional.

The other person there who caused change in my life was Major Ian Grimwood, a modest, quiet former Indian Army officer. We often met by chance at night, pacing the open-air corridors, as both of us were suffering from jet lag and sleeplessness. Strolling along, listening to Major Grimwood describe his field experiences in many lands, I gained tremendous respect for his practical and persevering manner of work. He spoke of his adventures as Kenya's Chief Game Warden; how he had rescued three of the last surviving Arabian oryxes (horselike creatures of steppes and deserts); ecological surveys he'd made in the Amazon jungle.

On two free days set aside for field trips, I joined my colleagues to visit Jim Corbett National Park and Bharatpur Bird Sanctuary. India's wildlife and wildlands are fantastic where they exist untouched and protected. At Corbett, I was hoisted up the side of an elephant onto a riding chair with six other people. We plodded through head-high grasses in search of tigers. The huge, pinkish-gray ears of our mount flapped nervously each time we surprised a black buck, chital deer, or blue bull. The landscape, seen from the back of an elephant, was dramatic. Swaying savannas stretched out on one side to a clear, foaming river. In the other direction, the forested foothills of the mighty Himalayas began. Only later, after we dismounted (we never saw a tiger) and the elephant padded softly away, did the park superintendent tell us of the plans for a dam and hydroelectric project which would inundate about half of the lowlands in Corbett National Park!

Our second field excursion to Bharatpur was even more spectacular. We headed south toward Agra (site of the Taj Mahal) and spent the night in ornate canvas tents outside the sanctuary. Everyone rose in the frigid dawn to enter the huge heronry. A stirring was already beginning in the marshes as skeins of gray-lag geese mounted into a tangerine sky. Parakeets, mynas, and treepies squawked atop the acacia trees. A Palas fishing eagle made its first stoop of the day. We climbed into a balky boat with two shivering boys to pole us through the swamps. Branches were bending under hundreds of nest platforms. Painted storks, white ibis, Eurasian spoonbills, shags, egrets, darters, herons were all awake and greeting the sun. The din was unbelievable on that frosty morning.

Two of our hosts at Bharatpur were Dr. S. Dillon Ripley, President of the International Council of Bird Preservation (ICBP), and Dr. Salím Alí, India's leading ornithologist. They took us to see the sarus cranes dancing and to observe in action a cooperative international bird-banding program (the Asian Migratory Pathological Survey) which in the last four years, had banded, examined, and released 80,000 birds of 1,006 species. On the less bright side, Dr. Alí pointed out the threats to this splendid sanctuary. People were draining it for more agricultural and pasture lands, deforesting it for firewood, poaching the animals, and diverting the present artificial water supply elsewhere. Furthermore, Dr. Alí noted, cattle and buffalo, which are sacred to 85 percent of India's people, were allowed to wander at will and often infiltrated and grazed within the refuge.

I was grateful that Dr. Alí was there to fight for Bharatpur—and even more appreciative when he received the J. Paul Getty Wildlife Conservation award in recognition of his labors.

These adventures almost persuaded me that India's wildlife and wildlands had a future and that her 5 national parks and 100 sanctuaries were fairly secure. But then came the drive back to New Delhi. Hordes of emaciated human beings edged the roadways, barely moving aside as our car blared its way among them. It looked to me as if they simply didn't care whether they lived or died. Outside the city the landscape was drab and devastated. Now and again I saw a dead or dying person lying beside the highway. Women were filling water jugs from poisonous-looking green irrigation ditches while a short way back in the fields men squatted to relieve themselves. One of the ecologists told us that 500 to 1,000 years ago this land had been forested and flowing with clear creeks. But now the *wadis* (gulches) were dry and barren. A pall of smoke and dust hung constantly in the air. This was a land one-third the size of the United States but with three times the number of inhabitants (700 million-plus people, increasing by 2.5 percent annually, as of 1969). Here stood 15.5 percent of the world's population on 2.4 percent of its surface.

Indians told me that government and private birth control programs could not begin to keep up with the population increase, and that 90 percent of India's wildlife has been lost in the last 25 years. A member of the Indian Planning Commission told our gathering gloomily, "The chief ministries have a difficult task to perform in their own states where population pressures tend to promote rather than check the constant encroachment of man on forest and wildlife. It is one of the greatest pities of democracy that trees have no votes and wild animals no constituency."

By the end of those 10 days in India I was sickened and discouraged. For the first time since becoming a conservationist I wondered if it was worth it. Nothing in any class or conference had prepared me for this shock. Yet it is something that every professional working with natural resources should be aware of. I became certain that the "triage" system of conservation priorities, as proposed by Dr. Thomas Lovejoy, is the most realistic way to save our natural heritage. With this method, India would have to be written off the list of places in which ecologists should devote time, energy, and money. How could conservation succeed where living skeletons roamed the land with the most desperate demands for food, water, and firewood? Conservation might be better achieved in young and relatively underpopulated countries like New Zealand, Brazil, and Iceland. Triage came as the most sobering thought of my entire conservation career.

The second international meeting which was to have a far-reaching impact on my thinking took place in Venezuela, the winter of 1974. The conference was convened by the IUCN under the sponsorship of the United Nations Environmental Program (UNEP). Financial support was given by UNESCO, the Swedish International Development Authority, and the World Wildlife Fund. It was the first such conference to bring together ecologists and planners, government specialists and officials dealing with agriculture, forestry, and land use. They came from all over Latin America, bent on devising ecological guidelines for use in developing the American humid tropics, especially rain forests. These would be published and presented to top decision-makers, urging their rapid implementation.

Rain forests are becoming prime targets for human intervention and exploitation aimed at transforming them or using the land for other purposes. Many development schemes have been devastating to these potentially renewable ecosystems. It was our hope that ecological guidelines would aid in the proper utilization of forests and thereby increase the long-term stability and well-being of tropical nations and their economies.

All too often ecologists are placed in the position of a medical doctor who is peremptorily summoned to effect a cure when the patient is nearly dead. Clearly, as M.D.s of the environment, we should be in on the diagnosis, or decision-making process, from the beginning. Ecological factors should be considered right along with political, sociological, military, and economic aspects in every project. That's what we were trying to do at this conference.

After we had finished the rough draft of our guideline report, the group was invited on two three-day field trips through the Venezuelan countryside. Both trips were organized for our benefit by CODESUR (Corporación del Desarrollo del Sur—Development Corporation of the South) of the Venezuelan Ministry of Public Works, and by CVG (Corporación Venezuela de la Guyana—Venezuelan Corporation of Guyana). We would be treated to a glimpse of the wet tropics where important development projects were being planned or implemented. This was my first visit to South America as a professional and the start of an awareness of its vast areas and the environmental problems. My world was widening. Central America and the Caribbean seemed almost miniature in comparison.

Our itinerary read like that of an Explorer's Club expedition. Our traveling home was an ancient but dependable DC-3. Its Plexiglas windows were cracked and split. We could spit right through them. All thirty-three participants had to strap themselves in sideways on bucket seats along the length of the plane. It hadn't been revamped one iota since World War II, when it was used to ferry paratroopers out on jumps. As we creakily took off from La Guaira airport at dawn, some of us remarked nervously on the possibility of crashing.

"If we do," said Dr. Gerardo Budowski soothingly, "we'd probably survive in good shape. Where else do you have so many of the world's top ecologists traveling together? If *we* couldn't figure out how to survive, nobody else could."

Conversation aboard the DC-3 flowed from topic to topic, continent to continent, as easily as flipping through an illustrated geography book. Every once in a while, a flurry of explanations broke forth and the plane took an unnerving dip sideways as all the passengers crowded on one side or the other to see some phenomenon below.

At Venezuela's newest and easternmost city, Ciudad Guyana

(not far from the island of Trinidad), we marveled at the then three-year-old settlement which had started from scratch and had already tripled its original population to 150,000. Once again I was witnessing the incredible human potential for reproduction and emigration. Not far away, along the grassy coastal plain of the Caribbean, we walked through a pine plantation of over 50,000 acres, with more trees being planted as we watched (as of 1978, there were 100,000 acres). The Venezuelan government was pinning its hopes on this gigantic monoculture of Caribbean pine in order to have a close and cheap source of pulp and paper products. Already some of the earlier plantings were eight years old and well over 25 feet tall. They could be cut within two to four more years. Yet foresters were worried lest an insect plague or disease strike the vulnerable exotic species before it matured enough to harvest.

As I went down the orderly rows of shimmering trees, I recalled a public square in Caracas. Newspapers lay scattered by the wind and discarded in trash cans. The cheaper restaurants and drive-ins served everything on paper. Supermarkets offered the same variety of tissues, paper napkins, toweling, and toilet paper as in the United States. The demand for disposable products was mounting at an extraordinary pace. Could huge monocultures satisfy these needs and cut down the import costs for the burgeoning Latin American populations? Only time would tell. The Caribbean pine has shown itself quite resistant to pests in experiments of over fifty years in Africa and so far has been doing well in Venezuela.

However, any single species growing alone in the tropics is normally headed for trouble from epidemics and infestations, whereas mixtures of species are far healthier and more resistant to disease. That was one of the ecological principles we had just finished writing: Diversity breeds stability.

Winging down to Canaima National Park, we sidetracked to view the Guri Dam—largest "black water" reservoir in the world. ("Black water" simply means clear, acidic water stained brownish or blackish by vegetation or bedrock.) As we flew over this impoundment, I saw it stretching for mile upon mile between forest-clad hills. Its hydroelectric power, reaching an output of 2,650 kilowatt-hours in 1977, and a projected 9 million later, will provide all of Ciudad Guyana's electrical needs. All this was especially interesting to us because no one knows what effect the impounding of black water will have. Normally clear or "white water" reservoirs silt up quickly, swift-water fishes die, water stagnates, become eutrophic, and may become the breeding ground for disease-bearing insects or snails. Such reservoirs lose their useful-ness quickly. However, this more acidic, dark-colored lake was a new experiment in the making. Ecologists would be watching it carefully.

Next we landed in Canaima–Grand Savannah National Park. The 7.5-million-acre park is now the largest in South America and one of the six biggest on earth. One of the reasons it is so large is to provide adequate protection and management of the upper Caroni watershed which heads up in the park and is vital to the Guri Dam and Ciudad Guyana industrial complex. Furthermore, the thousands of local and foreign tourists it draws each year have persuaded many Venezuelans that conservation *can* pay its way. To see the park's crowning spectacle, Angel Falls, we had to fly into the back country and view it fleetingly from our DC-3. Never will I forget the sight of that slender stream cascading 2,800 feet from the top of a table-topped, sandstone, steep-sided mountain, known as a *tepui*. A few milky clouds drifted across our line of vision, making Angel Falls seem even more mysterious and unat-tainable. Then, with one wingtip frighteningly close to the canyon wall, our little aircraft banked, turned, dropped, and roared away from the spectacle.

Now we continued south over Grand Savannah. This im-mense, undulating land flowed beneath us like tapestry, golden-tan in color and marked with monolithic tepuis and narrow black streams. The tepuis were a topic of keen interest and speculation among us. They are authentic isolated "islands in the air," rearing upward as high as 5,000 feet. Their tops support many endemic plants, including orchids and epiphytes, and dwarf forests. Most have never been explored by white people. Approximately ninety such mountains dot the Guyana highlands—one of the most gran-diose and magnificent geological sights in the world.

We leaped across Venezuela to the Rio Negro and the con-junction of this country with Colombia and Brazil. The meeting point is marked with one huge "sugar-loaf" mountain which we circled lazily like a giant, if ragged, vulture. This was my first sight of the Amazon basin—the enormous lowland rain forest which is the largest such tract on earth. The green carpet rolled out to the horizon on every side, cut here and there by sinuous brown rivers. Untouched, it seemed a living treasure house of natural diversity and beauty.

When we landed at San Carlos de Rio Negro for the night, we had the opportunity to inspect one of the "new towns" being built by CODESUR. The basic purpose was to draw together indigenous, free-roaming Indian tribes of the rain forest, settle them in cement-block houses, and give them a few civilized amenities, such as piped-in water, outhouses, transistor radios, and rough airstrips. Sociologically and politically, it appeared a great plan to integrate the nation. Not until our group of environmental doctors walked through the little hamlet did the medical and ecological drawbacks become apparent.

"Those cement floors and walls will cause health problems," prophesied Dr. Budowski. "It's been noted in other new towns in the tropics that babies and toddlers who lie on cold stone floors instead of bare ground become more susceptible to respiratory and urinary infections. When they go to the bathroom, the liquid and feces are no longer absorbed by the soil, broken down by bacteria, and eventually rendered harmless. Instead, the excreta puddles and piles until the mother cleans the floor."

All of us stopped to stare at the innocent-looking homes. Dr. Budowski continued, "We must remember that many indigenous people do not practice the same sanitary standards that we do in temperate climates. Besides, they probably earn less than one-hundred to two-hundred dollars per year. How can they possibly buy soaps, cleansers, disinfectants?"

We strolled on through the streets. "This new life style invites flies and filth," he went on. "Forest people have been semi-nomadic for centuries. They put up thatched huts with dirt floors, farmed and grazed as long as the soil held out, and then moved on to the next patch of wilderness to repeat the process. This simple way of life is sound for both humans and the tropical rain forest when groups are small. But when people are brought into these new towns, they are more or less trapped. They can't move the cement-block houses, yet the soil will wear out just as fast around the new town as it did around their jungle huts. Some towns are already experiencing desertification. Look here."

We had come to an overturned tree with its root system standing perpendicular to the ground. We could easily see that the top soil was a cap about 4 inches deep above sterile white sand, and that the roots had compensated by spreading out in a splayed, flat pattern.

"When soil is exposed like this," explained Dr. Budowski, "the water and sometimes the wind quickly strip it down to the underlying sand, then gnaw away at the edges, creating larger and larger sand patches."

"One more thing," broke in Dr. Ray Watters, a tropical ecologist from New Zealand, "it's been found that when thatched roofs are replaced by tin ones, many natural insect predators like spiders, lizards, and bats lose a home. Then insects increase around the human habitations and human diseases borne by them may also thrive. Malaria and dengue are two examples."

I found this conversation strangely disturbing. Around us the jungle pressed in—wild, fecund, teeming with life. Yet here stood these squat, conventional, concrete houses, rectangular lots, squares and streets, and a newly bulldozed airstrip large enough to accommodate a Hercules transport. Man had imposed a precise mathematical design and theoretical social order upon a natural, primitive, stable environment. It wasn't working exactly the way it should.

I knew that each of the South American nations which share the huge Amazon basin had plans to invade this "last frontier." Just as we "won our West," Venezuela is "conquering her South." She is trying to consolidate her native tribes and impart a nationalistic spirit through radio programs broadcast daily from Caracas and picked up by lonely radio towers deep in the jungle. Brazil was already embarked on a colossal program of colonization and highway expansion. Peru, Ecuador, and Bolivia had oil crews out searching for "liquid gold" in the western basin. Colombia and the Guyanas were pursuing trade in animal skins, diamonds, gold, bauxite, rubber, and other rain-forest products. The new town we were examining beside the Rio Negro was only one of hundreds of examples of twentieth-century developments infiltrating into Amazonia.

Clearly, our ecological guidelines were needed. But had we gotten them out in time? Would they be accepted and utilized?

Might the sights we were witnessing this week be forerunners of the same ecological and human devastation I had agonized over in India?

A third and most auspicious meeting took place in San José, Costa Rica, in December 1974. It was the First Conference on National Parks in Central America, to which came representatives from every Central American country, including Mexico, Panama, and Belize. Thanks to Rockefeller Brothers Fund financing, the crying need for parks in this part of the world was finally being acknowledged, considered, and contended with.

It was none too soon. With the shining exceptions of Costa Rica and Panama, attempts to establish national parks in the Central American isthmus had so far met with little success. A number of factors contributed to this: border squabbles, political changes, public apathy, a general ignorance about conservation and its benefits, plus a lack of training in the management of natural resources. Most areas declared parks or reserves were "parks on paper." Compared to the United States, Canada, and Africa, each with a long and proud tradition of national parks, and South America, with several newly protected areas, Central America was lagging far behind.

As I sat and listened, however, four delegates from each Central American country representing natural resources, tourism, culture, and central planning, began to formulate plans for "pilot parks," which would be the prototypes for each country. These would have easy access from metropolitan areas and contain outstanding natural and/or cultural features. The participants also made lists of other natural wildlands worthy of park status. In time, these would become "frontier" parks, wildlife reserves, biosphere reserves, marine national parks, multiple-use areas, and archaeological parks. This remarkable initiative was the beginning of a Central American system of true national parks. The enthusiasm of the delegates was noteworthy. Ninety days later they had an official request for assistance to Central America into the United Nations Development Program in New York. And in less than a year, they had written management plans for each of the pilot parks.

At the same time, with the generous support of the Rockefeller Brothers Fund, a Wildlands and Watershed Unit was agreed upon, to be housed within the Natural Renewable Resources Program at CATIE (*Centro Agronomico Tropical de Investigación y Enseñanza*—Tropical Agricultural Research and Training Center) in Costa Rica. The unit would assist the Central American governments in establishing these parks and managing their natural resources.

I had no way of knowing at this conference that my attendance would lead to a future consulting job at CATIE and then to a deep involvement in the entire Central American park system through a *National Geographic* assignment. Such are the surprise spinoffs of conferences.

After the official meeting, I joined a few colleagues for a trip to the 4,000-acre Monte Verde Cloud Forest Preserve in the Tilaran Mountains. How comfortable it felt to be back in one of my favorite ecosystems. We hiked down a muddy trail for a while, then I told my companions to go on without me. "I'll wait here and listen for quetzals," I explained, settling down on a moss-covered log.

I leaned back and relaxed. It was 4 P.M. Clouds and mist were enveloping the forest in an unearthly light. High above me the trade winds roared over the 4,000-foot crest of the mountains. The noise was as constant as sea surf. For six months, the winds blew thus. The other six months, rains fell and the winds were light and variable. From the top of a monstrous gnarled oak, I heard the familiar chatter of a male quetzal. A moment later, he swooped like a flash of green lightning across a clearing and up into another giant oak. As he passed, a shaft of sunlight streamed through the scudding clouds and lit up his crimson breast like a neon light.

Just to see that swift streak of splendor made the whole field trip worthwhile. I silently congratulated the World Wildlife Fund, USA, and the Tropical Science Center in Costa Rica for joining funds and forces to save this remnant wilderness when so much of the country's high oak and cloud forests are being cut and burned for charcoal and lumber. This reserve is bigger than my quetzal sanctuary on Volcano Atitlán and probably holds the largest remaining population of quetzals in Costa Rica.

Now the sun shaft switched off abruptly and a thick mist muffled the forest. I could feel my clothes dampening in the high humidity and could almost sense the mosses, lichens, liverworts, air plants, fungi, and trees around me absorbing the moisture. Monte

Verde was like one huge sponge, soaking up water and releasing it slowly throughout the year. The cloud forest made life possible downslope—a little Quaker colony making cheeses, the small farmers grubbing for corn and beans, and the wild animals drinking, bathing, and swimming. The last rays of the sunset probed up from the Pacific and dispelled the mist again. My friends returned. We stood silently watching the gilded moss, the bronzed trunks of oaks, ripe raspberries turned cardinal red. Then we descended slowly through that golden world, hearing the trade wind grow fainter and fainter above us.

There have been many other conferences in many different countries. Some people have called me an ecological elitist because I often trip to exotic cities and fare forth into beautiful hinterlands. Others have accused me and my colleagues of being "jet-setting, overeducated preservationists." Still, I'm convinced that conferences are essential to being a good ecologist. And no matter where I go and what I see, elevating or discouraging, two things stay with me: Mrs. Gandhi's undaunted tigress eyes and Major Grimwood's quiet assurance.

A Panda and Some Lions

One day toward the end of August 1974, I received a startling letter. Dr. Fritz Vollmar, then Director General of the World Wildlife Fund, International in Switzerland, was writing to invite me to the Fourth International Conference in Geneva, November 2–4, at which I was to be awarded the 1974 Gold Medal for Conservationist of the Year, in recognition of my work in Central America with the grebes, the quetzals, and Volcano Barú. I was astounded! I immediately wrote back, agreeing to come and accept this great honor.

Then, on October 2, while taking photographs in the woods

for a *National Geographic* article, I fell and broke my pelvis. Fortunately, I did not have to be in a cast, but I was kept flat on my back for three weeks. The doctor said I would be on crutches two months, could try walking after eight weeks, driving after three months, and expect full recovery in about six months. Those early days were among the blackest of my life. Would I be able to continue as an ecological consultant and nature writer? How could I earn my living in the interim? And how would I manage to accept my medal?

My physician, a good-natured and practical man, thought it over and gave his verdict. "*If* you promise to travel to Europe in a wheelchair, and don't go kicking up your heels, or doing any of the crazy things you like to do, you can fly by November first. But remember, those bones aren't knit yet. If you fall, you might be in trouble. If this accident had happened even a couple of days later, I could never have let you go."

Now that I knew it was possible to travel, I began realizing the logistics were almost too complicated to arrange. My heart sank. Who would drive me the 150 miles of bone-jarring roads from the Adirondacks to the airport? How would I pack? What would I wear, let alone could I dress myself? Could I get my hair done? Who would wheel me on and off the plane and meet me in Switzerland? Truthfully, setting off across the Atlantic in this totally helpless state seemed like the scariest thing I'd ever done. But I wouldn't consider *not* going. Not for a minute.

It all worked out beautifully. Thanks to wonderful friends who rigged a mattress in their van, an obliging beauty shop, and the courtesy of the airlines, I found myself aboard a Swissair jet the night of November 1, comfortably cushioned in an aisle seat. To my amazement, Dr. S. Dillon Ripley, Secretary of the Smithsonian Institution and my benefactor of the International Council for Bird Preservation (ICBP) during the Guatemala grebe campaign, was on the same plane, going to the same conference. He graciously kept an eye on me throughout the trip. I couldn't have been better cared for.

In Geneva, the morning of November 2, my friend Dr. Thomas Lovejoy of World Wildlife Fund, USA, wheeled me past customs, collected my baggage, and drove me to the hotel where the conference was already in session. Deftly, he pushed me into the back of the auditorium to a spot where I could hear the proceedings yet not be disturbed.

At once, I started surveying the room, calculating the shortest distance to the podium. It seemed miles away. Yet pride would just not let me be wheeled up there. I was going to use crutches as I'd been taught by the physical therapist. I looked at the highly waxed parquet floors. Definitely dangerous. Then at the gorgeous little Oriental rugs scattered here and there. They would have to go or I'd risk becoming a flying carpet myself. I'd have to ask for a high stool next to the mike, so as not to stand too long. And remote controls to the slide projector, by which I would illustrate my acceptance speech. I worked out my moves as carefully as a general deploying troops into a mine field. Only after I'd done this did I take a look at the conferees.

Again my heart gave a lurch. There at the head table sat Prince Bernhard of The Netherlands, then President of World Wildlife Fund, International, Prince Philip of England, the Maharani of Jaipur, India, assorted Ladies, Ambassadors, Barons, a millionairess from Canada, and Dr. Ripley. Among the audience were sprinkled other famous scientists and royal personages. It was the *Who's Who* of the international conservation world. How could I ever get up in front of such people in my condition? No way!

I motioned frantically to Dr. Lovejoy. "I can't go through with it," I whispered desperately. "You accept the medal for me and show the slides."

"Nonsense," snorted my sensible friend. "You've come all this way to get it. You can do it. You're just exhausted from the trip. Why don't we get you a room for a few hours, so you can take a hot bath and sleep a little? I'll come get you shortly before four o'clock, when the presentation is scheduled. You'll feel better about it then."

"But the rugs, the floor, the podium . . . ," I began. "It's all too tricky to navigate."

But Thomas was already wheeling me firmly to the front desk of the hotel. He arranged for me to have a room for six hours. A moment later I was inside an enormous high-ceilinged bedroom with French windows looking out on a rose garden still in bloom, blue Lake Geneva, and the snowy Alps behind. A crisply uniformed maid drew a hot bubble bath in the biggest tub I'd ever seen. She fluffed up those heavenly Swiss down comforters, opened the bed, and undressed me. Half an hour later I was fast asleep.

As Thomas had predicted, I felt a bit more confident in the afternoon. Yet when Dr. Vollmar called my name and I had to crutch my way forward like a hoptoad, I almost lost my nerve. But there was no running away. Shakily I balanced myself upright to face Prince Bernhard. I looked straight at him, noticing that he was a very good-looking man and that he appeared comfortably like a commoner in a brown plaid sports coat, slim-cut brown trousers, beige shirt, and soft tie. He smiled kindly at me as he read from a parchment scroll, then handed me a small royal-blue box. Trembling, I opened it. There lay a stunning round gold medal with the World Wildlife Fund symbol, a giant panda, on one side and my name and the date on the other. The Prince shook my hand warmly and gingerly gave me an embrace. I almost fell off my crutches. Then Dr. Vollmar stepped forward with a beautiful gold Rolex watch, again with my name and the date inscribed on the back. This was an extra little surprise and I was tongue-tied.

But the speech had to go on. Recovering my composure, I shared with the audience those months of conservation work in Central America. And then it was all over . . . the handshaking, the thank-you's, the cocktails, the accolades. Once again I was sound asleep among those cozy comforters while an early November snowstorm from the Alps dusted the roses outside my door.

Next morning, Thomas said casually at breakfast, "Why don't you come with us to London tomorrow? Remember, Mr. Getty is giving a small luncheon for the jurors of his new prize and those of us at World Wildlife Fund who administer it. You've been appointed a juror and you were invited. I'm sure he'd want you there, even like this. He's so proud of his new philanthropic interest."

I looked at him doubtfully. "Oh, I can't," I sighed. "It's so far and I feel so helpless traveling by wheelchair."

"You've already done more than that," he rebutted. "Albany, New York, to Geneva, Switzerland, is over four thousand miles.

London's just a hop and a skip away. Besides, I'll be along to push you around," he added impishly.

I grinned suddenly. Why not? Like receiving the gold medal, it was a once-in-a-lifetime opportunity. I was curious to meet J. Paul Getty, "richest man in the world." And really I was too tired to fly right home across the Atlantic. Perhaps I could rest a few days at the home of an old friend, archeologist Colin Wyatt, whom I had once met in Guatemala.

"Okay, Thomas," I said, "I'll go. Just let me wire a friend."

In London, I found myself with Dr. Ripley, Thomas, and the dashing Peruvian conservationist Felipe Benavides, then president of the Peruvian branch of World Wildlife Fund. "Please may I drive you all to the Getty place in my car?" asked Mr. Benavides gallantly as we came to the airport door. A long, slim, gray Daimler limousine with a uniformed chauffeur was waiting. I was helped into the back seat, while Mr. Benavides sat in front, turning at once to talk to us. As we drove through downtown London, he energetically regaled us with accounts of his work in Peru. His principal contribution had been saving the vicuña, once the prized beast of Inca royalty. The vicuña populations had fallen from an estimated 2 million animals ranging through the Andes Mountains to less than 7,000 scattered in the Peruvian highlands. Little wonder the ultra-soft fur was selling for $90 or more per pound. Under Felipe's prodding, the Peruvian government set up a 16,000-acre National Reserve in 1967 and signed a pact with Bolivia banning vicuña hunting for ten years. Mr. Benavides also was instrumental in saving other endangered animals and certain wildlands in the Amazon basin. His black eyes snapped and he minced no words in denouncing to us those countrymen who were exploiting wildlife. I was beginning to see that one did not "meet" Felipe Benavides, one "experienced" him.

Thomas turned to me and whispered, "Don't tell anyone, but Felipe will probably be the first winner of the new fifty-thousand-dollar J. Paul Getty Wildlife Conservation award."

My mouth dropped open and I listened with new respect to the elegant Peruvian. The miles slipped by. It was well past noon. My tummy was rumbling. We seemed to be driving endlessly through London. "I thought we were going to an apartment house downtown," I murmured to Thomas.

"I think Getty's home is on the outskirts," Thomas replied.

Now we were on a "dual carriageway" (superhighway), speeding smoothly through misty English countryside. The Daimler slowed and turned in at an imposing iron gate between high stone walls. A quaint cottage stood at one side and a cheerful woman called out through a loudspeaker, asking our identity. The chauffeur produced our invitations. We waited. Felipe fidgeted. Evidently, security was checking us out.

Then, with all the grandeur of a Hollywood production, the 20-foot ornate gate swung slowly open, and a guard beckoned us in. We followed a curving road through emerald fields where sleek horses grazed, past majestic oaks which might have shaded Robin Hood himself, up over a knoll with a sweeping vista of forest, fields, and "Sutton Place."

By rights it should have been called a baronial manor house, for it was a shade too small to be called a castle. Yet it was far too lavish and large to be anything else. We rolled up the circular driveway and parked beside other Daimlers, Rolls Royces, Bentleys, and Cadillacs . . . all quite different from my rusty 1967 pick-up truck at home.

Chauffeurs surrounded our car and helped us out; butlers opened doors and took coats; maids helped me to the powder room. Then I was in the drawing room, about to meet Mr. Getty himself.

I saw nothing at all imposing about the man at first glance. He didn't have Mr. Benavides' flashing eyes or his charisma; nor Dr. Ripley's gracious poise and patrician face; nor Prince Bernhard's sportsman's physique and charming manner. His suit was drab, his face dotted with blemishes, and his hands shook ever so slightly. The multimillionaire stood, slightly hunched like a hawk on a perch, awaiting his company. He seemed to be looking down at us from the height of his accumulated wealth and years. Then our eyes met. His were blue and as keen and penetrating as a falcon's. Crutching my way closer, I shook hands and sensed the tremendous concentration behind those hooded lids. I felt as if an electric calculating machine had just digested me.

Overtired from the trip, I asked to sit down. A butler helped me into a huge leather chair. A moment later, to my surprise, he assisted Mr. Getty to one beside mine. We looked at each other with a touch of chagrin: he for the toll of his eighty-six years, I for the aches of my accident.

Politely, I praised him for establishing the Getty award, largest of its kind in my profession at that time. He nodded. Then for want of anything better to say, I asked, "Would you like to see my medal?"

He nodded again. I reached for my handbag, then remembered I had left the box in the car. An ambassador was standing nearby, so I called to him sweetly and asked if he'd mind running out and getting it. (It wasn't every day I found such a fancy errand boy.) He literally rushed out the door and back to Mr. Getty's side. I opened the box and showed the magnate the 7-ounce circle of gold gleaming softly on blue velvet.

"Nice," he responded coolly.

After that, I could think of nothing to say. Mr. Getty, for his part, seemed glad of the silence. And, so, together, we rested and watched the buzzing cocktail company.

It was hardly what I'd call having "a few people in for lunch." When the head butler announced the meal, over thirty dignitaries trooped to a table longer than my entire log cabin. Mr. Getty presided at one end. There were so many pieces of silverware before me that my mother's carefully taught etiquette failed. All I could remember her saying was "Always start using your eating utensils from the outside in." I did so, wondering how I'd ever get through twelve pieces of silver without several faux pas. When the wine butler came to fill the first of three crystal goblets, I ordered milk. "Good for broken bones," I said apologetically, but I could have sworn he winced.

Course after course arrived on what looked suspiciously like golden platters. The meal took two and a half hours. I used only seven pieces of silverware. At the serving of demitasses and brandy snifters, Mr. Getty stood up, thanked us all for coming, and invited his guests to go outside to see his pet lions. Then he shuffled off, imperturbable, to take a nap. The guests started toward the back garden for this rare treat of lions after lunch.

Feeling unable to trust myself on crutches on a lion-filled lawn, I decided to obey my doctor's orders. Instead I hobbled from room to room in the mansion. Eventually I came to a huge living room with walls covered with enormous paintings. A great fire burned in the hearth, consuming not logs but whole tree trunks. I worked my way around the room, gazing up at Madonnas from the eleventh, twelfth, and thirteenth centuries. Gradually, it dawned on me that I was seeing part of a fabulous art collection. I had not realized that this was one of Getty's hobbies. At the head of the room, I came face to face with a very elderly man, bent like a fiddlehead over a cane, in the company of a gentle young woman. His progress about the chamber was as slow as mine. We stopped and his companion made the introductions. She pronounced my name perfectly with a French accent and then said, "Sir Julian Huxley."

The shock of white hair lifted, the kindest eyes imaginable looked into mine, and the tortured frame straightened for a moment. I sputtered, "Dr. Huxley! Oh, how *wonderful* to meet you! You don't know how I admire the work you did on the great crested grebes in 1914. It helped me so much with my research in Guatemala on the giant pied-billed grebes."

I stopped. I was sounding like a schoolgirl talking to a movie star. Yet how true it was. Out of that whole day, amidst the Bentleys and butlers, the priceless paintings and golden platters, the lions and wines, this world-renowned scientist was the greatest treasure I'd found. His early ornithological work had been a tremendous inspiration. It was like coming full circle. And how very opportune—just a few months later, Sir Julian died and the world lost one of its greatest humanitarians and scientists.

The day had been too much. While the other guests were still outside, I dialed my archaeologist friend Colin, to ask if he'd come for me.

"I've been expecting your call. *Of course* you can stay here just as long you you like," he said jubilantly. "We have so much to catch up on since Guatemala. I'll come for you right away. Where shall I pick you up?"

"At Paul Getty's estate in Surrey," I said.

My friend never missed a beat. "Righto," he said cheerily. "It's only half an hour from here. I know the place. See you." And he hung up.

Colin marched in just as the rest of the guests were filtering back, talking vivaciously. "Colin," I called from the depths of the leather chair I had returned to. I was struggling to get up, but then I stopped. The others had fallen silent and were all staring at the ramrod-straight, silvery-haired and mustached man. He was wearing plum-colored jeans, a flowery Western shirt, and a gorgeous embroidered shepherd's coat from Afghanistan. In that conservative gathering, he stood out like a hollyhock in a bed of ivy. Again manners failed me. What to do? Should I introduce him? How to explain my friend's predilection for traveling to the earth's most remote and bizarre places, clothing himself in native attires, and not giving a tinker's damn who saw him?

The day was saved by a voluptuous millionairess who cried out, "Oh, Colin, my dear! Why, I haven't seen you since St. Moritz three years ago."

Much hugging and kissing ensued. Colin had never bothered to tell me that he was a former ski-jumping champion. And then to his great glee, Colin was introduced to Mr. Getty, just back from his nap. The old gentleman merely nodded sleepily at this audacious newcomer.

Finally, Colin helped me tenderly out to the parking lot, ignoring butlers, maids, and chauffeurs. He opened the door of a 1964 Chevy with 1964 Wisconsin plates. He threw my overnight bag and medal box onto the back seat and helped me slide into the front. Rows of East Indian good-luck charms hung above the windshield. The seat was covered with a bright Mexican serape. He started the engine and we sped down the driveway, leaving a cloud of dust to sift over the startled chauffeurs.

I lounged back in my seat and let out a great sigh of relief. I was back with my own kind of people. Only after we got to Colin's house did I think to ask him how he got away with driving 1964 American plates in 1974 England. Then, as I crutched around the car toward his front door, I noticed the Spanish bumper sticker. It read: "FE EN DIOS Y ADELANTE" (FAITH IN GOD AND FORWARD).

That sentiment appealed to me. It had gotten me across the Atlantic and would get me home. It would put me back on my feet. Before Christmas I took my first steps without crutches, and after Easter was out doing field work again.

☒17
Manú

When J. Paul Getty established his annual wildlife conservation award worth $50,000, he made a magnificent gesture for the world's wildlife and wildlands. The public was suddenly made aware that conservationists' struggles to save rare and endangered species and places around the world deserved recognition. So I did consider it a special honor and pleasure to be one of the eleven international jurors who, under chairman Prince Bernhard, were to select the first recipient of the award.

The first year hundreds of applications poured into the World Wildlife Fund's office in Washington, D.C., the funneling and filtering point for the prize. It was agonizing to have to choose among the résumés of those dedicated human beings. The jury agreed that the first recipient should come from a Third World country, must have spent several years in conservation work, and preferably be a field person rather than an academic. Imagine my excitement when Felipe Benavides of Peru won, as Thomas Lovejoy had predicted.

A gala reception and dinner were held in Washington, with many Latin American dignitaries present. Nelson Rockefeller, then Vice-President of the United States, made a brief but brilliant appearance. After the official ceremony, Felipe and his stunning wife, Maria Louisa, joined me, Dr. Lovejoy, and a few others from World Wildlife Fund for a more intimate and informal celebration.

"You *must* come and review the wildlife work in Peru—the vicuña national reserve at Pampas Galeras, Paracas Marine National Reserve, our five new national parks, and most of all Manú," said the glowing Felipe. "Why not plan a trip in May during our jungle's little dry season? Thomas, you arrange it!" he ordered expansively. "Bring George Woodwell (Director of World Wildlife Fund, USA), one or two of the other jurors, and Anne. I want to use my prize money to build a wildlife research center out in the *campo* (field). You can all help me decide where."

Before the evening was over, he had set a date for four of us to fly to Lima, Felipe's home. From there we would go immediately to Manú National Park—the largest in the Amazon basin and at that time in all Latin America. It was as untouched and primeval a tract of lowland rain forest as one could hope to find.

As luck would have it, a few weeks later I received an assignment from *Audubon* magazine to do an article on the ecological situation in the Amazon. It would take me half a year to survey Amazonia (the Amazon basin), dividing it into three major segments. First, I would visit wild Manú in May with the man who had helped create it. Later, in November and December, the long dry season, I would take a 2,300-mile boat trip down the Amazon River. Finally, I would drive along the new Transamazonica and Belém-Brasília highways. All told, I would roam over 7,000 miles in the largest remaining chunk of lowland rain forest on earth—an area roughly equivalent to two-thirds of the continental United States (2,400,000 square miles), with new ecosystems, countries, and dimensions to be explored. All the assorted pieces—starting with my broken bones, the gold medal, the Venezuelan conference, and the Getty jury appointment—were falling into place in an extraordinary fashion.

One evening in May 1975 I jetted non-stop from New York City to Lima with our group, met Felipe and two government representatives, and continued at dawn to Cuzco along the rocky ranges of the Andes. At that high, windy airport we switched to a Twin Otter. My usual nervousness about flying turned to sheer panic as we rapidly spiraled up from 11,000 feet to over 19,500 and nosed into huge snowy clouds. The pilot ordered us to start breathing oxygen and pointed out two thin plastic tubes running along the cockpit ceiling. Thomas Lovejoy sat beside me, imperturbable as an eagle. Calmly, he passed the tube to me, waited as I sucked in a few breaths, then took it back. Breaks in the clouds showed a piercing brittle-blue sky above; cruel gray mountains laced with snow, ravines, and landslides below. Our plane was right over the great spine of the Andes, humming eastward, dauntless as a dragonfly in the face of that immense frigid world outside.

I broke into a cold sweat and began panting uncontrollably. Suddenly I had a flashback to my childhood. I was five, and my parents had taken me around South America on a four-month business tour. They had often described the rugged flight from Santiago, Chile, to Buenos Aires, Argentina, in a non-pressurized, twin-propellered plane of the 1940s. "You turned green," my mother told me, "and we had to give you oxygen. Yet you kept staring out at the mountains."

Now here I was, straddling the Andes and feeling green again. Then the altimeter began winding down—19,500 to 4,000 feet. My breathing slowed and that vision disappeared. The cabin became warm and humid. We broke through cloud cover and saw the Amazon forest spreading like a green carpet as far as our eyes could see. A few minutes later we were landing at 900 feet elevation beside a temporary oil-exploration camp not far from Manú. Here we would board City Service helicopters for the last leg of the trip into the park. The influence of Mr. Benavides, plus the coordination of the Getty and City Service oil companies and World Wildlife Fund, USA, had combined their logistic support with the Peruvian Air Force and Ministry of Agriculture so we could make the trip from New York City to Manú National Park in a miraculous 24 hours, instead of traveling with jeeps and dugout canoes for about two weeks.

An oil engineer and a geologist met the plane and helped us out. The pilots unloaded our backpacks, tents, and food supplies. Then we walked across the enormous airstrip toward the camp's mess hall. We passed bulldozers, generators, drilling equipment, cables, hundreds of pipes, and rows of air-conditioned trailers which served as dormitories and offices for the field staff.

"Would you like to see inside?" asked one of the men amiably. We walked around a huge Hercules transport plane unloading drilling equipment and stepped into a cool blast of air. Four bunks lined one wall, desks another, and a hot shower and modern toilet facilities were available.

"I can't believe all this luxury in the midst of untouched jungle," I exclaimed.

The engineer smiled and said, "We have to have it. Searching for oil in the Amazon is one of the most grueling jobs in the world. We work three weeks, then have nine days off with free air transportation to Cuzco or Lima. Besides the professional staff of engineers, geologists, and surveyors, there are over one thousand men here, most of them Peruvian laborers who cut trails for the seismic crews and do all the manual work necessary to keep a camp like this going. Remember, we have no roads, only the Manú River and the air."

We continued past huge sleeping sheds slung with hammocks where the workmen lived and a few private campsites where female camp followers stayed. At last we came to the mess hall. The two men welcomed us into the screened, open building next to the river. They set ice-cold Coca Cola on the tables. We were enjoying another one of the "miracles" of modern technology—cool, pure drinks in a land whose average annual temperature probably has not fallen below 70 degrees F for tens of thousands of years. Nothing ever tasted so good. As we sat sipping our Cokes, looking over the muddy Manú, a hundred questions ran through our minds. I started by asking, "How much does it cost a petroleum company to open and operate an exploratory camp like this?"

"About ten million dollars," answered the engineer coolly. "There are at least fifteen other private companies looking for oil in Peru alone, and there are others in Ecuador, Bolivia, Colombia, and Brazil. One of the most recent discoveries of petroleum is here in the upper Amazon. It might possibly yield four billion barrels a day by 1985. We're still not sure."

"How many acres does each company have?" asked Dr. George Woodwell.

"Around two and a half million," answered the geologist nonchalantly.

"But each one's almost the size of Manú!" Felipe stormed. "That certainly doesn't say much about our priorities."

"Not really," agreed the American engineer. "Anyway, each company leases a tract from the Peruvian government. Under their contract they can drill four test wells at two million dollars each and set up a base camp for another two million. They keep 46 percent of anything they strike; and the government receives the remaining 54 percent. A contract runs for about thirty-five years."

I was beginning to see why gasoline prices were rising in the

United States. I had never realized how much work and money went into just finding crude oil, much less transporting and refining it. "What about ecological damage?" I queried. "How bad is it?"

"We try to keep all pollution to a minimum," said the engineer. "There's usually not much large-scale damage to the forest itself, because the total area cut down for test wells, campsites, and the airstrip comes to only two hundred to four hundred acres out of the two and a half million. The hundreds of miles of trails cut by seismic crews grow up with jungle vegetation within four to six months. At the main camp, we normally build in a septic system and garbage dump. Organic materials rot fast out here and metals rust away in no time."

Felipe blurted out, "As I see it, the main threat to the environment is from surreptitious hunting and trapping by the laborers on their off time. It makes a bad drain on local fish and game."

A biologist-juror chimed in with, "Obviously the main ecological problem is not from oil exploration or drilling. It comes after the oil is found. There could be possible water pollution from leaking oil barges or pipelines. And air pollution from burning off the wells. Even more important are the roads. They infiltrate the forest and spread havoc by bringing in large-scale agriculture, ranching, lumbering, colonization, and other types of exploitation that the ecosystem cannot handle."

"Well, it's the same old story," sighed Felipe. "Overpopulation! Making a park like Manú is like trying to cure cancer with an aspirin. As long as the world population increases, we'll have more and more trouble saving bits of rain forest from people who need land for survival."

We all fell silent, drinking our Cokes and thinking of this global problem.

I was dying to ask a far different question. Blushing, I said, "Tell us about the camp women. How can you permit them at such a huge operation?"

"If we didn't, we couldn't control the men." The geologist grinned. "They have to have some release. The women have a good life out here. The laborers treat them like queens, and they make enough money to return eventually to their hometowns or go to Cuzco or Lima and buy a little shop and make a better life for themselves. No one is in it for any longer than it takes to make a bundle."

I pondered this unusual life style as I finished my drink. Then the screen door flew open and one of the pilots came in to announce that our helicopters were ready. We all paired off. Felipe and I squeezed ourselves and our gear into a small chopper. Our pilot, an Indian lad who looked about fifteen, smiled confidently and whirled us up into the sky.

We followed the brown Manú, which wound like an anaconda through the endless mat of trees. Not a sign of civilization. The park is roadless, free of airstrips, river ports, towns, and all other signs of human habitation except four small ranger stations. Eighty percent of the 3.8 million acres of parkland is lowland rain forest transected by the river, while the park's western border stretches up in the Andes to almost 12,000 feet.

Now we were landing at Pakitza, a ranger control station at the eastern edge of the park, at least 80 miles from the nearest permanent town, not counting the oil camp. We plunked down through the unbroken canopy and landed in a clearing beside the river. The helicopter pilot grinned good-bye and rattled away to shuttle the rest of our field gear here. We were in one of the most remote wilderness areas in the world. As the last chopper roared off, we were left standing with a mound of tents, packs, and canned goods.

A strangely silent jungle afternoon settled over us. Not a leaf stirred in the hot air. Not a bird called. Felipe broke the heavy stillness with characteristic humor. "Next to the Spanish conquistadores," he boomed, "we're the greatest explorers ever!" He tipped his safari hat at an even more rakish angle, tightened the belt on his khaki hunting shirt, and strode toward the station and the three park rangers who were hurrying down to meet us.

"How times and priorities change!" Felipe laughed delightedly as he looked at the rangers in brown uniforms with revolvers, the Peruvian flag with the World Wildlife Fund panda symbol above it, and the well-kept station house. Turning to us, he explained, "In 1966, Major Ian Grimwood came here as a wildlife consultant and completed the master plan for Manú National Park. World Wildlife Fund of Peru received twenty-five hundred dollars from the WWF in Britain to buy the first outboard motor and build a shelter here. Then on the seventh of March, 1968, President Fernando Belaunde declared it a National Reserve. In 1974, it became a National Park."

Although Felipe was being modest, I was sure that a man of his wit, stature, imagination, and political fearlessness had probably conceived of this enormous park and then fared forth fighting to get it. He kept on talking, as he stared up at the flags. "Meanwhile, World Wildlife Fund, USA, sent funds which helped build and equip the initial guard force. That enabled our government to get through its more time-consuming processes to accept the major responsibility of administration and protection through the Ministry of Agriculture."

It flashed through my mind that this was a repeat of my Guatemalan grebe strategy, only in gigantic terms.

Felipe climbed the steps and proudly opened the door of the station. "In 1975, the Peruvian government finally budgeted two hundred and fifty thousand dollars to run the park, train and support twenty-two guards," he said. "That's a hell of a long way to come in roughly twelve years!"

After a quick tour of the grounds, the others in our party prudently began setting up tents and unpacking boxes. Despite the tremendous trip, my fright of flying, and the fatigue of heat, I couldn't settle down. I was eager to explore the surrounding forest before dusk. Obligingly, two rangers offered to take me upriver. We eased into a dugout canoe with an outboard motor and knifed our way upstream. The setting sun shone golden-bronze on brooding jungle walls. Here and there a flame-colored flowering tree lit up the dark foliage. A few fingers of palm fronds quivered in the light breeze. My exhaustion seemed to slip away. Besides our boat, the only movement was the river itself. Turbulent currents and eddies swirled around jutting trunks and snags. The water was brown and totally opaque. This minor headwater of the Amazon— one of 1,100 tributaries—churned past us at 2 to 4 knots, although it dropped only a half-inch per mile all the way to the Atlantic, 1,700 miles to the east. At one curve in the river we came upon thousands of sandpipers swirling above a sandbank. Their slim silhouettes in flight made them seem more like bats than birds.

We returned to Pakitza safely before the light failed. As I walked toward the station, a pair of scarlet macaws swerved by overhead. The afterglow turned them acrylic red. For a brief instant they winged across the waxing moon, itself a three-quarter-full bud of camellia-white in a blue-black sky. I stopped in my tracks. A wave of reminiscence flooded over me. Back at my cabin, the white-throated sparrows would be singing plaintively from hidden balsam branches and spring peepers would be trilling in the misty marsh. How different this world was—dazzling, darkling, scintillating, somber, vibrant, vulnerable.

I found my companions sitting around a hissing lantern at a rustic table, discussing the oil camp we had visited earlier that day. In general, everyone had been agreeably surprised by the minimal environmental impact we'd seen, yet a sense of gloom was with us. To ecologists, oil crews and camps mean that civilization is creeping ever closer to the remaining wildlands. And the spin-offs of civilization often spell disaster in the tropics. By the time we stopped talking, it was very late. I crawled into my tent. Soft flutelike frog sounds came from the black forest behind me. The camellia-white moon threw strange shadows on the orange nylon walls. It was cool, damp, humid. I slipped into my sleeping bag for comfort. All·night, moisture condensed slowly on the walls and dripped silently on my head.

Early next morning, Adolfo Cuentas, the park administrator, and Bruno Sanguinetti, wildlife representative from Peru's Ministry of Agriculture, prepared a 43-foot dugout canoe with a 50-horsepower engine for our trip into the park. A 50-gallon gas drum and an extra motor were lashed aboard. Our tents, packs, and food were piled in the center and covered with a tarp. At ten o'clock we were ready. Traveling upriver, we surprised sixteen stately jabirus (large storks), stalking along a mudbank like so many preoccupied attorneys with their hands behind their backs. Every submerged log and stump seemed to hold turtles sunning and sleeping under a sun which seemed sizzling enough to cook them in their shells. Sandbars were crisscrossed with tracks and prints of shorebirds and mammals. Flocks of parakeets and tiny parrots flashed over the river course. No matter where we looked, some form of wildlife was evident.

We twisted and turned back on ourselves, following Manú's meandering curves. In midafternoon we stopped by the trail to Cocha Cashu. Here was another small ranger station and research facility beside a lagoon lake which is usually cut off from the main channel of the river except during peak flood time. Every so often, one of the river's ox-bow bends breaks through its neck and makes a new straight course. Then a *cocha* (lagoon) is left behind to stagnate and dream. The 3 P.M. sun struck the surface like a laser beam. We were half-blinded by the brassy glare, half drugged by the heat. Unanimously, our party decided to go back to the river, take a swim, pitch camp, and return to Cocha Cashu next dawn.

Trailing the group quietly through the high forest and listening for wildlife, I was impressed by the dimness after the open lagoon. One thin sun shaft fell on a mossy tree trunk. I held out my light meter. It gave off only a weak flicker. No more than 1 to 5 percent of full sunlight ever reaches the floor of a primary rain forest—one which has never been cut or burned in historic times. Its thick canopy, like a lofty greenhouse roof, shuts out the blazing sun, keeps the atmosphere cool and damp, and protects the ground from pounding rains.

We chose a broad white sand beach for our bivouac and soon had a cookfire blazing. Supper was canned ravioli, ripe mangoes, and cups of cocoa laced with *pisco*, Peru's very special brandy. An ocellated poorwill was wailing as I fell asleep.

At 5 A.M. it was still dark and completely silent as I crawled from my tent. A slight rustling came from the 15-foot canebrake that edged our sandbar. It's dripping dew, I thought, and slipped back into my sleeping bag for another snooze. Later, only 30 yards from the tent, I discovered the tracks of a large jaguar. No doubt the rustling had been this cat prowling by. I know that jaguars are very curious and do not attack people. Still this visitor made my night at Manú—at least in retrospect—one of my most memorable camping experiences.

As daybreak approached, I heard a distant humming like a generator starting or a high wind blowing through the canopy. It changed note, grew stronger, formed harmonics. I was puzzled. Just then Felipe emerged from his tent, tall and aristocratic, even in rumpled clothes and a new beard. "Howler monkeys!" he exclaimed. "What a nice reveille!"

Back at Cocha Cashu, white dawn mist still clung to the torpid water. The morning was clear, cool, and comfortable. Three of us crept into a shallow shell of a canoe, collectively clutching more than $5,000-worth of camera equipment. The donkeylike bellows of horned screamers resounded from the shores, while overhead the first petulant shrieking of parrots and macaws began. A few wild Muscovy ducks floated on the placid surface. Cormorants, herons, egrets, anhingas, rails, and kingfishers posed on damp branches. My head was turning this way and that so as not to miss a single new bird or a good camera shot. Suddenly we heard a loud splash directly ahead. We peered into the low-hanging trees. Two, three, four, no, *five* hoatzins (peculiar, primitive birds which resemble pheasants though they are not related and which have claws on their wings) stared back. A sixth young one was scrambling onto a branch like a lad about to dive into his favorite swimming hole. Three cameras clicked sideways in unison and the three of us almost tipped over the tiny canoe. I'd never been so close to these odd birds with their glaring red eyes, bare blue face patches, and crested heads. They reminded me of huge brown cuckoos—until I saw a youngster swim by underwater and then claw his way onto overhanging branches back to his nest! Circling Cocha Cashu we must have counted over thirty hoatzins and seen about 10 percent of all the species of birds indigenous to the Amazon rain forest. This watery remnant of the Manú River was my finest birding experience since, as an Audubon tour leader, I visited Corkscrew Swamp Sanctuary in Florida.

On our way back to the river the morning was climaxed once again by the sight of twenty-five *huanganas* (peccaries). They had dashed ahead of us, gaining a few minutes' lead. Yet before we could trace them to the bank, the spoor of a jaguar was already superimposed upon their tracks! Had my nocturnal visitor swum the Manú and decided upon pork chops for breakfast?

We continued upriver toward Tayakomé, the interior ranger station. That night we slept at the heart of the park, 100 miles from the closest settlement, perhaps 30 miles from a tribe of indomitable Amahuacas, and 2 miles from a village of peaceful Machiguenga Indians. Sometime during the night, ghostly sounds of a drum and rattles filtered into my dreams. At first I imagined one of our party had a transistor radio. Then reason told me the Indians must be having a celebration. Their primitive music added a new dimension to my Amazon impressions.

Indeed, their head man, or *cacique*, came to see us next day.

He was called Itayano and wore a black toucan-feather band around his forehead. He explained that he did not drink because he had to keep sober to look after the men, women, and children who often got dead drunk on *masato* and lay about the village.

The next morning I hiked alone into the dry-land rain forest, known as *terra firme,* to explore and photograph. "Be careful," Felipe warned me. "The terra firme makes up 90 percent of the Amazon basin, and it's terribly easy to get lost in there. Besides, there's nothing to eat or drink. A person can starve or thirst to death."

No doubt the Machiguengas would have disagreed with Felipe, but being unskilled in foraging for food in Amazonia, I heeded his words. I called out what time I expected to be back and double-checked my compass bearings.

Once I was inside the forest, a hundred shades of green engulfed me. Wild figs, *Cecropia,* cedrelas, myrtles, *Bignonia,* rosewood, lianas, air plants, ferns, vines, and orchids all grew beneath the 125-foot canopy composed of tall trees like the Brazil nut. Many palms grew in the understory. *Iriartia* had prop roots six feet long; *Astrocaryum,* wicked spines; *Sheelia,* long, arching fishtail fronds. Up in the pools of water trapped at the bases of bromeliads, more than sixty-five species of small plants and animals thrived. Fallen logs were clustered with creamy mushrooms, lichens, rust-red fungi, purple toadstools, yellow slime molds, pale water molds, and other saprophytes. Although the forest seemed dominated by the green producers, it was also an important place for decomposers. In fact, they are one secret of the rain forest's incredibly rich productivity and ultra-rapid recycling of nutrients.

Certainly Felipe was right. Of the biomass I saw in the dry-land rain forest 99.9 percent was vegetation; only 0.1 percent was animal. Putting it another way, for every 5,000 plants, there was 1 animal individual. Of course, along the waterways, the *igapos* (permanently flooded swamp forest), the *varzea* (annually flooded forest), and the cochas, fish, wildlife, and insect life abounded.

On the ground hundreds of ants and termites scurried about. Most evident were the big *saúbas* (leaf-cutting ants) so well described by Henry Walter Bates, the famous nineteenth-century English naturalist, who spent years in the Amazon. Columns of these ants were busily hauling bits of leaves to their subterranean galleries. Below a large mound of red earth lay deep shafts in which the leaf litter was used as a medium on which to grow fungi. This is the food of the ant larvae. Watching them intently, I now saw a slow-moving army ant wander past my boot. Hastily, I stepped back. Nearby, a thin line of fire ants was threading its way up a *Tachigalia* plant (member of the Leguminosae family) to their nests in the hollow petioles. This symbiotic arrangement insures that the ants have a home and the plant benefits by having the insects eat up other vegetation which tries to crowd it out. For a moment my imagination multiplied all the ants I could see in a 10-foot radius by the almost 2.5 million square miles of Amazon territory. The mathematics were awesome. Truly ants must outnumber in individuals all other terrestrial animals. Out of an estimated 12,000 species in the world, 7,600 kinds of ants have been described scientifically, and many of these live in Amazonia.

During my morning trek, two of the striking differences between tropical rain forest and temperate woodlands became evident. Any 5 acres around my cabin in the Adirondacks, or in New England woods, may have 10 to 12 kinds of trees growing; yet, here in the same-sized area, an average of 200 species can be found! Such a density means that individual members of any one variety are scattered thinly over wide spaces. I never saw a solid stand of any one tree, such as the balsam flats or birch groves up north. Yet the diversity and distribution result in healthier plants.

The other difference was the soil. Where a large tree had been uprooted, I noticed with astonishment that the layer of litter and humus was only a few inches thick. I recalled that the uprooted tree we had seen in Venezuela was underlain by sterile white sand, while here the lower layer looked reddish, highly leached, and infertile. The taproots of this forest giant had penetrated down only a few feet while laterals had spread out horizontally for at least 25 yards. Mycorrhizal fungi grew all over the roots and in the soil and humus.

Indeed, most nutrients in the tropical rain forest are not found in the soils as they are in the mid-western corn belt, for example, but in the vegetation itself. It's not the soil that's fertile, it's the foliage. That luxuriant, green, exuberant forest is totally deceiving. As Dr. Betty Meggers, famed Amazon anthropologist at the Smithsonian Institution, says, "It's a counterfeit paradise!"

At any given time, 70 to 90 percent of the total nutrient supply within the ecosystem is locked up in the foliage. Minerals are recycled directly from dead leaves, branches, and wood right back into living leaves, branches, and trunks. Those weird decomposers around me, especially the fungi, quickly break down organic materials and pass them into the roots. They do their job in about six weeks, as against the one year in temperate deciduous woodlands, or the seven years in northern forests, necessary to decompose tree litter. Less than 1 percent of the nutrients escape during this speedy, thrifty, "rot to root" procedure. Deep topsoils never accumulate. The forest survives despite its impoverished soils, not because of them. Their main function is to support, not to nourish. In fact, most of Amazonia is literally a desert covered with trees.

Exactly how many trees exist in the Amazon basin, nobody knows. About 25,000 have been identified. Perhaps as many more are still undescribed. Fortunately, a five-year forest inventory called "Amazon Flora Project" is going on now. It will accelerate collecting, identifying, and computerizing information retrieval. Meanwhile, the tropical rain forest performs its greatest service by buffering torrential rains (more than 100 inches per year) from the thin soils, and keeping ground temperatures low enough (below 77 degrees F), so that bacterial action and decomposition can proceed as they should. All this gave me plenty to think about on the way back to Tayakomé.

The next day we started back down the Manú, practically doubling our speed as we moved with the current. Sunshine, light showers, rainbows, and butterflies played over our canoe all day. We were treated to more wildlife diversions. A river otter scuttled down a bank. Five glossy capybaras bathed on a beach but bumbled off like big guinea pigs when they saw us. A bevy of little spectacled caimans (close cousins to crocodiles and alligators) slept upon a hot sandbank. In one clearing, four coppery-colored howler monkeys groomed one another with their prehensile tails curled up tight as watch springs. "Some people call this a Green Hell," exclaimed Thomas. "I call it Green Heaven! We're seeing the richest forest fauna and flora in the world."

"Right," chimed in Felipe. "At least 10 percent of our planet's species are living right here in the Amazon basin."

As the heat of the afternoon peaked, we sprawled out in the dugout. Bruno Sanguinetti, standing tall and looking cool in a white shirt, engagingly explained the new forest and wildlife law signed into existence by President Juan Velasco Alvarado on May 13, 1975. For the first time, Peru's natural resources (including animal products and ornamental butterflies) are now declared public domain and protected in varying degrees. "It took three years and all·our Peruvian experts on fauna and flora to make this law," said Bruno proudly. "Fortunately, most of the resources in this country are still so wild that they merely need protection, not management."

"I'm not so sure about *that!*" snapped the indefatigable Felipe. "Colonization and civilization are spreading faster than you think, my friend. If Manú were opened to roads or airstrips, its vegetation, wildlife, fish, and soils would be destroyed in twenty years. The resources would never recover. We need not only protection, by plenty of management and good land-use planning."

I sat up straight in the canoe. Felipe must be exaggerating. Twenty years to wipe out this immense tract of rain forest? But my travels were to show me that even his estimate was optimistic.

No one talked any more. A sense of uneasiness had seized us. Sunset was coming. We all stared up at the skein of clouds turning from cerise to maroon to gray. The river was lit with a saffron sheen. Directly ahead, an almost full moon edged through heaps of cumulus clouds. They were milky marble dappled in slate-black, pearl, pewter, and cream, and shot through with streaks of shiny silver. But the lightning was far away. We continued running downstream by moonlight as our ranger-boatmen skillfully navigated the deadfalls and snags. One wrong turn and we could be toppled into the water and swept downriver. To regroup and make an emergency camp soaking wet and without gear would have been a formidable task.

Before midnight, we were all safely asleep in our tents at Pakitza, and next day we regretfully prepared to leave Manú. However, instead of the three choppers that had delivered us, one lone whirly bird arrived for us in the afternoon. The pilot explained tersely that one of the machines had crashed, another was on an urgent medical run into the jungle, and only his could be spared. "I'll have to make three or four trips," he reckoned, gauging the pile of camping equipment and our assorted weights. "Well, come on," he motioned to Thomas and me. "You two are the lightest. We'll fill 'er up with as much gear as possible."

Half an hour later we were dumped unceremoniously on the heliport of the oil camp. It was 3 o'clock. The delay meant we couldn't possibly all fly out to Cuzco before dark. The airport there had no night facilities. The camp was abuzz with activity— mechanics hurried about the makeshift hangars, drivers ran bulldozers up to a gigantic Hercules transport and disappeared into its guts to offload heavy equipment, workers tugged on lengths of pipe and bunches of couplings. No one paid the slightest attention to us. Thomas and I strolled closer to the plane and watched in fascination.

The muffled clacking of a helicopter grew louder. I glanced up expectantly. "That sure was a fast turnaround flight," I said. "Maybe Felipe and George will be aboard."

But it was a different chopper that landed. Slung from its frame was a stretcher with an injured Peruvian workman strapped in. I edged nearer; Thomas hung back. "Better not get in the way," he warned. "We're really only guests here."

"But maybe I can help," I argued. The man was critically wounded, having fallen backward onto a sharp stump he had just cut along the trail. The point had rammed into his anus and ripped the large intestine. The man needed surgery and massive doses of antibiotics as soon as possible, but the camp had no doctor or nurse. The only hope for him was to fly him out at once in the Hercules to get him to Cuzco before dark. Otherwise, by morning, shock and infection would surely have set in. I walked over to the engineer in charge and asked if anyone would accompany the poor fellow on the flight.

"No," he muttered. "I can't spare anyone here. I'm the only one really who could get away, and I shouldn't."

A daring plan grew in my mind. "I'll go!" I volunteered. "I recently finished a course to become an emergency medical technician, so I can at least watch out for shock or hemorrhage. I speak Spanish, too, so I can talk to the patient. I'll stay in Cuzco tonight and meet the others there in the morning after the Twin Otter brings them up."

He stared at me gratefully and then nodded agreement.

"Okay, but the Hercules is hardly a commercial jetliner, you know."

"It doesn't matter. It'll get us there," I reasoned. "How soon are we leaving?"

"Right away." The engineer shouted more orders and the man was carried inside and laid on the floor of the plane. I followed hesitantly. A hundred men gathered around the rear door and huge loading ramp to gaze at me. I was the only woman there except for the camp followers.

Inside, I looked around in dismay. The Hercules was totally empty and as large as a house. There were no windows, benches, or carpeting. The metal floor was smeared with axle grease, motor oil, and clumps of mud. The poor Peruvian lay impassively on an aluminum stretcher. Somehow I would have to fasten him down. Then my mind started working. Throwing shyness to the winds, I turned and crisply demanded blankets, ropes, and drinking water. One of the geologists started off to get them. But the Hercules' props were already turning and the giant doors shutting. The pilots were motioning everyone off the field. Only an hour and a half of daylight remained and the flight took over an hour. The door banged closed. I was alone with the injured workman without a single medical supply.

Kneeling beside the stretcher, I swiftly ran down a mental list: Reassure the patient. Keep him warm. Make him immobile. Maintain an open airway. Check pulse frequently. All I could do was try. I spoke calmly in Spanish to the man and was rewarded with a weak smile. Taking off my light jacket, I covered his chest and loosened his belt. I felt beneath his buttocks for blood. Nothing yet. His pulse was faint but normal.

Now the plane was moving. An incredible vibration filled the hollow chamber, and I had an awful vision of the stretcher sliding clear across the floor during the steep angle of takeoff and smashing the laborer against the rear door. Somehow I had to hold it in place. Groping in the filth on the floor, I found a recessed ring used for tying down machinery. I gripped this firmly in my left hand, grabbed the stretcher with my right, and spread my knees to steady my body. How could such an enormous hulk ever become airborne, I wondered. My fear of flying welled up. No way to see outside. Nothing to do but shut my eyes and hang on for dear life.

Miraculously the Hercules lifted, smoothly, ponderously, without a shudder. The vibrations ceased. The Peruvian and I stayed in one place. I opened my eyes and saw a few overhead lights had come on. I could see my watch. Time for a pulse reading. Take the vital signs (just like television's *Emergency*).

After half an hour, I was sure the man's condition was stable and that the cargo plane could fly. I spoke to him comfortingly and got up to find the cockpit. A steel ladder led forward to another level, so I climbed up it. Suddenly I was dazzled by the setting sun spearing straight into the cockpit. Between me and the awful Andes were only two instrument panels, two sheets of Plexiglas, and two Peruvian pilots. They turned to greet me. One set up a jump seat between their chairs; the other placed his headset over my ears. A tango drowned out the motor roar.

The last rays of sun were splendid. They turned the massive snowfields below us to gold, then backlit the towering, jagged ranges with electric lavender. All at once, I was no longer afraid of these mountains; I was totally transfixed.

"How long to Cuzco?" I managed to ask.

"Too long." The captain frowned. "A headwind is slowing us down. We'll land with only about ten minutes of light to spare."

"Can you radio ahead for an ambulance and doctor?" I urged.

"Already did," answered the co-pilot. "But that doesn't mean they'll be there."

"Well, let's hope so. I'd better get back to my patient. Thank you."

He was still satisfactory, so I stroked his head and told him about Manú, to try to take his mind off the pain. What his chances for recovery were, I didn't know. Surely he was in for a severe infection with the contents of his large bowel loose in the abdominal cavity. I hoped there was a good hospital and competent surgeon at the other end of this flight.

After circling Cuzco, the plane landed as neatly as an Andean condor. The rear doors opened and four mechanics carried the stretcher and man out. The pilots switched off engines and lights and appeared ready to leave for home. I searched the grounds for an ambulance. Nothing. "Call, please call, as soon as you get home," I begged the two men.

Then I was sitting alone, with the Peruvian lying on his

stretcher, upon a cold cement sidewalk in the dark outside a closed airport. The chill night wind whistled down from the mountains and turned our corner eerily. I shivered uncontrollably. Compared to the heat and humidity of the Amazon, this felt like Alaska. Finally, after what seemed like an eternity, an ambulance arrived and two attendants carted the workman off. I never knew his name or what happened to him. All I know is I met him at Manú.

Four years later, most of the exploratory oil camps were gone. The rich promise of petroleum—the "black gold"—had petered out. The pipeline from the upper reaches of the Amazon to the Pacific brought a mere trickle to tankers. The City Service outpost is abandoned, its trails and airstrip slowly growing back to jungle.

My Green Heaven

After I got back from Peru, I spent the summer and fall impatiently at my Adirondack cabin, waiting for the long dry season in the Amazon. It was a time of high anticipation. I steeped myself in books and articles about the area. I fell asleep at night imagining the mighty river, and the strange animals I'd see, the new people I'd meet. And, as always, it would be an adventure just to be aboard the MS *Lindblad Explorer*, on which I had traveled three times before as staff ecologist on natural-history cruises. Yet, somehow, I didn't quite believe that the trim, 250-foot, red-and-white, world-circling ship would actually poke her bows up the Amazon River and travel three-quarters of a continent inland to Iquitos, Peru. However, the 2,300-mile stretch of river between Iquitos and the Atlantic is technically considered an oceanic waterway and can accommodate, year-round, boats with drafts to 20 feet.

In November I flew to Lima, then doubled back over the

Andes to Iquitos, just 500 miles from the Pacific Ocean. This was the "jump off" port. My first sight of the *Explorer* with her halo of lights glowing in the hot, humid Peruvian night made me catch my breath with admiration. She would be my home for a month. I climbed expectantly up the gangplank and opened the door to the main deck. A rush of air-conditioning and the chattering of seventy-five passengers washed over me. Everyone was having a pre-midnight snack, getting acquainted, and waiting for the ship to cast off her lines and head out onto the mightiest river on earth.

I shook hands all around and began mentally categorizing the passengers and staff. Some were old friends from other cruises I had worked on. Others were "regulars"—ardent amateur naturalists and nature photographers who often sailed on the *Explorer*. A few were nervous newcomers, not really sure what they'd got into or if they could take the Amazon. Most of the passengers were retired couples or widows, well-to-do and well-traveled, although one couple had scraped and saved for months to afford this luxurious floating nature tour.

One passenger stood out from the rest. He was a striking blond Finn in his thirties, impeccably dressed in tailored slacks, knit sportshirt, and sleek boots. His green eyes were slanted like a Lapp's and he had a disconcerting way of constantly flicking his eyes around the room. He just didn't look the "Lindblad type." He appeared to be neither bird-watcher, photographer, skin diver, nor nature-lover. He looked as if he belonged at an elegant bar in some sophisticated European city.

The ship's siren blew, and we heard the great engines start to purr beneath us. Fifteen minutes to departure! We all hurried on deck and lined the railings. Heavy hawsers dropped with splashes from the moorings and the gangplank was laboriously cranked up tight against the ship's side. A few sleepy but curious Peruvian longshoremen stood on the dock to watch the pretty little vessel depart. Otherwise, no fanfare, no waving, no farewells. At midnight sharp, the bow slowly veered sideways, and an ever-widening slice of black water appeared between ship and dock. I could feel the current catch and pivot the ship. Five minutes later we were headed downstream into the dark jungle night.

Passengers began going to their staterooms or into the bar for a nightcap. I walked forward and climbed to the deck above the bridge. Alone up here, I could be fully aware of the whole river, could absorb its smells and mood undisturbed. Two huge spotlight beams probed across the swirling surface, searching for small fishing boats, dugouts, drifting logs, and uprooted trees. Hundreds of insects had already discovered these lights and had formed miniature swirling snowstorms around the glass. Back home, I thought, it would actually be snowing. I inhaled deeply. The air was heavy and laden with pungent odors of living and decomposing things, different from anything I'd ever smelled before. This air was *alive*. For an hour, hair streaming, nostrils flaring, absorbing the Amazon night, I rode right at the front of the ship. Then a spatter of rain began. I turned and groped my way back toward the narrow inner stairway. As the door swung open, a band of light shone out onto the deck. I glimpsed the red glow of a cigarette and the gleam of a well-shined boot propped against the rear deckrail before the door swung shut behind me.

Early next morning the ship anchored off the main channel and we made our first side trip. Daily we left on explorations like this up tributaries, using rubber, inflatable landing craft called Zodiaks. Six staff members swung six of these down from the top deck with hook, winch, and kingpole, and drove them to the gangplank to onload the eager passengers. I helped twelve people into my raft and sat them along the rubber sides. Then we set off upriver. We soon discovered that the Upper Amazon has many moods. At sunrise, with mist hanging over the water, it looked like a large, shallow, summery Wisconsin lake. As the day cleared, the skies became changeable. Great cumulus clouds built up dramatically, then dissipated. At different quarters of the horizon, squalls would form, blacken, dump heavy loads of rain, and move on. By evening, the red ball of sun would hang in hazy solitude, undisputed, then disappear.

I could see that the Upper Amazon (called the Solimões above Manaus, Brazil, and the Marañón in Peru) is as muddy as a cup of coffee with cream; I nicknamed it the "milk-coffee-river-sea." Everywhere one looked, the water was moving, moving, moving, despite the vast flatness and distance from the Atlantic. I filled a glass and let it settle for half an hour in the bottom of my Zodiak. It changed from café-au-lait to the clarity of what one might expect out of a New York City water tap; however, as wild river water, it was probably purer than city sources; even with that sediment, it could be drunk fairly safely. Most water in the Amazon basin is still uncontaminated by man-made pollution except just below the large cities and towns. Even the raw sewage of Manaus (over half a million population) and Belém (over a million) is quickly digested and diluted by the enormous liquid mass of this river. Whatever bacteria and viruses might be present are scattered, oxidized, and settled out by the sediments.

We returned to the ship for lunch and a nap in the heat of the day and set forth again that afternoon. The tributaries we traveled were low, since this was the main dry season. Looking upward as I steered the motor, I could see dead branches, grasses, and roots hanging from the high-water mark along the banks. Six months from now, in rainy season, the river level would be 30 to 35 feet above our heads.

The Finn was in my boat. He was wearing the skimpiest of bikinis and a superb tan. He lolled on the rubber bow with his camera exactly as if he were on a beach on the French Riviera. All eyes were directed either to him or to the bushes which lined the narrow channel we were threading, where new species of birds and amphibians might lurk. No one bothered to look behind us until an ominous roll of thunder boomed. We turned and saw a leaden mass of clouds laced with lightning covering half the sky. It seemed to have come out of nowhere and was moving fast. I revved up the motor and began looking for overhanging trees under which we might shelter—there was no chance of getting back to the *Explorer* before the deluge hit. The squall line approached, and the older ladies began cowering under beach towels or windbreakers. I should have brought plastic tarps for my passengers. It was a good lesson never to trust the Amazon. I found a tree, tied up to a stout root, and watched in fascination as the squall raced toward us. The surface of the stream turned from brownish-blue to silvery black. A sheet of rain as solid as cotton pushed over us. And finally a gust of wind buffeted our bodies. The temperature dropped 15 degrees in 10 minutes and an inch of rain fell in the first half-hour. It was my first experience with an Amazon cloudburst. Little did I know that such storms can release forty times as much water as an average rain in the northeastern United States. But most are short-lived. Within an hour the sky and stream looked much as they had before. The only change was that twelve passengers and one staff member were sodden and shivering with cold.

"Whoever thought we'd be chilly in the Amazon?" I joked, trying to cheer up my miserable crew. I cruised hastily downstream toward the main river. "Brandy and hot coffee coming up," I shouted encouragingly. A few people smiled. The rest remained glum. But the Finn flashed his even white teeth at me, although his flesh was prickled with goose bumps—and no wonder, with what he had on.

As we swung into the Amazon itself, two other Zodiaks neared us and we headed for the ship together. But the placid mirror-mood of morning had been replaced by a frothy tumble of mud-colored waves. Now we were soaked from spray. I slowed down. At this rate, the *Explorer* was at least an hour away. I began to think of hypothermia, pneumonia, bronchitis, arthritis, and all the other ills that might crop up from this sudden chilling, especially for the older people. Still, there was nothing I could do but steer and get us back safely. This was all part of a natural-history cruise.

Ahead of us some sort of floating building was moored to the bank. Another fishing shack, I thought, until one of the Zodiaks steered toward it. Paulo, our Brazilian interpreter, was piloting that boat. He beckoned imperatively at us to follow him. When all three of the Zodiaks were jostling alongside the shack, Paulo clambered out and disappeared inside the building. Two minutes later he came out of the floating store carrying three quart bottles of what looked like patent cough medicine. A broad grin split his face. "*Cashasha*, everyone! Good Brazilian firewater. Bye, bye, cold shivers. Drink so you won't be sick."

A bottle was passed around each Zodiak. People sputtered and gasped as the fiery liquid hit their stomachs and bloodstreams. Then they asked for seconds. Before long, three very tipsy boatloads of people were bucking down the Amazon river, laughing and singing. And no one became ill—perhaps because of our cashasha remedy.

As the ship traveled downriver, I began to notice changes. The river widened, deepened, seemed less closed in by the exuberant rain forest. Whereas the Manú had been a single meandering channel bordered by dense vegetation, the Upper Amazon was beginning to braid and channelize. Daily the horizon receded and diminished. Islands came and went. Swamps, igapos, canebreaks, and mudbars edged the river. The only thing that never changed was the color.

This far inland it was all muddy, or "white," for the waters come rushing down from the Andes rich with suspended particles of eroded soil and minerals. They are low in bacteria and almost neutral on the acid-alkaline scale (pH 6.6 to 7.0).

Further downstream we would encounter "black" waters the color of strong tea. These originate from impoverished sandy forest soils far away from the main river itself. "A black river is a starvation river," say the natives, because it is marked by a paucity of fish, insects, and aquatic life. The water is very acidic (pH around 4.0). Clear blue and green waters flow down from the ancient granite highlands of central Brazil and the Guiana region. These are also poor in animal and plant life and have pH values of 6.00 to 6.5. Thus the chemical makeup of Amazonian waters indicates the type of landscape from which they come. Most are poverty-stricken and infertile. White, black, blue, green, all these waters meet, sometimes in fluid patterns like watered silk, and finally mix. Eventually 200 to 500 billion cubic feet of water and 106 million cubic feet of sediment surge out to sea each day from the Amazon's mouth. Churning, eddying, eroding, sucking, pulsing, whirling, and roiling inexorably eastward, these turbid, untamed waters drain four-tenths of South America and carry 20 percent of all river water in the world.

One afternoon, our Zodiaks left the *Explorer* for a fishing spree at Campinhas, a white-water lagoon. Several of us were determined to catch piranhas. Our good-natured chef had offered to fry them for supper. We sat jigging with simple hand lines and baited hooks. By now, I knew the Finn would be in my boat, scantily clad, snapping pictures of everything, and charming the lot of us. Today was no exception.

Within minutes he had hooked the first piranha. It fell snapping and thrashing into the Zodiak. Twelve pairs of bare feet jerked up. Despite their small size (7 to 17 inches), each of the four species of piranhas has super-sharp teeth which can take a grape-sized chunk of flesh. However, piranhas normally attack only bleeding, ill, or thrashing prey, or bite in defense—as they would now. In fact, we often swam in clear black-water tributaries with piranhas and no one was bitten. The Finn dispatched his fish. Feet went back down. Fishing resumed. In two hours we had enough piranhas for all seventy-five passengers and six staff members. Delicious! Mysteriously the Finn produced a bottle of cashasha. That was enough firewater to send us singing and shouting back to the ship. From then on, our group felt a special kinship, and many jokes revolved around the Finn's piranha party.

The fish life of Campinhas lagoon was really extraordinary. Hundreds of walking catfish swirled the water with their hard fins. One throw of the round casting net brought up thirteen catfish, a black piranha, a wolf characin, and a gorgeous brown-and-yellow tucunaré (a cichlid).

This abundance of fish life was attributable to the dry season. Lowering water levels were constricting the aquatic habitats and their denizens were crowded together like meat and vegetables in a soup pot that has boiled too long. Come rains and higher water, these creatures would scatter out over a huge area and be far more difficult to catch. In fact, many of the large characoids and other major food fishes would head up tributaries to the inundated floodplain forests. There they would feed and fatten on fruits and seeds that fall into the water. Both adult and young fish would find valuable nourishment in these flooded forests.

More than 2,000 fish species have been recorded in the Amazon basin—more than from any other river system on earth. Louis Agassiz, the nineteenth-century Swiss-American naturalist, noted that the Amazon contains more fish species than the Atlantic Ocean from pole to pole. Certainly fish is a prized form of protein along the entire waterway. Every town, huge or tiny, that we visited had a fish market filled daily with fresh catches. I was told that commercial fishing operations between the Rio Negro near Manaus and the Amazon have until recently netted 1,000 pounds per morning. Unfortunately, heavy logging activities and agricultural disturbance of the river floodplain forests for rice and water buffalo may be reducing the food supply of fruit-eating (frugivorous) and seed-eating (granivorous) fishes. When river banks are deforested and swampy lowlands flooded, not only trees but their fruit and seeds disappear. Fish which eat these food items may die or move away. This could be the reason the fishery is decreasing.

Also, overexploitation may be affecting fish populations. Between 1968 and 1975, the number of commercial fishing boats jumped from 82 to 748.

On our cruise down the Amazon, in contrast to the Manú, we did not see a single turtle or large caiman. Hunters have been destroying these animals along the major waterways for decades. The farther downstream we went, the more despondent I felt about the exploitation of the river turtles: the large *tartarugas* (*Podocnemis expansa*), the smaller *tracaja* (*P. dumeriliana*) and the *iaca* (*P. sextuberculata*). In *The Naturalist on the River Amazon*, Bates wrote of the plentitude of turtles. He estimated that in the 1860s 48 million eggs laid by almost half a million females were harvested yearly by natives for food and oil. Hundreds of thousands of adults were killed for meat and shell. Now, not 120 years later, we naturalists aboard the *Lindblad Explorer* did not see even one turtle along the 2,300 miles of main Amazon channels. As for caimans, the tanning factories in Manaus alone are reported to have handled 5 million skins of black caiman annually until 1971. Bates wrote, "Alligators were seen along the coast [banks] almost every step of the way, and the passengers [aboard river boats] amused themselves, from morning until night, by firing at them with rifle and ball."

We took the Zodiaks into isolated backwaters one night to search for caimans. We startled a few small specimens but none measured longer than 1 foot—quite a contrast to the 20-foot creatures mentioned by Bates.

Manatees were also seemingly nonexistent. They have been coveted by Indians and *caboclos* (mixed-blood Brazilians) for centuries. People used them for meat, hide, lamp oil, and bone tools. In the late 1700s, for example, 8,500 animals were slaughtered at a single hunting station, and the meat and oil exported to Holland and her colonies. But between 1950 and 1954, the number of hides taken in the whole state of Amazonas in Brazil diminished from 38,000 to 5,500.

In 1971, Brazil passed legislation protecting both river turtles and caimans and the principal nesting beaches of turtles. (Only about 10,000 females still use these sites.) However, there are only about fifty Amazonian game wardens covering this gigantic area. Poaching continues. During the whole 2,300-mile voyage downstream by ship, I never saw a single turtle.

Both Brazilian and Peruvian laws have protected manatees since 1967 and 1975, respectively, and have declared the animals officially endangered. But insufficient enforcement presents the same problem as with turtles and caimans.

Shortly before we arrived in Leticia, Colombia's Amazon port, we made a short stop to see a band of Jivaro Indians. On the jungle trail to their camp, I found myself walking with Rolf, the Finn. We chatted about the cruise so far, and I was surprised at his enthusiasm. He obviously knew nothing about natural history, seemed to be a terrible photographer, and hated to get his hair wet. Yet he went out, bikini-clad, on every field excursion and then appeared each evening in the ship's lounge attired in the finest tailored European clothes imaginable. He always invited everyone at his table for drinks and dutifully asked the older ladies to dance. He conversed knowledgeably in five languages on many subjects. But when I asked about his profession, he spoke vaguely about "being in finances."

I was intrigued. Somehow he didn't ring true, but he was most attractive. Why would a good-looking man like this be walking half-naked through the Amazon jungle to see equally naked Indians?

Then we were at the Jivaro camp, gawking at the bare-breasted women, the grass-skirted men, the red-painted faces, the tooth-and-claw necklaces. Cameras clicked and whirled. Indians posed nonchalantly, then sullenly put on a demonstration of their shooting accuracy with 8-foot blowguns and feathered darts.

"They use curare on the dart tips to kill game," whispered Rolf, pressing softly against me. "It's a nerve poison which kills an animal in just minutes." I looked at him in surprise. How would a Finnish financier know something like that?

In the stilt-legged huts, women suckled babies on the floor and old men slept in hammocks; outside, kids followed the passengers, begging for candy and coins. The whole Jivaro settlement had an unreal quality. Later our staff anthropologist told us that this particular band no longer lives off the land and the river; instead they live off the tourists. Enough of the travelers who pass this way know of their existence that the Indians can afford to dress up, paint their faces, and hang around camp all day. They survive on the tips and bribes paid them for photographs. Remembering the Guaymi of Panama, I realized that I had just seen another rare and endangered group of humans. In fact, I learned later that the number of Amerindian tribes in Brazil alone has plummeted from an estimated 230 to 143 since 1900, as a result of diseases, persecution, and ecological problems caused by official relocation.

The Finn and I wandered through the camp, he taking hundreds of photographs. Jokingly, I said, "I'd love to have one of those grass skirts to wear around my cabin on hot days."

"So would I," he replied. "And why not? Let's buy two. In fact, let's buy the whole costume—men's headpiece, the wristbands, women's grass breast covering." He grinned infectiously. "We could wear them to the masquerade party tomorrow night."

So we bargained for and bought the outfits. Then we started back along the trail, looking for achiote bushes. The seeds inside the prickly pods of these plants are used in cooking and also yield a greasy red pigment that is extremely durable on human skin— much better than lipstick. The next night we went into his cabin and painted each other's faces. The Finn asked me to decorate his back with symbols and signs. Laughing hilariously, I applied achiote to Rolf's smooth tan skin and tied a headpiece around his neatly coiffed hair. His eyes lingered on me as I worked. I began to feel self-conscious. "That's enough," I decided. "You look like the tattooed man in the circus. Let's put on our grass clothes now."

Of course, we won the best-costume prize, a magnum of champagne. I was giddy with laughter and wine. This was the most fun I'd had in ages. When the party broke up about 2 A.M., Rolf saw me to my cabin door and asked if he could come in for a nightcap.

"Oh, no," I groaned. "I'm so tipsy now I can hardly keep my eyes open, and tomorrow we have a dawn birding trip. I'll never be able to run my Zodiak. Some other night, Rolf."

He nodded politely and leaned forward just far enough to brush my red-striped cheek with his lips. "See you tomorrow, love," he said softly.

I fell on top of my bunk, grass skirt, achiote, and all. He liked me! The beautiful, mysterious Finnish financier liked me! I tingled from head to foot. Wild visions of us traveling around the world flashed through my head. Then cold reason cut in. I didn't want a shipboard romance. They always ended in tears and the two people never saw each other again. Besides, I was here on assignment in the Amazon, not to party around. The next thing I knew, I was fast asleep. The red dye that came off on the pillowcase did not endear me to the ship's Chinese laundrymen next day.

When the *Explorer* stopped at Leticia, once a notorious Colombian skin- and animal-trade center, I combed the small shops restlessly, looking for contraband. About five years ago, the sale of many kinds of pelts became illegal here. Furthermore, the United States passed its Endangered Species Act, prohibiting the importation of certain animals. Peru was the first Latin American country to ratify this Washington convention. Were these laws being obeyed in Colombia, I wondered? I had to see for myself.

Every shop was jammed with toucan feather necklaces, butterfly wing trays, letter openers made with baby alligator heads, crocodile wallets, turtle-shell combs, stacks of hides, piles of dried birds, and piranhas mounted above ashtrays. But no skins of the large spotted cats seemed to be available. Each time I casually asked a shopkeeper for a jaguar skin, he immediately rolled his eyes skyward and righteously proclaimed, *"Esta prohibido, Señorita!"* Even so, somewhere on a colorful sidestreet near some houses of prostitution, a tall mulatto sidled up to me and asked, "You want a big yellow one?"

Had I been male, I might have thought he had other merchandise in mind. But it could mean only one thing—jaguar skins! How I wished Felipe Benavides were with me. I could just hear him thundering, "If you let just one jaguar or ocelot become a coat, they'll want more, kill more. Wild animals should not be bartered, exchanged, or sold. There are other ways to make a living." He would have shaken his fist at the mulatto, then softened his explosion with a smile and a winning, "Señor, conservation is not a rich man's hobby. We all benefit. What are you doing about it?"

Lacking Felipe's flair for extemporaneous speaking, I merely shook my head and walked on. But I felt sure now that a black-market trade still exists along the Amazon, especially in Colombia, despite the dedication of patrol officers. In the 1960s, before the laws, the annual kill of jaguars and ocelots in Brazil was estimated at about 15,000 for jaguars and 80,000 for ocelots. It has probably dropped to half these figures. One estimate is that a quarter of the riverboats carry illegal fauna, either for food or commerce. This is not surprising, given the immensity of the basin, the inhabitants' meager incomes, and the fact that many European countries have not yet outlawed imports of threatened species, including spotted cats and caimans.

The Finn was walking with me, obviously unconcerned about the animal products we saw for sale. Probably all his girl friends wore jaguar coats and carried crocodile bags and reveled in them, I thought maliciously. I remembered seeing stunning ocelot coats for sale in elegant shops not far from World Wildlife Fund headquarters in Switzerland. And I'd watched stacks of furs and hides, bound for Mexico and then Europe, being loaded at jungle airports in Guatemala, Panama, and other countries. Clearly, multinational legal action is needed to stop the collecting and selling of Amazon wildlife. Morosely, I turned back toward the ship. This part of the trip was making too deplorable a contrast with the wildlife I'd marveled at in Manú National Park.

"Where are you going, my dear?" asked Rolf. "Come on, there's so much more to see."

"No, thanks, this port depresses me. All the dead animal curios. You stay, Rolf, and enjoy the town. I'm going back to the library on board."

"No way," he announced stubbornly. "We have to take more photographs. Look, Anne, sunset is coming. Let's go up on that hill and watch. We don't sail till 10 P.M., so we can sample the local beer and have a steak dinner." He coaxed me up a side street, snapping pictures all the while, and then down a quiet path to an overlook above the river. Huge flocks of green parakeets were streaming across the sky. Clouds were turning scarlet and the Amazon was rippled in black, orange, and blue. A lone palm made a fantastic framework for our photographs. A few dugouts described delicate silhouettes on the river's satiny surface. Gradually I regained my good humor. Leticia was attractive, even if it was the Mafia-like capital of animal contraband in the Amazon.

A little later we sat with two of the ship's officers and a few passengers at a sidewalk café. The Colombian beer was cold and delicious. Motor bikes, many carrying two young girls, kept scooting by and some stopped right beside our table. The girls eyed the men saucily and accosted them in rapid Spanish. The Finn was the only one who clearly understood what they were saying. "They're propositioning us fellows," he laughed. "The brothels are just up the street and they open at 8 P.M. Shall we go?" He winked at me.

I stared at him in disbelief. The officers, shy Swedes, looked embarrassed.

"I mean it," insisted the Finn smoothly. "In these countries it's quite permissible to visit such a house, have a drink, look over the merchandise, then stay or leave."

"But they'd never let a woman in," I began, utterly fascinated by the idea. In my line of work I'd never been near a brothel, let alone inside one, and I was burning with curiosity.

"Of course they will. You're no competition. You're with me." Rolf grinned in his infectious way. "Come on. Let's eat our steaks and go."

And so, along with all the ecology, fauna, and flora I was seeing along the Amazon, I also had the opportunity to observe the oldest profession in the world. I came away surprised, chagrined, elated, and sad. Surprised, because the girls were so young, pretty, and courteous to us. No sequined G-strings, only light blouses and slacks. Chagrined, because all my life I had considered prostitution to be evil; in Leticia, I saw the other side of it. These young women provide, for a brief time, human warmth, touch, and attention to the lonely men who work up and down the many rivers. Far from home, illiterate for the most part, beleaguered by heat, disease, and the ever-dangerous waters, men flock to these young women for solace. Elated, because I'd finally seen a side of life I'd never been exposed to. And sad, because there was no other opportunity for these girls to "get ahead in life." Most came from the simplest jungle hamlets and had no education at all. They could marry, have kids, and live out their lives in the forest, or they could become prostitutes. There seemed to be little else they could do to survive. Like the camp followers at the oil camp, most wanted only to earn enough money to buy a little shop somewhere and become independent.

As we strolled back to the ship shortly before 10, I looked up at the Finn with new admiration. He was the first man I'd ever met who would dare suggest a thing like that. How worldly he was, how cultured, how sure of himself. Perhaps he might be the kind of partner with whom I could share my life. Someone like Rolf would understand my professional career and zest for travel and might learn to be concerned about conservation. Surely he would not be jealous, as Armando had been, not so parochial in his life style. I started to think of Rolf in a new light, looking at a possible future beyond our idyllic cruise down the Amazon.

The next day we were in Brazil. The farther downstream we went the wider grew the floodplain, the varzea. More people lived and farmed here, as this was the only truly fertile land in Amazonia. Although the varzea occupies only 2 percent of the entire basin—twice the area of Holland—it is infinitely more productive than the banks of the Upper Amazon and the endless hinterlands of terra firme which cover 90 percent of this region. Fresh alluvial soils, brought down and deposited on the varzea by the annual white-water floods, give a life-sustaining quality to the varzea. Since 1 acre may receive as much as 4 tons of sediments containing precious nutrients, varzea soils can yield two, three, or four times the quantity of crops and cattle as terra firme.

We were due in Manaus the next day. Everyone was excited about visiting this city, now a free port and in the late 1880s the sixth richest port on earth by virtue of the fact that this area was then the world's only source of rubber. Situated 1,000 miles up the river, Manaus once boasted magnificent plantations, resident billionaires, cobblestoned streets, electricity, streetcars, and entire buildings shipped over from Europe and England. Rubber barons were said to be so wealthy that they lighted their cigars with paper money, sent their dirty laundry to Paris by ship, built châteaus of imported European bricks, and entertained friends at the lavish Teatro do Amazonas, an opera house which seated 1,600 and rivaled La Scala.

A few passengers planned to disembark at Manaus, and spend some time there, flying to Belém to rejoin the *Explorer* before she headed for Rio de Janeiro. A special dress-up dinner and dance was planned for the night before our arrival.

Rolf (whom I now thought of as "my Finn") asked me to be his date. By coincidence we both wore white. He, in a hand-stitched suit of lightest wool with a black-and-white polka-dot tie, looked like an early Manaus rubber baron, save for the blond hair and slanted green eyes. I wore a long gown of sheer dimity with puffed sleeves and low neckline and had abandoned pigtails for an upswept bouffant hairdo, bare feet for high heels. When we walked into the lounge together, a hush fell, then the old ladies started whispering. Like it or not, as far as they were concerned I was having a shipboard romance. The dinner was as elegant as any I'd ever attended. We sat at the captain's table. The wine master doted, the maître d' hovered. The dance music was slow and romantic. Glancing at my tall, slim escort, I could think of nothing but our days ahead in Amazonia.

Next morning, I had to take a group of passengers shopping in Manaus, so I didn't see Rolf. When we returned at noon, I went straight in to lunch and didn't go to my cabin until well after 2 P.M. A note and a bulky plastic bag were on the bunk. The note read, "Hi, Love. I received a cable from my company. Have some urgent business to attend to. Will try to join you in Belém. Keep the grass skirt. It wouldn't fit in my luggage, and it may remind you of me. Love, Rolf."

I was stunned. Why hadn't he told me in person? What could be so important in Manaus that he couldn't wait? I rushed back downtown to the main tourist hotels. Rolf was not registered at any of them, although one desk clerk remembered that a tall blond man had made an overseas call there.

"Where to?" I asked breathlessly.

"Who knows?" he shrugged. "It could have been New York or Berlin or Paris or . . ."

"Are there any planes out today?"

He scanned the airlines guide. "Yes, flights to Rio, Caracas, Miami, and Bogota."

There wasn't time to go to the airport, as the ship was due to sail at 5 P.M. I went back and spent a nerve-racking afternoon in my stateroom, hoping he might come back to the *Explorer* to say good-bye. But when the vessel pulled out into the Rio Negro's black waters, the dock was empty. And then when it curved back into the mainstream of the muddy Amazon again, Manaus simply faded from the horizon as if it had never been there—just like Rolf.

The night before we reached the mouth of the Amazon a week later, I stood on the top deck one last time. I was wildly impatient to reach Belém, yet nostalgically trying to capture the essence of my month-long trip. I thought of pink fresh-water dolphins rolling in the blue waters of the Tapajóz River under a rosy sunrise; the precise smacking of three spade-shaped paddles dipped by Indians into a jade-green jungle streamlet; giant *Arum* and *Victoria amazonica* waterlilies in a Rousseau landscape; black nunbirds, a green araçari, two cream-colored woodpeckers, spangled cotingas, and masked crimson tanagers all feeding together in a giant ceiba tree; too, too many beautiful, brown-skinned, sloe-eyed children waving from stilt-legged shacks. Then I thought of the sullen Jivaro Indians with their blowguns—and the splendid new luxury hotel at Santarém, as plush as any in Acapulco.

Actually it was easier to think of what the Amazon is not, than what it is. It's not just a river. It is vastness. Vastness coupled with brooding peacefulness. This peace has a deceptive quality of foreverness. Perhaps this comes from being the earth's oldest and most complex ecosystem; or a 60-million-year-old rain forest; or the mightiest river in the world.

Then I thought of Rolf. Who was he? A young, spoiled financier, bored with it all, taking exotic tours around the world? Or a man with an unhappy past, trying to forget? Or a secret agent? Why had he taken so many pictures of just about everything? How come he knew such interesting facets of life in Latin America? Perhaps I'd never know. If my Finn didn't meet me in Belém, would I ever see him again? Meanwhile, the river pushed inexorably to the sea. The *Explorer* would dock in just 8 hours. I had better come off cloud nine and think seriously about my *Audubon* assignment. After all, I'd be completely on my own now. Best to forget my fantasies and hopes—they were somewhat out of character for a wildlife woman. Yet I couldn't stop the stray tears that rolled down my cheeks and blew away into the tropical night.

The Transamazonica

After leaving my compact little stateroom on the *Explorer,* I found myself the next morning in a spacious suite on the seventeenth floor of the Hotel Excelsior Graō Para. I peered out nervously at Belém's skyscraper skyline, silhouetted against the rising sun. Below, a glut of traffic nudged past the proud old mango trees around Plaza Republica. What had happened to the sleepy jungle port? The population explosion had happened, plus construction of the Belém-Brasília Highway, BR 101.

The highway was devised to link Brazil's capital and the highly industrialized south to her major Amazon port and the markets of Europe and the Americas. The 1,100-mile paved road makes sense commercially and in this context has been a success. But in terms of environmental degradation, it may have been unwise or even worse.

Before I could travel out on BR 101 to evaluate the ecological situation for my *Audubon* assignment, I needed to find a good Portuguese interpreter-guide-driver. I spent several days in the steamy city looking for one. Finally I decided on Raymond, an elderly North American expatriate who worked for one of the leading import-export companies. He assured me that he could take some time off from his job and would enjoy driving into the hinterlands.

On Saturday morning, in a rented Volkswagen, Raymond and I started out on BR 101. My mood was glum. How much nicer it would have been to be sitting beside Rolf instead of this portly, pockmarked man who talked incessantly, though knowingly. Trucks roared past constantly. Service stations, bars, restaurants, and shacks flashed by continuously. I saw tropical woods and imported goods from Belém heading south; cattle and cars from the states of Goais and Minas Gerais, and the city of São Paulo going north. People were clustered everywhere beside the macadam. It almost looked like India all over again. My guide explained that over 120 small towns had grown up along BR 101 in the eleven years since it opened. More than 2 million people, many of them *posseros* (squatters) have settled haphazardly along its flanks. There has been no such government control over colonization along the Belém-Brasília Highway as there has been on the Transamazonica Highway. I was to find the contrast in settlement patterns and numbers of immigrants along the two roads quite startling.

Even more amazing to me was the amount of clearing that had

taken place during the highway's existence. Mile after mile of range met my eyes in areas where rain forest had been the original natural cover. Only scattered patches of trees remained or, far back on the horizon, a thin line of forest vegetation. Raymond told me that 5 million cattle roamed the ranches which lined both sides of the road.

We drove nearly 200 miles without stopping. My guide had arranged for me to visit two ranches belonging to friends of his and to see firsthand how beef-growing is done in Brazil. The first ranch belonged to a wealthy family from Belém who used their property chiefly for weekend relaxation. They maintained a few cowboys to round up the animals and do the chores. Land had been cleared by the traditional slash-and-burn system. Grass seed had been sown desultorily, much of it obviously too long after clearing. Sturdy weeds and scrub trees had taken hold of the land before the first grass shoots appeared. Good pastureland lost out. I could tell that the onslaughts of rainy seasons had already caused a lot of erosion. Reddish gashes gouged out many slopes. The ranch owner complained that a once-perennial stream had almost dried up except during the height of wet season. As I gazed out from the handsome ranch house, I saw a few scraggly patches of forest and some thin cattle scuffing over sun-baked, cement-hard ground. Yet the drinks were strong and the table loaded with delicious food. Four well-groomed horses stood tied by the door for anyone who wished to go riding. The owners were only "playing" at ranching. They were not even aware of what was happening outside their windows. I felt that if I tried to play environmental doctor and warn them of the ecological changes taking place, they wouldn't even be concerned.

At the second ranch, owned by two brothers, also from Belém, I found a pleasing contrast. Although the land had been partially cleared, farmed, and abused by squatters for seven years, the brothers were waging a vigorous battle to reclaim it.

"We've planted kudzu and other leguminous species on the old cut-over places," explained the younger brother, "and sowed *capim colonial (Bracharia mutica)* and *para (Panicum maximum)*. Those two grasses make the best fodder and have deep root systems which help hold the soil." He guided us through his stables and stockyard. "Wherever we prepare new pastureland during dry season, we plant those grass seeds immediately. That way they get full advantage of the open soil and early rains." He pointed toward a herd of cattle and continued, "We graze our animals lightly and rotate them often from field to field. Most of our land now has regained green cover after four years. In fact, some patches of kudzu are ankle deep."

His older brother chimed in enthusiastically. "We're trying to think ecologically. We leave large stands of forest to shade the cattle, keep the stream banks and hillsides vegetated, and protect our wildlife. Most people think we're crazy."

A giant bull ambled up while he was talking and began grazing at our feet. The younger man ran his hand appraisingly over its shiny shoulder and nodded at his brother. "Not bad, not bad, eh, Joachim? At times, I'd like to move back to Belém, but when I see results like this it seems worth staying. Besides this land takes a lot of attention." Turning back to me, he went on, "Research done at INPA (*Instituto Nacional Pesquisas Amazonica*, National Institute for Amazon Research) at Manaus shows that soil permeability drops dramatically when trees are removed and replaced by grassland. A primary rain forest can absorb three and a half inches of heavy rain in seven minutes, but an equal acreage of five-year-old pasture can handle only half an inch in the same time. All the rest becomes run-off. Really, the cushioning effect of forest canopy is astounding." He gave the bull a slap on its rump and turned to show us the feeding pens. "So my brother and I want to supervise all cutting here ourselves. We don't want to leave it to the laborers and just check in on weekends. We have eighty-five inches of rain a year out here. That could mean our land might lose as much as forty-five tons of soil per acre if it were cut bare. It is better for us to keep it well vegetated. Wooded hillsides, they found at INPA, lose only half a ton at most."

"But we're not sure how much longer we'll succeed," mused the other man. "Some ranches along BR 101 are already exhausted five years after removing the jungle. That ranch you saw earlier? We give it one or two more years before it is completely unproductive. Their range capacity has dropped in the last three years from one head per two and a half acres to one per twenty-five."

Raymond was quiet all the way back to Belém, so I had time to watch the sad landscape and ponder its ultimate end.

Next day I decided to have a bird's-eye look at the Belém-Brasília Highway and environs. I rented a light plane for a few hours. My pilot, Pedro, was a wiry, crew-cut, sunburned, skilled man who had been flying for over thirty years in the Amazon. "It's changed a lot," he remarked casually as he belted me in to his aged plane. "In the old days I flew for hours over virgin jungle. We used to say, if you had engine trouble and landed alive, wild animals would eat you. If you landed dead, they'd still eat you. So what the hell difference did it make? If those engines failed, you were done for."

He propped open the cockpit cover with a two-by-four so that I would be able to take photographs unobstructed by glass or metal. Then we were taxiing down the field, and in a moment we were off. He leaned toward my ear and yelled, "Now there's habitation everywhere. You'll see. Emergency strips, radios, pastures to land in if necessary. I give the Amazon another twenty-five years and it'll be all used."

Our flight path took us in a great arc south of Belém. The first 20 miles had been cleared of trees and planted in small oval vegetable plots. Farther out we passed neat square fields of black pepper, truck crops, and small pastures. Most of these were managed by Japanese farmers. Their industrious and integrated methods of agriculture are about the only ones that produce crops consistently and seem to put little stress on the environment. Not until we were 75 miles from the city did we fly over truly untouched lowland rain forest. Then, angling east toward BR 101, we began to see huge tracts of burning trees. Visibility lessened abruptly. Pedro reached up and slammed shut the cockpit cover. I stared with disbelief at the flames licking up the forest.

I recalled hearing rumors that the Volkswagen Company of Brazil had defoliated, cut, and burned a piece of land roughly 100 by 100 kilometers (3,600 square miles) for cattle ranches in 1974. It has been called the largest man-made fire in the world. Satellite photographs from 940 miles out picked up the smoke which rose tens of thousands of feet. This apparently happened in spite of the fact that Volkswagen had signed an agreement, as per Brazilian law, to cut only 50 percent of the area and leave the other half in forest. Although VW claims it abided by this law, it is widely believed that it did not. The company now has approximately

300,000 acres in ranch land and is one of the largest cattle operations in the world.

Pedro was pointing down at the Belém-Brasília Highway now, and minutes later we were circling over ranch land around Paragominas. He shouted, "Four years ago this was wild forest. It sold for fifteen to twenty-five cents an acre. Now it's worth four hundred dollars per acre as improved land *without* cattle."

"Can I take some pictures?" I yelled.

"Sure." He reached up and slid back the cockpit cover, propping it open again with the board. "Ready?" He leaned the single-engined plane on its side, allowing me a clear shot of the ground. Absolutely sure I would fall out, I nevertheless snapped several shots. But my stomach was turning upside down and I felt queasy. Pedro leveled off again and shouted, "Next year I'm going to talk to some ranchers about hiring me to spray defoliants on their land. Using hand labor, it costs them about two hundred to two hundred and fifty dollars an acre to cut, burn, and seed. The biggest trees may not catch fire or fall down for years. Using Vietnam defoliants, I could cover fifteen hundred acres in an hour. It would be much cheaper and all the trees would be down within two to four years."

I turned a horrified look at Pedro, but he didn't notice. He went on shouting companionably. "After the burning, I could come back and sow grass seed by air. It'd be a good pot of money for me."

I was beginning to feel nauseated and despondent, so I motioned Pedro to head back to Belém. Vietnam defoliants! How widespread was their use down here? Was there no law to protect the environment from this kind of chemical abuse? By the time I arrived back in my hotel room, I was both airsick and sick in my soul. I was coming to realize that Amazonia was in for big trouble.

The next place I wanted to fly to was the huge Jari holding northwest of Belém. It is considered to be the largest and most grandiose private forestry-agricultural-mining enterprise in Amazonia, and possibly in the world. Jari Forestry and Agricultural Enterprises is owned by an 81-year-old American industrialist, Daniel K. Ludwig. It covers about 3.75 million acres, an area roughly the size of Manú National Park. The organization's propaganda claims fabulous accomplishments following an eleven-year period of development. There are 225,000 acres of rapid-growth *Gmelina* (an Asian hardwood tree) and Caribbean pine, kaolin mining and processing of 220,000 tons per year, and 12,500 acres of high-yield rice cultivation producing a staggering 4 tons per acre per year. In addition, Mr. Ludwig had a $200 million floating pulp mill built in Japan and towed 15,000 miles by sea to Jari early in 1979. Moored in the Jari River, it will be used to process pulp from the *Gmelina* trees and pines. The mill boilers will be fired with the residue wood from cutting and clearing virgin rain forest at the rate of 10,000 acres annually.

As an ecologist, I was anxious to see these undertakings and judge the effects of such megatechnology upon the land and its natural resources. Having heard harsh criticisms of Jari, I wanted to prove for myself where the truth lay. Many scientists have been deeply concerned about the long-term hazards to climate and ecosystem health of destroying huge patches of primary forest and replacing it with monocultures of exotic species. Also, what about the open strip mines and the disposal of mill and human wastes? The mill is supposed to process 750 tons a day, and about 18,000 people live on Jari properties. Are these wastes having a deleterious effect on the fisheries, the native peoples, and the water quality downstream?

I used every possible contact in Belém to gain entry to Jari. I was politely refused. So I can only wonder what is really going on at Jari. Is the company taking a responsible role in the ecology of the area? Are the trade-offs of facial tissues, coated paper, and newsprint worth the elimination of a stable, healthy, natural environment? If development is inevitable, is this the best way to handle the land?

Instead, three days later, I took off for the Transamazonica Highway, the notorious BR 230. The National Department of Highways (DNER) of the Ministry of Transportation had kindly provided me with a pickup truck and a driver to cover the 195-mile section between Altamira and the crossroads of the new Cuibá-Santarém-Surinam Highway, BR 163. I was burning with curiosity to travel this part of the "Transam" and see what was happening out on Brazil's last frontier. As it would have been impossible for me to cover the entire 3,500-mile stretch in the short time I had available, I had chosen this central and most heavily colonized section as being the most interesting. Although the Transamazonica officially starts as a paved road at the Atlantic coast, in the Zona Bragatina, it peters out to a mud track somewhere near the Peruvian border.

I flew off one morning by commercial jet from Belém to Altamira, a dusty, TV-Western-type town of about 8,000 people. I envisioned endless miles of jungle, no eating or sleeping places anywhere, so I had purchased a dozen large bottles of guaraná (Brazil's equivalent of Coca Cola), and cheese, crackers, and chocolate. I went to the market for a hammock, mosquito netting, and two lengths of rope. Then I bought a big burlap coffee sack—an acceptable piece of luggage in Brazil—and stuffed everything inside it. I was fully prepared to sleep between two trees during this adventure.

At Altamira, the DNER truck was waiting, equipped with two spare tires, an extra 20-gallon gas tank, a shovel, and chains. I assumed we were in for a rough ride.

The Transamazonica has been called everything from an "unqualified and victorious success," to "a road from nothing to nothing," to "Transmiseriana." The project was sparked off impetuously in 1970 by former president Emilio Garrastazu Medici after a visit to drought-stricken northeastern Brazil. One-fifth of its then 23 million (now over 30 million) people were close to starvation. Suddenly the sparsely settled Amazon basin was seen as a means of easing pressures and famine in northeastern Brazil through colonization. The "conquest of Brazil's last frontier" made a strong rallying point. Other justifications were access to untapped mineral resources, agricultural and ranching development, new commercial connections to the remote towns on the southern Amazon tributaries, and, most important, national security. Brazil, after all, borders on all other South American nations except Chile and Ecuador.

Naturally it was hoped that BR 230 would be a commercial success comparable to BR 101. Initial plans were to construct 3,500 miles. Other major Amazonian highways were also planned, the longest being the Perimetral Norte (Northern Perimeter Road). This was to run north of the river and link towns with the capitals of French Guiana, Surinam, Guyana, Venezuela, and Colombia. Eventually, this 14,000-mile network might conceivably connect Brasília to the capitals of seven other South America countries.

To my surprise, the DNER driver maintained a steady 40 to 50 miles an hour (except when we crossed the many bridges) along the superbly engineered dirt highway. We soon arrived at one of the much-touted small-scale colonization projects sponsored by the National Institute for Colonization and Agrarian Reform (INCRA) and the Amazon Development Agency (SUDAM). This was the hamlet Agrovila Carlos Penha.

Unlike the area along the Belém-Brasília Highway, where settlements were simply allowed to spring up spontaneously, here colonization had been to a large extent planned and controlled. A 60-mile-wide strip bracketing the highway—a total of 360,000 square miles, or roughly eight times the size of New York State or Guatemala—is federal land. And a settlement—*agrovila* (rural hamlet), *agropolis* (rural town), or *ruropolis* (agricultural and commercial center)—was planned or had been built every 10 kilometers along certain stretches of the Transam.

My driver asked if I'd like to stop. "By all means," I assured him enthusiastically. I saw forty-eight frame houses with outhouses flanking three sides of a large clearing in the jungle. I noted a tiny elementary school, chapel, clinic, small store, soccer field, and water tank. The agrovila is the basic unit where colonists live and from which the farmer walks out to his plot of land. Each family is given 250 acres of virgin rain forest, worth about $700. The government was providing transportation, six-month loans for hand tools and crop seeds, and even some simple farming instruction.

Ten kilometers farther on at Agropolis Brazil Novo, we stopped again. About 100 homes were occupied, although plans had originally called for 1,000 families. Here I saw a larger school, clinic, sawmill, gas station, and the INCRA administrative offices. Stepping into the director's air-conditioned office to introduce myself, I was almost ashamed of my appearance. Indoors, old field clothes, boots, and pigtails seemed foolishly out of place beside a stylish young secretary in 6-inch-platform shoes, mini skirt, and dangling earrings. She greeted me cordially, however, and made me feel right at home by saying, "We try to keep up the city ways out here in the country. There is so much work to do. We *have* to have discipline, otherwise . . ." She shrugged helplessly.

We also stopped at small roadside stalls for tiny cups of sweet Brazilian coffee. Everywhere I listened to "Transmiseriana" tales. At one place, a couple related, "The first year here we thought we could grow everything. Two years later we abandoned our farm and set up this little store. We couldn't grow anything." At another stop, an almost-toothless man in his forties grinned wryly as he recounted his experiences. "Bananas were two feet long the first year. The bananas were one foot long the second year. The bananas were six inches long the third year. The fourth year? No bananas."

And yet the colonists between Altamira and Itaituba near the crossroads are luckier than most. Here the Transam fortuitously runs through a narrow band of fairly good soil, called *terra rosa,* whereas 80 to 90 percent of the rest of Amazonia's soils are classified as "poor" (low fertility) with only 10 percent suitable for agriculture. As living proof, instead of the 100,000 immigrants expected by 1975 (half a million by 1980) only about 45,000 had arrived by the time I was there. Many have already moved back whence they came, discouraged by the heat, humidity, diseases, insects, poor crops, and isolation. Their farmland was simply abandoned. Colonization west of Itaituba has been officially halted. The soils are just too poor. And as of this writing, almost all small colonization schemes have been discarded by the Brazilian government.

I was chilled by the treatment of the environment on those working farms we passed. That first day we drove off and on for 12 hours, and almost every mile of forest was in flames. Each colonist was taking advantage of the dry season to clear some of his 250 acres. By law, half the plot had to be left in forest, or it could be sold. This loophole effectively cancels out the conservation purpose of the forestry law. Moreover, the farmers seldom comply precisely with the law. The cleared half of the land is planted with subsistence crops of manioc, rice, maize, beans, bananas, yams, and a bit of coffee or guaraná on the side. Here again was another trade-off: green timber for kitchen crops. As one astute Brazilian, F. C. Camargo, wrote in 1948, "The felling of the forest [is] destroying gold; and producing manioc meal, rice, and other cereals [is] producing silver."

Camargo didn't mention sugar cane as one of the "silver-producing" crops because he never could have visualized in 1948 the vast fields of it which would be planted along this Highway. We stopped at an enormous plantation and mill where cane was being processed into raw sugar, molasses, and alcohol. I gazed spellbound at the huge juice heaters of bubbling liquid. My nose wrinkled with the heavy, redolent, sweet odors. I watched my driver turn a spigot and catch alcohol in his hand. "This will be used to mix with gasoline to make gasohol for our vehicles," he explained. "Regular gas is just too expensive out here."

The mill was in its second year of operation and doing well. Several hundred acres were under cultivation and more was being planted all the time. Filters, boilers, evaporators, and other machinery steamed and throbbed at the plant. The whole place looked efficient and up-to-date. But I couldn't help casting a speculative eye at the soils and wondering if it might be another story like that of the bananas.

Cane crops normally require large amounts of nutrients from the soil and permanent soil fertility is usually maintained by heavy applications of fertilizers. However, Amazon soils don't take kindly to these. Chemical fertilizers are often nearly useless because they volatize quickly under the hot sun or leach out with the heavy rains. Also they often cannot become "fixed" in tropical soils because of the absence of colloids. As for natural fertilizers, the Transamazonica was probably too recently settled to have manure and compost available to the sugar plantation.

By nightfall, after driving through flame and smoke for hours, we reached Ruropolis President Medici, the only one completed so far. Trucks and buses were continually rolling into the town, dropping off supplies and people. My driver said that at least 100 vehicles passed this stretch of highway every twenty-four hours. However, farther west toward Peru, travel was still minimal and the road was often impassable during rainy season.

To my utter astonishment, the ruropolis had a small motel, swimming pool, dining room, church, social services center, and several stores, although it was still less than a year old. All the electricity came from an old wood-fired locomotive engine. That night I left my hammock, guaraná, cheese, and crackers in the pickup and rented a room. Apart from having to kill a 6-inch hairy spider on the wall, I was as comfortable as I might have been at any roadside inn Stateside.

Gorillas and Jaguars

The next morning I strolled around the ruropolis chatting as best I could with its inhabitants and transients. All the people I met seemed enthusiastic about being pioneers on the Brazilian frontier. They made me think of what our early Westerners must have been like. It was heartwarming to listen to their dreams and see their dedication.

By noontime I was ready to travel on and see more, so I persuaded my driver to forgo lunch at the motel, drive on to the crossroads, and take the new Cuibá-Santarém-Surinam Highway, BR 163. "We'll find something to eat along the way," I prophesied recklessly. In the short time I'd been here, I was reassured that wherever humans went in Amazonia, there would most always be food, shelter, and drink of some sort available. Sure enough, before we'd been on the road half an hour, we spotted a tiny, open-air café flanked by uncut rain forest. For 60 cents, we had a full-course lunch with ice-cold guaraná—chilled in a dilapidated kerosene refrigerator. Only the zillions of flies on the table made our repast less than appetizing.

The Cuibá-Santerém Highway had been opened only a few weeks so no settlements had begun along its right-of-way. Consequently it gave me a perfect comparison with the small-colonization pattern on the Transamazonica and the large-scale ranching scene along the Belém-Brasília highways. The contrast in environmental vigor and health was obvious. Here dense forest hugged the red dirt roadside. The route ran straight as a die over rolling hills and vales, empty of traffic as far as I could see. This is what BR 101 and BR 230 had once looked like, I imagined.

Now I could clearly understand that simple, low-key, slash-and-burn agriculture is the best of all traditional methods in tropical forested regions—*if* it is done by very small groups of semi-nomadic people in very large tracts of forest. This ancient farming practice is almost like having natural tree falls with resultant small openings in the jungle. As long as natives cut tiny plots, plant a diverse mixture of crops which really mimics the forest's diversity, and move on in two to three years, this is the most ecologically sound system. Nomads usually don't return to their fallow patches for 50 to 100 years. By then, the nearby forest has grown back and healed the pinprick of an opening in its canopy. The microclimate has not changed. Soils have not washed away or baked hard. The coolness, dampness, shade, and species diversity and composition are all intact. This type of slash-and-burn subsistence living can be repeated indefinitely, given a small human population and vast acreage.

No sooner had we left the café than we experienced a bizarre event that could happen only in Amazonia, where one soon grows accustomed to strange happenings of all sorts and learns to shrug them off. This time a traveling circus had broken down on the highway. A rough-looking, bearded man was lying on his back under a van, alternately arguing with a beautiful girl in tights (probably the trapeze artist) and swearing at a gorilla in a small cage. We braked to a stop and tried to help, but the van was so rusty and rundown, and the parts so damaged, that all we could do was promise to send out a mechanic from Santarém later.

My heart went out to the animals, broiling in the midday sun, cooped up behind wire: a margay cat, several snakes, some jungle fowl, the inevitable monkeys, and that poor African primate. The gorilla was so far from home and doomed to a life without proper food, mates, or exercise. I tried to engage the girl in conversation to see if we could rig up some shade over the cages, but she was too upset by the delay and concerned about getting sun on *her* skin to bother. Finally, I offered the creatures some water from our tank and cautioned the man not to neglect them. "Ahhh, they'll be all right," was his tart reply, as he struggled with a wrench.

My driver motioned to me to leave, and we started off again. After a short silence while I grieved for the animals, I asked him, "Do you ever see jaguars out on the highways?"

"Sometimes at night," he replied, "where there's still wild land on both sides of the road. But never where the farmers are."

I told him about my experience with one in Manú. Then I fell silent again, remembering how large a range one pair of the spotted cats needs—at least 100 square miles. Dr. John Terborg, a professor at Princeton University who has spent thirteen summers and one full year in Manú National Park, estimates that parks and reserves of 1,000 square miles are necessary to prevent extinction of neotropical birds in lowland rain forest. Anything smaller will confine and restrict them and cause slow extinction. Obviously, large mammals like jaguars, pumas, giant river otters, and tapirs, can never survive in small, disjunct sanctuaries; they will not be able to encounter enough food, water, mates, or territory. They'd be little better off than that poor gorilla in its cage. Few large-animal populations can maintain themselves on less than 2,000 to 5,000 square miles of land. Therefore, the designing of national parks in the Amazon basin will need to take into consideration the minimum critical size of the largest and most actively ranging species.

Unfortunately, along the major highways and cities in the Amazon basin, human populations are becoming rapidly larger and more sedentary. Areas cut and cultivated are expanding; the forest is retreating. The 50 percent-cut and 50 percent-saved forestry law is not really working. Most wildlife has little chance.

To be more precise, the Brazilian government, mainly through SUDAM (Amazon Development Agency), has been encouraging large-scale farming and ranching projects with lots averaging 250,000 acres in size. More recently, it announced a new program that will level about 100 million acres (roughly the area of California) for timber. With a national debt of $41 billion, this is one way to pay off. Brazil offers fine tax exemptions, or "risk contracts," for multinational corporations moving into the Amazon basin. Moreover, a new thrust called "Polamazonia" is already creating fifteen "poles of development" for towns, agriculture, and industry. These poles will level thousands more acres of land.

There seems no way for the rain forest to keep a normal microclimate or reseed itself under such gross changes. On large clearings, estimates are that it may take 100 to 500 years for soils and rain forest to recover, if they ever do. Closer to the truth, I believe, is that once razed in such grandiose style, a rain forest cannot ever be restored by man. In comparison, it appears that these new maxi-programs of exploitation will be far more destructive to the environment than all the small colonists put together.

And all this is happening—just as surely as our West was "won." No longer is the question whether Amazonia will be developed, or if it is morally right to practice such giant environmental manipulations. Rather, the question is: who will do it, and how?

Still one more amazing site we visited on the way to Santarém was a large hydroelectric dam being built on the Curía Una, a tributary of the Tapajóz River. Somehow, the idea of harnessing the water power of the Amazon basin had never occurred to me. The rivers seemed too wild, too unmanageable, too prone to fluctuation. Yet here was a dam to rival any medium-sized one in the United States, with turbines and other machinery all manufactured in São Paulo, Brazil. I wondered if the government would prohibit colonization along its shores. Far too often, when settlers or squatters move in and cut the forest, erosion and siltation begin, the reservoir loses 10 to 40 years of its potential life span, new dams have to be built sooner, and the price of energy rises. And, in the Amazon, it can have another detrimental effect. Fruit- and seed-eating fish may lose their foraging grounds when river banks are deforested and swampy lowlands flooded. When the trees disappear, so do their fruits and seeds, and then these valuable, edible, fresh-water fish die or move off.

At sunset that day we reached Santarém. Once again I gazed out at the blue Tapajóz and the incredible "milk-coffee-river-sea." Even here, 500 miles from the Atlantic, tides came and went. I could barely glimpse the far horizon. Banks of ivory thunderheads towered over the rain forest, slowly changing colors as the sun sank—old-rose and beige, strawberry and lavender, ice-blue and mauve. The wind was fresh and cool. It felt good to be back on the river once more.

I found an airy room in a local inn overlooking the water; the plush new Hotel Tropical seemed too luxurious and touristy after my adventures. I collapsed on the bed under a filmy mosquito netting. Memories of the *Explorer* and Rolf flooded into my mind, making me toss fitfully. Would I ever sail aboard that ship again? Would I ever see my Finn again? Because of them, Amazonia would always be a bittersweet place for me.

Sometime late that night, a bit of the timelessness and peace of the river seeped into my soul. It was as if the Amazon were saying, "Be patient. Everything works out in time: your problems, my problems."

Black Pepper

When I checked back into the Hotel Excelsior Graõ Para in Belém, it was almost like coming home. By now, everyone knew me; I was the "American *menina* (young lady) who was writing something about the Amazon." The bell boys smiled, winked, and hurried to open doors and elevator. The chambermaid brought fresh flowers to my room. The European manager kindly invited me to join him for dinner. Brazilian cordiality can be wonderful, and here at the oldest and best hotel in Belém it was a tradition.

After resting and writing up my notes about the Transamazonica Highway, I decided to go to the Zona Bragatina during the few days I had left on my *Audubon* assignment. The last outpost of Amazonian rain forest before the Atlantic Ocean, the Bragatina covers about 10,000 square miles and has been under cultivation since the Portuguese arrived in the 1500s. It has been called "the most disturbed ecosystem in the Americas."

I wanted to compare this much-utilized region with the newly settled lands I had seen along the highways and the virgin country of Manú National Park. Only then could I really draw conclusions about how much ecological change is occurring in Amazonia. I had a melancholy drive in drizzle from Belém out to the Bragatina. The landscape was monotonous and desolate. Only 5 to 10 percent of the zone is left in original forest; the rest is mostly *capoeira*, a worthless scrubby woods of second-, third-, and fourth-growth palms, weeds, *Cecropia*, coarse grasses, and small trees. Could the Bragatina be a preview of what might happen along the Belém-Brasília and Transam highways?

I wryly recalled the predictions of the English naturalist Alfred Russell Wallace in *Travels on the Amazon and Rio Negro*, published in 1853. Following extensive field excursions, he raved, "I fearlessly assert that here the primeval forest can be converted into rich pasture land, into cultivated fields, gardens, and orchards, containing every variety of produce, with half the labor, and, what is more important, in less than half the time that would be required at home." Poor Wallace. If he could have seen what I was seeing, how he would have been disillusioned.

One of the biggest shocks for me were black-pepper farms, which represent an incredible trade-off in the Amazon basin. The behemoth buttressed trees are being swapped for tiny pepper-corns—giants for grains, ancient irreplaceable forest for brief-lived bushes. The ecosystem which has taken 60 million years to evolve and reach a steady-state equilibrium is being razed for small, short-lived plants which yield no calories or nutrition. Of all the sights I'd seen in Amazonia so far, this trade-off seemed the most outlandish and foolish.

I knew now from my travels that every twist of a grinder, every dusting of pepper on a salad or soufflé, every tasty mouthful, represented the whack of an ax, the slash of a machete, the strike of a match, as virgin tropical rain forest was cut and burned for farmland. That day, I decided never again to eat black pepper: my small gesture of disapproval of the unwise exploitation of the Ama-zon basin, my minuscule sacrifice for its conservation. Until proper land uses are in effect, I can live without pepper.

In the three months' total time of my assignment I had gone from the euphoria of seeing magnificent conservation in action at Peru's Manú National Park to depression over rampant develop-ment in Brazil and other countries. Development seemed to me to have the upper hand. Venezuela was pursuing her own *Conquista del Sur,* conquest of the south; Peru and Ecuador were looking east for oil; Colombia had her lingering market in animal trade and may also find oil; Brazil was ramming roads and ranches into her frontier with alacrity. More than sixty foreign companies were bidding for forestry, mining, and ranching contracts in that country alone, and, reputedly, 20 percent of her Amazon land was spoken for. The whole world seemed to be pressing in on its last great tropical wilderness—Amazonia. Never since the Ice Age had she faced such a juggernaut.

I remembered that Pedro, my pilot, had predicted that within 25 years the Amazon will be all used up. I had also read the predictions of many scientists who specialize in tropical rain forests. Dr. Thomas Lovejoy feels that the primary forest is within a few years of being 80 percent nonexistent. Dr. Ghillean Prance,

Research Director of the New York Botanical Gardens and an expert botanist, had told me somberly, "I estimate that 24 percent of the Amazon basin has already been 'disturbed.' I predict another 24 percent will go—soon. The other half? I *think* we'll live to see that half saved." Dr. Robert Goodland, co-author with H. S. Irvin of the controversial book, *Amazon Jungle: Green Hell to Red Desert?*, warns that the desert is only decades away.

If they are right, we will lose the largest tract of tropical woodland in the world. Already satellite pictures going back 10 years (1968–1978) show that 200,000 square miles of the basin have been deforested. It will be well over 10 percent by 1980, and at that time it is estimated that 1 percent of Brazil's rain forest—an area roughly the size of Indiana—will disappear each year. Dr. Otto Huber, scientist with Venezuela's CODESUR, said gloomily, "Anne, I'm convinced we're the last generation to see virgin rain forest in the Amazon."

A major change in overall climate may be underway. Fifty percent of the rain in the Amazon basin is generated by water evaporation from the trees themselves and cycled directly through the forest. If the trees are cut, rainfall may be reduced by as much as 30 percent. Moreover, humidity is reduced and more solar heat is reflected, especially from fields. This changes air circulation, wind currents, and weather patterns. In time, it may start an irreversible drying trend. What rain does fall will run off faster and cause floods and siltation of rivers.

I heard one outstanding scientist say, "We don't really know how large an area of rain forest should be preserved in order to maintain the maximum recycling effect which guarantees a wet climate. By the time we find out, it may be too late. It's like trying to stop a supertanker under full speed from hitting something right in front of it. By the time it slows down, the tanker may have traveled ten miles and left the pieces far behind."

There is fresh concern that such a drying trend could result in automatic loss of the remaining Amazon forest and cause climatic changes far beyond the tropics. If rainfall were to *decrease* in the equatorial zone, it would probably increase between latitudes 5 and 25 degrees north and south; then fall off again between 40 and 85 degrees north. This could be critical for the great grain-growing regions, especially Canada, Russia, and the United States.

A second worrisome consequence of deforestation and climatic change is the build-up of carbon dioxide in the atmosphere. Tropical forests hold an enormous pool of stored carbon, the largest on earth. Since the 1950s CO_2 has been increasing in our atmosphere, mainly as a result of increased burning of fossil fuels and of forests. If great pulses of this gas are released because of ambitious Amazon development projects, the environment could lose its ability to absorb and buffer carbon dioxide. Sudden climatic changes might occur, most probably a warming trend in temperate areas from the "greenhouse effect."

The third, and most unpredictable, danger is to species and genetic diversity. Should we lose a million species, we will deplete our earth's catalogue of fauna and flora by about one-fifth. What's lost will be lost forever. Among those million tropical living things there might be potentially beneficial medicinal plants, such as those already in use—alkaloids for the treatment of heart disease, curare in anesthetics, and certain plant chemicals in contraceptives; new foods as nourishing as palm oils; other plants as useful as the rubber tree; and insect predators and parasites which could serve in biological control of pests. As it is now, 40 to 50 percent of all medicines are derived from plants, most foods go back to wild plants, and woods, dyes, resins, and much more are direct gifts of the forest. With these gone, our planet will be less able to support mankind. Evolutionary processes will slow down. And economic hardships will intensify.

According to Dr. Norman Myers, we could already be losing two species a week in the Amazon. Quite possibly, he estimates, this rate could escalate to one per hour by the late 1980s—a biological debâcle.

My drive back to Belém was as dismal as the trip out. I had gone from the best (Manú) to the worst (Bragatina). Then, as I walked disconsolately through the lobby, the debonair hotel manager of the Excelsior Graõ Para asked to see me.

"I'm so terribly sorry," he began, "but my staff is not always as well-trained and intelligent as I would like."

What was he leading up to?

"While you were away this time," he said apologetically, "a new front desk man came to work. He straightened up everything and sorted through all the old unclaimed mail. He found a cable for you that had been posted under B instead of L. I do hope it isn't something urgent that you'd been waiting for."

I started to tremble inside. It had to be from the editor of *Audubon* . . . or from Rolf.

It was from Rolf and had been sent the day after he disappeared from Manaus. It simply read: "Meeting impossible Belém. Will call you New York after return. Miss you. Love, Rolf." At least he had tried to leave a message. However, the cable gave no explanation of why he left the ship so abruptly or of who he was. But he did plan to see me again. That was heartwarming. Did I want to see him? Was there any future with my Finn? Probably not. Perhaps I should just write it off as a shipboard romance. After all, doesn't every woman deserve at least one in her life? I thanked the manager warmly and went up to my room to think.

Strangely enough, my melancholia began to lift. I had been from the best to the worst, literally speaking, both ecologically and romantically, yet I was determined to be positive. Perhaps, as the Amazon had whispered to me that night in Santarém, things would work out.

First, I would find out what was being done to *save* Amazonia before I wrote a biased article. (I'd decide about Rolf when I got back home. I might not have been only a passing fancy on his part, after all. But I was sure he was more at home with elegantly turned-out women than with muddy-booted ecologists with sunburned noses.) I started interviewing a handful of scientists and bureaucrats, asking them about ways in which the Amazon might be developed along sound ecological lines. Bit by bit, I found there were a few organizations and people working for conservation and on techniques which might have minimal environmental impact on the delicate Amazon basin.

The most intriguing office I visited was RADAM (Radar Amazon) of the Ministry of Mines and Energy. In 1971 it had begun one of the biggest programs ever undertaken to map the earth's natural resources. Using side-looking radar images, full color, infrared, and black-and-white aerial photographs, RADAM was covering 2.5 million square miles, or 46 percent, of Brazil's so-called Legal Amazon. At key sites ground survey teams were dropped in by helicopter, usually in places where no non-native person had ever set foot. This huge reconnaissance effort was not without perils and casualties. At the time I interviewed RADAM officials, forty persons had been lost in accidents with helicopters and river rafts. Nevertheless, RADAM had been amassing maps and data on geology, geomorphology, vegetation, and soils. Technicians were drawing up land-use plans of the entire region, including areas for national parks.

Another group doing noteworthy research is the government's National Institute for Amazon Research (INPA) in Manaus, which I mentioned earlier. It is one of the few organizations dedicated to the nondestructive utilization of the rain forest. INPA was looking for products that could be extracted harmlessly, so that the forest canopy, soils, and nutrient/rainfall recycling would be preserved. There are choice tropical hardwoods, latexes, ornamental plants, orchids, gums, waxes, barks, roots, nuts, oils, fruits, medicinal plants, seeds, honey, and resins which can be harvested. Some day, the forest may produce methane and alcohol for fuel, leaf proteins as food.

The former director of INPA was Dr. Warwick Kerr, a dynamic scientist and administrator—perhaps the academic Benavides of Brazil—who was pushing conservation in Amazonia. Over 200 researchers are working at INPA on various aspects of Amazon agronomy, biology, medical science, and technology.

Dr. Kerr told me reassuringly, "We can do a great deal to manage our resources in a sound way, but we can't control ecological exploitation and damage by multinational corporations. Sixty percent of Amazon development is now being done by outsiders, 30 percent by southern Brazilian companies, and only 10 percent by Amazonians."

"What kind of damage are you referring to?" I asked.

"A good example is a foreign company that is interested in building an aluminum plant on a major tributary of the Amazon. The pollution from mica wastes could destroy the aquatic ecosystem up to three hundred miles downstream. What about the poor caboclos who depend on fish for food? Another example is a timber outfit with new tropical chippers capable of rendering an entire forest into bits and pieces. What about trees for firewood for the native residents? You can be sure that most multinational companies will not offset the deficit cost to the environment with any of their profits from the projects. Now I call *that* ecological imperialism!"

A third encouraging effort that I discovered was the Brazilian Institute for Forestry Development (IBDF), which, with additional input from RADAM, FAO, and the United Nations Development Program (UNDP), is working to establish national parks in Brazil. An American international parks consultant, Dr. Gary Wetterberg, had been loaned to the government to assist with a master plan for the Amazon. And just in time. The current status of parks is precarious. Only two areas are officially managed—Pico da Neblina, covering 5.5 million acres, and the Amazon (Tapajóz) National Park, 2.5 million—but they are still mostly parks on paper.

However, the future outlook is more encouraging. Brazil could create one of the best designed systems of conservation units in the world. The work is being chiefly directed by the professional skills and mettlesome temperament of Maria Theresa Jorge Padua, now head of Brazil's national parks service and probably the highest-placed woman in any conservation office in the world.

To identify top-priority areas, researchers are incorporating a lot of fresh scientific evidence and recommendations by other organizations such as RADAM and Polamazonica. One criterion is vegetational diversity. Although terra firme covers 90 percent of the basin, there are several smaller areas of high interest, such as swamp forests, bamboo glades, mangroves, and savannas, each worthy of representation in the park system.

Among the top-priority areas are Pleistocene refugia, places formed when the last Ice Age (circa 18,000 years ago) caused a drier, cooler climate in the tropics. During this time the jungle shrank and savannas covered much of Amazonia, but some remnant patches of rain forest persisted. Within these refugia many birds, butterflies, plants, and lizards were "trapped" as if on ocean islands. Later, when the climate warmed and the forest again expanded, many of these animals and plants survived but remained clustered at or near the Ice Age locations. These rich centers of diverse endemic species would be ideal components of national parks.

The stickiest consideration of all is the minimum critical size of conservation units. Some fauna and flora are distributed over hundreds of miles, yet with only one individual per square mile. Others are extremely restricted in range. Thus, in designing parks to preserve as many species as possible in good health, the smallest possible territory for all the creatures must be taken into account. Studies by World Wildlife Fund indicate that most parks must be very large—at least 800 to 1,000 square miles.

Very recently, Sra. Padua has planned that roughly 47 million acres, as a minimum, be set aside for future national parks in the Amazon region. This means that 5 percent of Brazil's Amazonia would be protected. If all the criteria are followed, the park system could preserve up to 75 percent of the species that exist in the basin on a mere 5 percent of the land!

Other South American countries have already achieved some conservation successes, perhaps because their holdings are smaller and fewer organizations are competing for the environment. Venezuela has four new national parks and two national monuments touching on part of Amazonia and totaling 9.2 million acres. Colombia and Ecuador each have two parks; Peru has three; Bolivia, one. Not all these, however, observe the aforementioned criteria or minimum critical size. None has addressed the problem of how much land is needed for the proper recycling of rainfall.

Strange as it sounds, cities and tourism are considered to be another way of saving the Amazon countryside. The cities must be self-contained—company-town types of communities—supporting light industry and artisan shops. Food and other life necessities would have to be imported from southern Brazil. Creeping colonization or slums festering into the forest could not be allowed.

As Dr. Myers puts it, "The only long-term solution to saving tropical forests is rapid urbanization with decent standards of living and expanded trade between rich and poor nations. Light industries like making shoes or assembling TV sets are better alternatives than putting chainsaws and matches to the forest."

Utilization of existing fish and wildlife is another wise strategy. With proper management there can be game cropping and aquaculture of animals such as the manatee (which is more nutritious than beef), tapir, agouti, capybara, turtles (the so-called cattle of the Amazon), and nutria. Surplus numbers of primates, caimans, and tropical fish could be exported for medical research, leather, and pet shops. Fish, the greatest food resource in the Amazon, can continue to feed protein-deficient people, provided that swamp forests are not destroyed by lumbering and large-scale agricultural projects and the resource is not overfished commercially.

On my next-to-last day in Brazil, I stopped at EMBRAPA (*Empresa Brasileira de Pesquisa Agropecuária*, Brasilian Company of Agronomy Research), which gave me a guide for the day— Miriam, a pert, intelligent soil scientist who had done work in the Bragatina. She introduced me to two types of agriculture that seemed to be causing minimum environmental impact in the Amazon.

The first was a black-pepper farm run by an industrious Japanese family. These fields looked entirely different from the sun-baked plots of yellowing bushes that I had seen elsewhere. Tall mounded rows of pepper bushes were interspersed with mats of thick grasses. These cushioned the pounding rains and kept soil temperatures low. Chickens, pigs, and cows wandered around the farm. The Japanese farmer used the animal manure which was absorbed better and lasted longer than any artificial fertilizer. He imported his animal fodder from southern Brazil and exported eggs, milk, and meat. These paid the farm's basic expenses. The real cash crop was the pepper, which brought in about $2,000 per acre during its usual four years of good production.

The second type was illustrated by another small farm where "agri-mazonia-culture" was being practiced. Miriam explained to me that the large Amazonian family which owned it didn't realize how ecologically sound their system was. They were growing a pot-pourri of native crops—rice, beans, corn, squash, manioc, coffee—all mixed together on varzea soil. They grew only enough for their own needs. The variety of plants mimicked the diversity of the forest in miniature. These people were not practicing super-technological agriculture to make lots of money; rather they were surviving in a simple, healthy life style. To Miriam and to me this made sense.

At the end of the trip, my conclusion was that no matter what type of development takes place, Amazonia should be kept in *as natural a state as possible*. The ultimate goal should be not millions in profits on quick trade-offs but environmental stability and self-sustainment of human life. After all the Amazon was not made for exclusive use of the First World.

I left Belém on a Sunday night at 2 A.M. It was hot, muggy, rainy. I was tired after my long assignment, yet, curiously, I had a light heart. I just could not believe that the Amazon's future is entirely bleak. For one thing, Latin American countries are keenly sensitive to foreign criticism and world opinion. Possibly all the finger-pointing in the press, negative as it may be, will force government decision-makers to pay attention to the environmental warning signs. Then, too, *Amazon Jungle: Green Hell to Red Desert?* has finally been translated into Portuguese. Its revelations of the ecological facts of what's happening in the Amazon basin should have beneficial effects.

Within Brazil and Peru, there have been caustic remarks made by leading citizens. For example, the late José Piquet Carneiro, former head of the Brazilian Foundation for the Conservation of Nature, protested in 1974 against "crimes to nature." In a newspaper review he said, "Developers are turning the Amazon basin into another Sahara, destroying the forest, up to a million trees a day, rivers, and animal life."

Another reason for my guarded optimism that night was the small but growing amount of good research and land-use planning being done and the number of environment-minded leaders in Latin America. There is now a Special Secretariat for the Environment (SEMA) in Brasília, who can relate directly to high government levels.

As I boarded the plane, I clutched my burlap coffee sack firmly under my arm. It was too precious to check in as baggage. In it I had stuffed the Jivaro grass skirts that Rolf and I had worn to the ship's masquerade party, a pod of achiote, the hammock I'd taken out on the Transamazonica Highway, a dried piranha, and some fine Brazilian coffee. The great jet slowly gained altitude and turned out over the 200-mile-wide mouth of the Amazon River. I gazed down onto blackness and wondered: Will environmental concerns within each nation save Amazonia? Will economics—the soaring costs of roads, petroleum, machinery, and construction—slow down development? Or will Amazonia save herself? Perhaps after 60 million years of adapting the perfect ecosystem for that harsh environment, she has more resiliency than we realize. Her built-in survival mechanisms may minimize the intensity of human exploitation. Certainly we are already seeing many negative feed-backs—erosion, compaction, climatic changes, flooding, disease. People have come, people have gone, people are going. Amazonia has already weathered booms and busts in rubber, gold, oil, and colonization.

But it's too early to tell. The real crunch will come in the next five to ten years.

Now we were high in the sky and headed for Miami. I lay back in my seat and relaxed. My long trip was over: Manú, the Amazon River, the highways, and the Bragatina. Three months. Seven thousand miles. I had seen many places and many moods of Amazonia. A slow smile spread on my lips as I suddenly realized what a long way I'd come. My path had started with the miniature microcosm of Lake Atitlán with its flightless grebes and rustling reeds and had unfolded and evolved to the vast and complex Amazonian rain forest. In coming to know something of the ecology of each, and all the places in between, I had glimpsed the world at large. I'd been privileged to be made aware of the ramifications of all that can happen when wildlife and wildlands are not treated wisely. Truly, we humans *must* be the stewards of our planet.

Wildlife Woman

To be a professional ecologist, conservationist, or environmentalist means an on-going, lifelong commitment. Each of my former projects has assumed an identity and life of its own. Moreover, some of them have managed to overlap or connect in strange ways. For example, a great many events have continued to shape the Lake Atitlán grebe campaign since I left Guatemala in 1968. I had just returned to Cornell University to finish my doctoral dissertation when word reached me about plans for a $115-million hydroelectric plant to be built at the lake. The plan proposed to use the lake as a natural reservoir. The lake's extensive surface, great depth, elevation, and proximity to the Pacific slope meant that a fall of roughly 2,000 feet could be achieved by using underwater outlets to the Pacific slope tunneled through the escarpment near Roberto's coffee farm. In addition to the reservoir and outflow scheme, four diversion tunnels would convey water from four rivers into Lake Atitlán to compensate *in part* for the intentional lowering of the lake by 27 to 40 feet temporarily and 23 feet permanently. The project was planned for development between 1970 and 1980. It would result in a power capacity of almost 500 megawatts and an annual output of 1,000 gross watts per hour, or 10 to 12 percent of the projected power demands of Guatemala in 1972.

When I heard this, I was thunderstruck, raging and fuming inwardly, casting about for what I could do. Such a project would also bring severe and irreversible changes to the lake's aquatic ecosystem and hydrology. And it might have repercussions on the resident Indian population of 50,000 within the watershed.

If the water level dropped too quickly the shoreline vegetation and submerged aquatic plants might be reduced or eliminated. The drawdown could prove to be more than the reed and cattail beds could withstand or accommodate. Second, turbidity was bound to increase from the excavation of tunnels, ditches, and engineering rubble. Silting and degradation of water quality could be expected from the four river diversions, which I suspected would introduce bacterial contaminants, possible undesirable aquatic life, and more silt. This would cause gradual eutrophication and diminishing of Lake Atitlán's crystal aquamarine aspect. Indeed, a report in 1971 stated that it would take no more than 77 years to replace the existing water in the 1,200-foot-deep lake completely with diverted river water.

Therefore, the physical, chemical, and biological characteristics of Lake Atitlán would no longer exist. These changes would threaten the Indians, waterbirds, and fisheries. I further reasoned that one of the costs which might be incurred beyond the $115 million would be the extinction of the Atitlán grebe.

One day I met with a professor on my committee and glumly

told him of my fears. "If only I could do something," I wailed, "and stop that damn plant."

"Why don't you?" he asked.

"How can I fight a power project two thousand miles away? And I don't know anything about hydroelectricity."

"Find out!" was his direct reply. "You're at one of the best universities in the world to get information and mount an attack. Look, here's what we'll do."

Before an hour was up, he had called some colleagues—hydrologists, engineers, limnologists—and set up a meeting to discuss this potential threat to Lake Atitlán. When that meeting was over, I had the combined objective opinions of twelve experts on the effects of this hydroelectric scheme and their promised assistance in preparing an open letter of protest. I also had a basic working knowledge of power plants and could write intelligently about the subject.

My letter, outlining point by point the ecological hazards of the project, was sent to various dignitaries and famous scientists such as Prince Bernhard and Prince Philip of the World Wildlife Fund, Sir Peter Scott, Dr. Dillon Ripley, and others for their endorsement. Then the epistle was mailed to the President of Guatemala, the head of the National Institute of Electrification (INDE), and to the Guatemalan Tourist Institute (INGUAT). I hoped that with those prestigious names backing it, the letter would reach the highest decision-makers smoothly and swiftly.

None of us, to my knowledge, ever received a reply. Yet word filtered back within the year that the project had been temporarily halted and alternate solutions were being investigated. How instrumental our appeal was I'll never know, but as of this writing, twelve years later, no plant has been built at lovely Lake Atitlán.

This ecological case history doesn't end there. I returned every year or two to re-census the grebes. They were steadily increasing until they reached a high of 230 individuals. I noticed, however, that vacation homes and hotels were also on the rise. Well-to-do Guatemalans were purchasing plots of land from the Indians, first for a few hundred dollars, then for two, three, four, five times as much. Real-estate values on that spectacular shoreline skyrocketed because of the burgeoning population, higher affluence of middle-class and upper-class people, greater ease of travel, and the willingness of local Indians to sell their cornfields and other properties. (Unfortunately, they didn't always think ahead as to where the corn and beans would come from without agricultural land to plant.)

In 1968, I had estimated that there were 92 vacation homes around the lake; there were only 28 when I first visited Atitlán in 1960. In 1972, I counted 110 such homes; in 1973, 140. Moreover, boathouses, docks, beach huts, and retaining walls were often built. Many owners cleared the entire shoreline of reeds and cat- tails to make beaches or in an effort to eliminate mosquitoes and water snakes. Sewage facilities, even at the hotels, were question- able. I wondered how many residences were polluting this clear body of water. Simultaneous with this real-estate development was increased recreational use of the lake by vacationers and tourists, especially for motorboating, waterskiing, skin-diving and scuba- diving. Not only was this a new nuisance factor for the Indians, but it created the possibility of oil slicks, wake turbulence, and further pollution in the lake.

By 1975–1976, the number of houses was well over 200. Also several new hotels had been built around Panajachel and a huge, twelve-story, two-tower condominium was rearing its walls nearby. Once again I was dismayed, but helpless. The threats here were so insidious—gradual pollution and contamination from the introduc- tion of artificial fertilizers, pesticides, sewage, and herbicides into an ecosystem which had been remarkably free of such materials because of its largely Indian population.

This time I wrote to the National Planning Council and to INGUAT, pointing out the need for a regional land-use plan and sanitary code. I also urged that the Indians' way of life be pro- tected against absorption into the Spanish life style. Those twelve lakeshore villages with their distinctive costumes, dialects, and cottage industries could all too easily be swallowed up by west- ernized jobs, clothes, and language. Not only would the Mayans lose dignity and a traditional way of life, but tourism would also suffer. Again, I never had an answer and I doubt that this letter did any good at all.

In February 1976 a terrific earthquake hit Guatemala. It lev- eled many towns, killed over 20,000 people, and opened up un- derground fissures beneath the great volcanoes which backdrop

Lake Atitlán. The water began seeping out. In the four years between 1976 and 1980, the lake level has dropped over 13 feet. Some reed and cattail beds started to dry up and die. Slowly, the grebe population decreased as its principal habitat diminished. Our refuge is completely dry now.

In 1978 the game warden took action. Gathering a group of Indian reed cutters, he commenced a campaign of transplanting the shoreline vegetation from shallow to deeper water. It was done as much to save the fisheries and the reeds as the grebes.

Most recently, the draining of the lake has slowed somewhat. The birds seem to be holding their own at about 150, and the fisheries are still intact but not plentiful.

Even now, I can't relax. Lake Atitlán illustrates perfectly why continued concern, support, and vigilance are so important in any conservation project. Next year I may hear that some new contaminant is causing a decline in the grebes, just as DDT once did to bald eagles and ospreys, and acid precipitation seems to be doing to loons in the northeastern United States today.

As for the private quetzal reserve on Volcano Atitlán, it's still there and the birds are doing well. The landowners have an official tax exemption and continue to support the wardens. Just ten years after David Allen, Armando, and I had agonized over the *National Geographic* assignment, a Guatemalan photographer, Diego Molina, obtained photographs at the same spot. It took him a lot longer than it did us, but ultimately he came out with the first set of exclusively Guatemalan photographs of the national bird. He displayed them most attractively at the Banco Industrial in 1979. Since few Guatemalans read *National Geographic*, thousands of them saw pictures of the life history of their revered bird for the first time.

As for little Anegada Island, no new development complexes have been tried. The first was stopped, as was a second similar scheme. Some of us who went there to survey the island published our data, which is now in general use and which is much more extensive and of better quality than had previously been available in the literature. Island Resources Foundation is operating in St. Thomas and is the chief listening post and conservation watchdog of the Caribbean.

The Volcano Barú project is in a long-drawn-out process of

becoming an outstanding national park. After our initial survey and report, it took four years until the area was officially declared a national park by President Omar Torrijos. (The rumor was that the lengthy and byzantine negotiations for the Panama Canal may have played a part in the delay.) The new lower border is set at 7,500 feet and will enclose 35,000 acres. In my opinion, this boundary is far too high. The land below it has already fallen into ranching, farming, and lumbering hands. I hope the government will be strong enough to defend that border and keep out squatters. A park administrator has been assigned and work is underway on basic visitor facilities and interpretive displays. Benjamin is still the official guardian. He married the young Guaymi woman he met at the hospital in David and they live happily in Boquete.

Meanwhile, the copper mine and the hydroelectric plant on or near the Guaymi reservation are both functioning, but I have not been back to see what sociological changes these have made among the Guaymi or what the environmental impacts have been.

Panama has shown a strong interest in at least two other parks. One is the Darién National Park, consisting of about 1,125,000 acres. It is at once the largest proposed conservation area, the most ambitious plan, and perhaps the most important biological region in all Central America. The Darién is one of the last great tracts of undisturbed tropical forest in the Isthmus.

Tremendous attention and land-use pressures will soon be focused in the Darién upon completion of the Pan American Highway. At present, the only stretch missing between Alaska and Tierra del Fuego is in the Darién Gap, but once it is finished, as it is expected to be in the 1980s, the region will become dangerously vulnerable to ecological abuses, loss of native cultural values, infiltration of squatters, and the spread of animal and human diseases. For these reasons, the proposed Darién National Park has been given top priority. Its goals include saving representative samples of fresh-water, terrestrial, and marine ecosystems; protecting the many watersheds; safeguarding the future scientific, aesthetic, historical, and educational values of this wildland region; preventing the spread of hoof-and-mouth disease from South America into Central America; eliminating the illegal entry of immigrants from Colombia into Panama; and preserving the indigenous cultures and life styles of the colorful and independent Choco and Cuna Indians. Both tribes are "ecosystem people," living in stable harmony with the land and the jungle.

The other park is the newly conceived Friendship Park between Costa Rica and Panama. The presidents of both countries met in March 1979 to inaugurate Latin America's first binational water and wildlife preserve. The nearly half-million-acre area straddles 20 miles of border in the Talamanca Range. It will protect Panama's extensive water reserves, hydroelectric potential, nine of Costa Rica's twenty ecosystems, and supposedly Central America's greatest concentration of quetzals.

As for the Dominican Republic's proposed Parque del Este, it's still in limbo. The only development is that the National Parks Service has been upgraded and has a new chief and plans for improving the existing parks.

The sea turtle situation there and on many other Caribbean islands has not improved. In general, despite the many conservation projects that have sprung up round the world in the last fifteen years, not one single species or colony has been rehabilitated. All sea turtle species now are threatened and endangered and are protected by international regulation.

What have I learned from these experiences? What methods and techniques can best be used in establishing successful sanctuaries for wildlife and wildland? What inferences can I draw from my ecology-conservation field projects?

In all five cases, the work took place in developing countries where little expertise existed in wildlife management, ecology, or conservation. All the areas contained rare and endangered wildlife with unique qualities and touristic value, and good examples of their habitats. In order to save any one species, I had to preserve the habitat it depended on. Yet, in each place, even whole ecosystems were threatened.

At Lake Atitlán, introduction of largemouth bass, reed cutting, and poaching were factors jeopardizing the endemic flightless grebe and its shoreline habitat. In the virgin cloud forest on Volcano Atitlán and in the Cuchumatanes Mountains, private plantations, slash-and-burn agriculture, and resulting wildfires were destroying acres of quetzal habitat. Moreover, natives were killing the birds. On Volcano Barú, agriculture, ranching, and lumbering were nibbling away at the prime montane forest both inside and outside the proposed park and endangering resident wildlife. Anegada Island was singled out for a major tourist resort–retirement complex which would greatly change the character and quality of two-thirds of the island, especially the beach-dune ecosystem and the "bush" in which the rare Anegada iguana lived. As for the Dominican Republic park area, a combination of small but significant abuses were occurring—burning trees for charcoal, overharvesting of conchs and lobsters, cutting fan palms for thatch, and over-shooting white-crowned pigeons. These were taking a cumulative toll of the natural resources. In every case, data on the local ecology and natural history were limited, and outside funding and expertise were needed. Each project had to be approached differently. Methods ranged from a one-woman, trial-and-error, lengthy coverage, to a concerted and sophisticated team effort using the finest equipment available for a short period of time. I would say that three of my projects were successful—namely, the small and modest government wildlife reserve for the grebes, the private quetzal sanctuary in Guatemala, and the Volcano National Park in Panama. One, Anegada, really never got off the ground. The last, in the Dominican Republic, had all the elements of a super-successful project but was aborted due to a miscarriage in the economy of a multinational corporation.

Nevertheless, from these experiences, I was able to draw certain conclusions about accomplishing conservation work. First of all, whenever possible, a rare or endangered species should be chosen as a key symbol upon which to focus public attention. Animals have an exceptional emotional appeal to people and can be used to enlist public sympathy. Such sympathy is crucial to the success of the project. For example, the quetzal, national bird of Guatemala, became the *raison d'être* for establishing the cloud forest reserve, and those birds may be the main attraction to tourists at Volcano Barú National Park. Similarly, the Atitlán grebe was used to arouse national pride in this uniquely Guatemalan species and as a motif for three airmail stamps, for arts and crafts, and for conservation education among the local Indians.

Second, it must be recognized that while enthusiastic personnel from outside sources may be needed to provide professional expertise at the beginning of any project, the real initiative and management must come from within the host country. A conservation unit cannot and should not be established if it runs counter to national and local interests.

National and local talent should be involved with the project from the beginning with on-site practical training. This will instill pride and prestige, gain publicity for the program, and at the same time decrease apprehension and dependence on outside assistance. Since most developing governments are characterized by a centralized decision-making system (as opposed to a grass-roots, democratic one), some scientists and government workers who stand far down in the hierarchy are often not recognized and never get to make a contribution. Their expertise and help may be extremely useful.

Professionals working outside their own countries should place great emphasis on diplomatic interpersonal relations. Every effort should be made to create an atmosphere of equality and ease with native colleagues and to avoid "paternalism" or "scientific imperialism." It is almost essential that the outsider speak the native language, develop a sensitivity to the existing time dimension, and understand the local customs and mores.

Technical advice and equipment brought into the country should be simple, inexpensive, and easy to operate. For example, an inexperienced game warden—like the one we had first at Lake Atitlán—should not be given a high-horsepower motor and speedboat to use if he or she does not know how to run it, fix motors, or swim. And modestly trained technicians should not be given fancy tape recorders or sampling equipment to operate when there is no way to obtain batteries, electricity, or repair services. Furthermore, clear explanations should be offered to co-workers and laborers when new materials and machinery are used. Witness the two fiascos I endured at Lake Atitlán with our fish reclamation ("poison pills") and night-lighting equipment ("man-eating monster").

Accurate and lively news coverage must be obtained, if possible, during the establishment of any wildlife or wildland unit since this is one of the fastest, cheapest, and most effective ways of educating the literate people in urban areas. Such publicity often leads to excellent support from unexpected sources in terms of loans of equipment, contacts to high-level officials, and so on.

I believe that outside funds and international cooperation should be used judiciously. They definitely add dimension to any project, give a psychological importance to the cause, and often serve to stimulate matching funds or fund-raising campaigns within the host country. This certainly proved true with the various grants I obtained for Operation Protection Poc in Guatemala.

Once the reserve or park is established, full responsibility for its administration and funding should be turned over to the national organization or organizations in charge. Foreign professionals should not prolong their stay, "baby-sitting" as it were, no matter how attached they are to the cause. This shifting of responsibility should be done with a certain amount of ceremony, as was our inauguration under the rainbow at the grebe reserve. Also press releases and official visits by government dignitaries are useful. This way the act of assuming responsibility becomes psychologically important and enjoyable.

The foreign professional, however, can and should maintain contact with the project. This can be done by arranging beneficial publicity abroad and forwarding it back; sending congratulatory letters from foreign dignitaries; mailing books, reprints of pertinent papers, and small pieces of equipment to reserve or park personnel. Such "rewards" have an invigorating effect. Likewise, the foreign professional should try to return occasionally to the conservation unit and the people in charge. For instance, I go back to Guatemala every year or two to help re-census the grebes and to obtain more data from the quetzal preserve for papers about cloud-forest conservation. This sort of thing can be done without embarrassing or offending the local personnel, and it often has a tonic effect on the entire project.

A fact which should always be born in mind is that the most realistic justifications for establishing wildlife and wildland areas in Third World countries are increased economic benefits and national pride. The benefits include protection of watersheds and soils, tax exemptions, and recreation for the people. I learned early in my first project that arguments based on aesthetics, morals, pure preservationist philosophy, scientific research, and ecological diversity cut no ice. They are arguments of an affluent society, and most developing countries have not arrived at the point where they can incorporate them or even understand them.

Lastly, the greatest thing I learned is, "*The price of conserva-tion is eternal vigilance!*"

I wouldn't be able to say that one project approach is more successful than any other. What is important is that both foreign professionals and local personnel be willing, competent, flexible, and enthusiastic; that the nation is ready for conservation; and that cordial and helpful relationships are nurtured and endure across the miles and years.

On a personal level, I discovered the power of a woman in Latin countries. The Latin male tends to be consistently chivalrous and attentive, and I never felt any antagonism toward my profes-sional attainments or jealousy about my skills and contacts, whereas these attitudes are often all too possible toward a foreign male. Whatever the reason, my dealings with male professionals in Latin America and the Caribbean have been full of respect, appre-ciation, and cordiality.

However, anyone who thinks that the life of a wildlife woman is all glamor, romance, exotic locales, and jet-setting travel is somewhat mistaken. For every hour in the field, I must count two to three at a desk writing reports, researching, reviewing litera-ture, referencing, captioning photographs, and writing letters. And for every three days at conferences and meetings, listening to dull papers and debates, I consider myself fortunate if I get one day out on an exciting field trip before or after. Furthermore, when I'm abroad I have to count on a 30 percent chance of getting sick with either gastroenteritis of some sort, a respiratory or flu infection, or an unexplainable fever.

One of my small shocks has been finding out that a college ed-ucation and science background are not always useful or even ap-propriate for handling certain problems. There is a whole non-scientific realm operating in the world: witch doctors, shamans, ESP, superstitions, psychological motivations, intuition. At the risk of making my hard-core scientific colleagues snicker, I'll say that these forces *do* exist and must be reckoned with objectively in one's work.

And I have also learned the tremendous gratification that comes from meeting a challenge and solving problems, however bizarre they may be. I have chances to exercise all the native in-telligence and ingenuity a human is capable of in my work. All this is quite a bit more satisfying than the average desk job with a regular paycheck. Also, the excitement of travel and strange adventures is always exhilarating. I have never regretted my early decision to assist developing countries in their environmental needs and ambitions. These many wildlife assignments have provided me with a sense of having made some small contribution to keeping this world wild and wondrous.

Predictions

When people ask me how I feel about the fate of our earth in terms of the environment, I say, "Pessimistic, but hopeful."

Basically I see our world as one giant ecosystem in which each part is dependent upon the others, one way or another. Mankind cannot be divorced from this ecosystem, or from ecological laws, or from environmental causes and effects. Natural life-support systems keep us alive—the recycling of water, the trapping of energy from the sun by plants, the production of soils, the flow of energy through ecosystems, the decomposition and cleansing of dead organic materials, and the regulation of global climates.

Until a few years ago, environmental problems tended to be localized and regionalized. Thus, they could be set right fairly easily. Today, however, we are faced with such sweeping exploitation and contamination that we can be affected by events taking place thousands of miles away. Just three examples will indicate the scope of our environmental problems: deforestation, desertification, and acid precipitation.

Deforestation is occurring on a massive scale, far greater than that I witnessed in Amazonia. It is happening chiefly along the 3,000-mile-wide belt of tropical forest which stretches around the world. No amount of reforestation, to date, can keep up with deforestation. It's proceeding at a calculated rate of 50 acres per minute—over 72,000 acres per day, more than 25 million acres per year. Some of the land goes into farming and ranching, some is lumbered for commercial uses, and some is wasted with wildfires and erosion. Deforestation promises to increase. By the year 2000, the world will have consumed an estimated 300 million cubic meters of hardwoods. Only one-third of the existing rain forest cover will be left.

The results? I described some of them in the Amazon chapters: loss of potable water and watersheds; loss of potential hydro-electric projects; siltation of rivers, lakes, and reservoirs; suffocation of marine estuaries and reefs with their resident fishes and shellfish, where muddy waters flow into the sea; the extinction of 1 million to 2 million species; the probable alteration of local and quite possibly of global climates.

All this in an ecosystem which has not had any great shake-up since the time of dinosaurs, which has evolved into a complex, stable, balanced, beautiful natural system. Yet man is creating changes in an area about which he is still quite ignorant—just look at the mistakes made in a few years along the Transamazonica and Belém-Brasília highways. If he keeps up this major scalping, the chances are that the tropical forest will never regenerate itself and we'll be left with meager sorry remnants and dangerous side effects.

The spreading of deserts (desertification) is roughly the same sad, worldwide process of destruction. We are losing to drought and sands hundreds of square miles of grasslands and savannas. These dry but productive areas have always been like a tension zone between forests on the one side and deserts on the other. But now the tension zone is breaking. The Sahara is expanding southward. The *sahel*, as it's called in Africa, is engulfing hundreds of thousands of acres. The Thar desert in India is advancing, amoeba-like, at the rate of half a mile a year along its entire perimeter. Two thousand years ago, ancient records tell us, it was jungle, and rhinoceroses and tigers roamed here. Desertification is much less often caused by climatic changes than by overgrazing, overbrowsing, trampling and concentration of too much livestock, ill-planned agriculture, charcoal-burning, and other abuses of the land around the edges of deserts. Soon, soil compaction and erosion take place until nothing but thorny, drought-resistant, bushy desert plants can survive. Sands begin drifting, dust blows, water-courses dry up, gullies deepen, and other desertlike conditions appear.

As with the destruction of rain forest, the damage may be permanent. Even those of us who have never seen a desert are affected. Again, local and possibly global climatic changes occur, livestock production decreases both for domestic consumption and for export, and our taxes go up to help support huge programs to combat this worldwide problem.

The third example, acid precipitation, is a fairly new environmental threat. The greatly increased use of fossil fuels since the 1950s has led to mounting air pollution with distinctive fallout patterns. Mountainous, forested areas having high rain and snow falls, shallow bedrock, acid soils and waters are prime targets. In the United States and Europe, the Adirondacks of New York State and the mountains of Scandinavia, respectively, are hardest hit. The prevailing wind and weather patterns carry air pollution from heavily industrialized regions directly to these places, even from 1,000 miles away.

Acid precipitation is rain and snow contaminated chiefly with sulfur dioxide and nitrous oxides in the atmosphere which form dilute sulfuric and nitric acids in solution. "Normal" rainwater has a pH of 5.7 (pH is a measure of acidity or alkalinity). Before the Industrial Revolution, acid precipitation as we know it today was probably nonexistent, and certainly it was rare before the 1920s. But measurements taken now, as compared to the 1950s, show pHs of 4.0 to 5.0, or on the order of twenty or more times acidity.

The obvious effect of these low pH values has been the reduction of trout and other fish in Adirondack lakes and in Scandinavia, where 75 percent of the trout and salmon fisheries have been lost. Moreover, little aquatic life survives in these regions, and fish-eating animals like loons, otter, eagles, and herons may become scarce.

Preliminary research in Scandinavia indicates that acid precipitation is reducing tree vitality and causing an over-all growth loss of 1 percent per year of the normal growth gain in timber. There is a new suspicion that acid rain and snow are lowering the resistance of trees to various diseases and parasites.

As for wildlife, the overall effect of acid precipitation is not yet known, but studies on deer in Poland showed changes in hormone levels with resultant stunted body growth and loss of antler growth (up to 30 percent) in animals browsing on vegetation contaminated by acid rain and snow. Amphibians, which form the basic links in many food chains and act as important insect controls, are also very vulnerable to acidic conditions.

Acid precipitation may change soil chemistry and cause a breakdown in the function of microorganisms in topsoil. This could lead to a slowdown in the decomposition and recycling of dead organic matter and litter and, possibly, a reduction in nitrogen fixation. This would lead to decreased soil production and productivity.

Even drinking water may be affected. Samples of Adirondack ground and surface spring water have been found to contain lead and copper levels at or slightly above the recommended safe drinking-water standards because of the leaching out of these heavy metals from municipal and private metal water lines and/or from bedrock and soils.

Thus parts of the world which depend on natural resources for their economy, tourism, and well-being and are innocent of any pollution are being dumped upon by neighboring industrialized areas. They are suffering the consequences of far distant air contamination and have no recourse. There appears to be no long-term or permanent solution to the acid-rain phenomenon other than cleaning up the point sources of pollution in this country and others.

Today no part of the world is really safe from environmental damage. Our super-technology and overpopulation are creating environmental effects of monstrous proportions.

Today any ecosystem, no matter how rich and resilient, can be pushed to the point of no return. Beyond that threshold, recovery can become impossible. Perhaps given geological time frames of thousands of years, the earth could gradually heal its wounds, but it could never do so in terms of a human life span, or even two or three.

So how can I be hopeful about the future of wildlife and wildlands? I need only look at three movements—national parks, World Wildlife Fund projects, and the support system among conservationists which nurtures and inspires us.

The national parks idea actually began in 1872 with the creation of Yellowstone, the world's first true national park. Just 100 years later, this idea has become an international movement with over 1,200 parks or equivalent reserves set aside around the world. In the United States there are more than 285 different kinds of park units totaling 30 million-plus acres and clocking some 200 million visitor days per year.

The concept of parks varies from country to country, but basically parks function in three ways: to conserve, to welcome visitors, and to provide raw material for ecological research. A detailed definition exists. It was written out by the International Committee on National Parks of IUCN and adopted at the General Assembly in New Delhi in 1969 (the one I attended, when I met Mrs. Gandhi). Most national parks conform to this definition, although there are also many "compromise parks," such as small sanctuaries and nature parks.

As I look at the impressive network of parks around the world, it seems to me that six factors have been at work:

One is that most industrialized, First World countries are very enthusiastic about the national park idea.

Second, the developing nations have begun to realize the economic benefits of having fine parks to attract tourists. Figures from Kenya, Tanzania, and Uganda with their giant game parks illustrate this point perfectly.

Third, there has been a large increase in the amount of foreign financial aid and expertise provided to countries starting park systems. The FAO is probably the most generous organization.

A fourth factor affecting the enlargement of the world park network is the creation of "marine parks" with accompanying protection of coastal strips, coral reefs, and islands.

The fifth is the sporadic appearance of tenacious, stubborn decision-makers who believe in parks and are willing to struggle against political and public apathy or private interests to achieve conservation. Costa Rica's former President Daniel Oduber, for example, created Corcovado National Park, a pristine coastal area of 113 square miles, and promoted several of the other parks in his country. Because of this, he was selected for the New York Botanical Gardens 1977 Green World award. At present, Costa Rica has twenty-two conservation units (mostly national parks) and is the shining example of this movement in Central America. Another such leader is former President Carlos Andrés Pérez of Venezuela, who pushed for parks, advocated the rational use of natural resources, and stanchly blunted the thrust of CODESUR to carve more "new cities" in Venezuela's virgin frontierland, changing its orientation to basic ecological research and conservation efforts. Furthermore, he put a temporary moratorium on killing all wildlife and harvesting trees for commercial use in the Amazon territory.

The sixth and last important factor in the success of the park movement is the many regional conferences set up by IUCN to arouse support for nature and natural resource conservation. These have been held in Africa, southeast Asia, Argentina, Madagascar, New Delhi, and more recently in Yellowstone National Park on its hundredth birthday.

I am optimistic, too, because of the involvement and achievements of World Wildlife Fund, a non-government organization with many appeal groups. Not only have they helped the establishment, expansion, and maintenance of national parks throughout the world—a total acreage of 50,000 square miles—but since 1961 they have provided grants of more than $30 million to almost 1,000 projects in nearly 100 countries. These funds help in such diverse ways as protecting wolves in Italy, tigers in India, and California condors in the United States; building wildlife education centers and training wildlife personnel in Africa; conserving coral reefs in the Red Sea. WWF also supports in part the TRAFFIC (Trade Records Analysis of Fauna and Flora in Commerce) group, which was set up by IUCN in 1976 to help monitor the international trade in wild animals and plants and their products. On the basis of data collected, TRAFFIC can make recommendations for action to control or stop trade detrimental to certain species.

And, of course, there are many more organizations, governmental and non-governmental, at work saving wildlife and wildlands, ecosystems and eco-people.

The international network of conferences, awards, publications, and reports also gives me cause for hope because we conservationists are now a cadre of highly motivated and united professionals. We keep in touch and learn at our conferences and congresses. One could spend the entire year jetting from one meeting to another. Few do. The secret is to pick those most pertinent to one's topic or cause, or those providing the best contacts, and to spend the rest of one's time doing conservation work, rather than talking about it.

The Getty Wildlife Conservation award is still being given each year. In addition, there are at least ten other important prizes being offered for distinguished environmental service. These range from plaques or watches to a maximum cash award of $150,000. This kind of positive reinforcement seems to me one of the best psychological boosts to our cause.

Also inspiring and educational are the growing numbers of journals, newsletters, books, and magazines in this field. Two I consider particularly efficacious are the journal *Environmental Conservation* and the series of books in Spanish on national parks of Latin America. The former is an international journal devoted to maintaining global viability through exposing and countering environmental deterioration resulting from human population pressure and unwise technology. The latter is a group of gorgeous color-illustrated books published by INCAFO which proudly present for the first time the parks of countries in Latin America: Costa Rica, Venezuela, Peru, Mexico, and Brazil have been covered to date. Again, the psychological impetus to be gained from this type of publication is inestimable.

Then, too, our little corps can gain perspective and a look at the "big picture" through various special reports. Two which promise to lay out the future and fate of our global environment are IUCN's *The World's Conservation Strategy,* which will include a means of ranking the most effective solutions to environmental problems and crises, thus helping to initiate action, and AID's *The Year 2000.*

I'll not presume to comment on these up-coming world predictions, but I would like to offer my own prognosis about what's happening. I believe that there is a bright side. Although people have been the culprits, it is people who are going to make the difference between ecological disaster and well-being. I think that the women and men fighting for conservation may tip that balance the right way.

Maybe some folks think that we ecologists, environmentalists, and conservationists are just little kids sticking our fingers into holes in the dike to stop the impending flood. But I think we're more than that because we have a reverence for life. I feel that it is totally indefensible to allow decimation or extinction of a species to take place as a result of greed, ignorance, political ambitions, apathy, or just poor judgment. Such eradication is justified only when large-scale human suffering is in question.

We can *all* do something to save wildlife and wildlands, in our homes and front yards right up to an entire nation. But we have to fight and we have to be vigilant—constantly. We environmental doctors cannot save every ecosystem and every species, any more than physicians can cure every patient. And here's where an element of unscientific faith comes into play.

A popular saying in Brazil is "God is a Brazilian." Maybe people say that God is a Peruvian in Peru, an Anegadan in Anegada, a Guatemalan in Guatemala, and so on. I don't know. All I hope is that whatever or wherever, he, she, or it, God is a multinational conservationist and will be watching over Lake Atitlán, Amazonia, the world, and whatsoever things wild.